PENGU

THE STRANGE DEAT

'Brilliantly acerbic . . . what ma   wonderfully easy, amusing style. It abounds with memorable phrases and rich pen-portraits' Leo McKinstry, *Literary Review*

'Discursive and anecdotal, rattling through the party's history of reinvention with [an] irreverent eye' John Campbell, *Independent*

'Witty and thoughtful . . . irresistible' Christopher Hudson, *Daily Mail*

'Most political historians pride themselves on being bland, dogged and clichéd, parading their dullness as a badge of their seriousness. Wheatcroft is quite the opposite . . . his prose shines brightly, shedding new light on old faces . . . His anecdotes, too, are perfectly picked' Craig Brown, *Mail on Sunday*

'Accurate, intelligent and fair-minded' Andrew Roberts, *Evening Standard*

ABOUT THE AUTHOR

Geoffrey Wheatcroft was born in London in 1945. After reading Modern History at New College, Oxford, he studied typography before spending several fruitless years in publishing. In 1975 he departed the book trade involuntarily but gratefully, and joined the *Spectator* as an assistant editor, subsequently becoming Literary Editor, leader-writer and columnist. He left London in 1981 for South Africa, to report and research his first book, *The Randlords*, an American History Book Club selection. Wheatcroft returned to work as 'Londoner's Diary' Editor of the *Evening Standard*, whose opera critic he later was, and then wrote for the *Sunday Telegraph*, the *Guardian* and the *Daily Express*. His book *The Controversy of Zion* was published in 1996 and won an American National Jewish Book Award.

Politics aside, Wheatcroft now writes about sport for the *Daily Mail* – his book *Le Tour: A History of the Tour de France 1903-2003* was shortlisted for the NSC Sports Book Prize – and contributes frequently to the *Spectator*, *The Times Literary Supplement* and *Prospect* in England, and *The New York Times*, *Wall Street Journal* and *Atlantic Monthly* in America, where he lectured recently at the University of Texas. He is married to the painter and fashion designer Sally Muir, and they live with their young son and daughter near Bath.

GEOFFREY WHEATCROFT

The Strange Death of Tory England

PENGUIN BOOKS

To Sally

PENGUIN BOOKS

Published by the Penguin Group
Penguin Books Ltd, 80 Strand, London WC2R ORL, England
Penguin Group (USA) Inc., 375 Hudson Street, New York, New York 10014, USA
Penguin Group (Canada), 90 Eglinton Avenue East, Suite 700, Toronto, Ontario, Canada M4P 2Y3
(a division of Pearson Penguin Canada Inc.)
Penguin Ireland, 25 St Stephen's Green, Dublin 2, Ireland
(a division of Penguin Books Ltd)
Penguin Group (Australia), 250 Camberwell Road,
Camberwell, Victoria 3124, Australia (a division of Pearson Australia Group Pty Ltd)
Penguin Books India Pvt Ltd, 11 Community Centre,
Panchsheel Park, New Delhi – 110 017, India
Penguin Group (NZ), cnr Airborne and Rosedale Roads, Albany,
Auckland 1310, New Zealand (a division of Pearson New Zealand Ltd)
Penguin Books (South Africa) (Pty) Ltd, 24 Sturdee Avenue,
Rosebank 2196, South Africa

Penguin Books Ltd, Registered Offices: 80 Strand, London WC2R ORL, England

www.penguin.com

First published by Allen Lane 2005
Published with new material in Penguin Books 2005

1

Copyright © Geoffrey Wheatcroft, 2005
All rights reserved

The moral right of the author has been asserted

Typeset by Rowland Phototypesetting Ltd, Bury St Edmunds, Suffolk
Printed in England by Clays Ltd, St Ives plc

ISBN-13 978–0–141–01867–6
ISBN-10 0–141–01867–4

Contents

List of Illustrations

(Photographic acknowledgements are given in parentheses)

1. An election poster for Sir Alec Douglas-Home surrounded by election posters for Iain MacLeod, 1964 (Getty Images)
2. Edward Heath, Sir Alec Douglas-Home and Harold Macmillan, c. 1972 (Getty Images)
3. Baroness Margaret Thatcher and Sir Edward Heath, 1998 (Camera Press/*Guardian* Magazine)
4. Keith Joseph, 1979 (copyright © Hulton-Deutsch Collection/CORBIS)
5. Enoch Powell, 1978 (copyright © Hulton-Deutsch Collection/CORBIS)
6. Margaret Thatcher, rejoicing, 1987 (copyright © Reuters/CORBIS)
7. Margaret Thatcher with Sir Geoffrey Howe, 1983 (Camera Press/Erma)
8. John Major and Lady Thatcher (Camera Press/Graham Turner/*Guardian* Magazine)
9. Margaret Thatcher and Michael Heseltine, 1981 (Camera Press/Lionel Cherruault)
10. Michael Portillo, 2001 (Camera Press/Martin Argles/*Guardian* Magazine)
11. William Hague, 2001 (Camera Press/TSPL/Ian Rutherford)
12. Ian Duncan Smith, 2003 (copyright © Reuters/CORBIS)
13. John Redwood surrounded by his supporters, 1995 (Mirrorpix)
14. David Davis and Michael Howard, 2004 (Camera Press/Rota)

Preface

To look back over the past century is to see hopes and fears confounded again and again, and every confident prediction falsified. The only 'lesson of history' we have learned is that history does not follow a foreseeable course.

A hundred years ago this winter the Conservative government resigned and the Liberals called an immediate general election, which was a landslide victory for them and a rout for the Tories. It seemed a new dawn for the forces of progress, which were surely now unstoppable. Who would then have guessed that within fewer than ten years the last Liberal government would have passed from the scene, that the party would never hold power again, and that the Tories would be in office for thirty-two years out of the first half of the twentieth century?

Sixty years ago this summer Labour won another historic landslide and the Tories suffered another rout. It was the high tide of socialism, and very many people, Conservatives among them, assumed that state control and a command economy were the irresistible wave of the future. Who would have guessed then that the Tories would return to hold power for thirty-five years out of the second half of the century, and that, after adopting what many had regarded as the utterly discredited doctrines of the competitive free market, they would moreover hold office for a longer period, and win more consecutive elections, than any party since the Reform Bill?

Twenty years ago, that new tide seemed to be sweeping all before it after the Tories had won two elections, and the Labour party appeared to be on the point of collapse or even extinction. Who would have guessed then that by the first decade of the twenty-first century a Labour government would have been in office for eight years, after winning not one but three easy victories to crush the Tories, and that by now it would be the Tories who seriously wondered whether they had any future, or whether they might follow the Liberals into oblivion? The great thing about history is that it keeps us on our toes.

This narrative, of how what was meant to have been a progressive twentieth century became instead the conservative century, but how at the end of it the Tories declined and fell, is one of the most fascinating stories of our age, and it was time someone told it. My credentials for doing so are mixed. Born in the year of Major Attlee's landslide and the longed-for coming of a New Jerusalem, I grew up in its shadow and in its spirit, reared in the bosom of the Labour party and in the progressive tradition, in an enclave of professional-intellectual north London which might have been a Welsh mining village for all the Tories one was likely to meet. Nor indeed did I know many, although I knew several members of Harold Wilson's Cabinet, one of whom had taken me as a schoolboy to the Commons, where I saw Churchill plain.

Soon I was in reaction to my circumstances (and anyone whose boyhood was spent being taken yearly to the Hampstead Garden Suburb Labour Party Garden Party might be forgiven for reacting against that): in the 1960s at an Oxford full of public-school Trotskyists and play-acting revolutionaries it seemed more amusing to affect romantic High Toryism. The idea that there might be an honest radical non-interventionist tradition had not occurred to me, and the notions of individual freedom and responsibility which were later to resurface were then still deeply submerged.

Thirty years ago my first, brief and inglorious career in publishing ended abruptly. The *Spectator* had just changed hands, and Alexander Chancellor, its new editor, rashly offered me a job. As described later, the magazine was held to have played some part in the revival of libertarian and individualist politics. Whether we deserved the glowing tribute *The Times* paid us in 1978 I am not sure, but working there was fun. I thought of taking up political journalism as my trade, but Alexander decided otherwise by making me literary editor rather than political columnist, and I suppose I should thank him for sparing me many long hours in the press gallery and in Annie's Bar. Instead I went off to South Africa to write a history book about that country, before returning to London for a sojourn in Fleet Street, at the *Evening Standard* and then the *Sunday Telegraph*. By this time I knew plenty of Tories, socially as well as professionally, Members of Parliament, ministers in Mrs Thatcher's Cabinet, some of them older men one met in Clubland as well as in the Palace of Westminster, but also a number of my contemporaries who were now conspicuous in politics, and although I was not a lobby correspondent I had a close view of, for example, the Westland affair and the fall of Mrs Thatcher. All of this provided me with material which I stored for this book long before I knew I was going to write it.

Then I wandered off again, popping in and out of journalism while writing other books, a collection of biographical essays, a study of Zionism, and a history of a bicycle race (a list which might suggest polymathy, although short attention span seems to me another way of putting it). Only now in what has to be called later middle age do I for the first time attempt a book on English history. I am by the way grateful to George Dangerfield for giving me a title to adapt, even if I have mixed feelings about his famous 1935 book *The Strange Death of Liberal England* (and even if 'Strange Deaths . . .' will soon be a drug on the market). At least he made it possible for me to keep 'England' in my title in an age when that name has been almost extirpated: English History in the Oxford Modern History syllabus has become British, books are published on 'Britain' in the Middle Ages when that is simply a misnomer, and a voice-over on a television advert intones, 'This blessed plot, this earth, this realm, this Britain'. On my title page at least there remains a corner which is for ever England.

Many friends and colleagues helped me write this book, whether they knew it or not, and I have obviously benefited from talking to numerous politicians, not only recently but over very many years. I had thought of listing names but, given the title and theme of this book, plenty of those thanked would not thank me in return. The Tories have got enough problems as it is, so I hope that they will accept my generalized gratitude. Two old friends in particular have given invaluable assistance. Robert Harris has retired from the journalistic fray to write novels and to live spiritually in Ciceronian

Rome, and who can blame him? But even from afar he remains one of the most knowledgeable and astute observers of British politics, and I greatly esteem his encouragement and insight. No one has suggested more sources or lent me more useful books, except of course for the incomparable London Library, to whose staff I am as grateful as ever. After writing a weekly column for more than forty years, Alan Watkins must now be called the doyen of the London political commentariat. It was said of the first Lord Camrose that he chose to 'resist the Fleet Street trend towards younger staffs, preferring to make the fullest use of older men of long service and experience', and I trust his example will not be forgotten. For at least thirty of those years Alan has been a friend who has shared his matchless understanding of Westminster, and he saved me from error when he read this book in proof.

For an author to thank his publisher may seem both ingratiating and superfluous, but this is a special case. My book was mooted eighteen months ago, when I had just published another. It was proposed by Gill Coleridge, whose virtues as an agent I have known to my benefit for many years, to Stuart Proffitt of Penguin Press, whose virtues as an editor I had heard sung by others and can now sing myself. It was commissioned and begun early last year, a large part of it was delivered in September, followed by the rest, and then the whole was revised under Stuart's watchful eye. Plainly the book had to be published either before the coming election or after its result had been digested. We went for before, but that has meant that everyone had to work very hard against the clock. Proofs arrived on my birthday, two days before Christmas, but the Epilogue was still to be written, the references assembled, and the pictures found.

All this required great professionalism and sheer toil from all concerned: Stuart and his colleague Liz Friend-Smith, our copy-editor Janet Tyrrell, Auriol Griffith-Jones who compiled the index, Amanda Russell who researched the illustrations at the shortest notice, and very far from least Richard Duguid, Andrew Henty and their colleagues in production at Penguin, who just about kept their nerve and their temper under extreme pressure while January turned into February and the book tensely neared the moment when it could go to press. They all deserve more than a few formal congratulations. Perhaps I could add here 'E&OE', the old commercial mark for 'errors and omissions excepted'. This is not an academic history of the Tory party, or of England, in recent times, and there are gaps and lacunae of which I am conscious. Despite the best efforts of many people, I shall be surprised if this book contains no errors, and delighted to have any such pointed out. I am grateful to Ian McIntyre, Richard Ollard and Francis Wheen for having done so when the book first appeared.

After looking back at events of forty or twenty-five years ago, I think also of the summer day in Siena fifteen years ago when I married Sally Muir, and what we have one way or another been through since. Guiltily contemplating my fatigue and tetchiness as the new year began, I realized that this wasn't quite inexplicable, since I had written two full-length books within the space of two and half years. But it is the author's wife and children who have to put up with his irritable moodiness and, although this is not the time to say 'Thanks for the memory', I hope that Sally, Abigail and Gabriel might be able to echo the line Shirley Ross sang in that lovely song, 'You may have been a headache but you never were a bore.'

Since meeting Sally, I have published books dedicated to a friend, to our children, and to my mother-in-law. Polly Muir died last October after a gruelling illness bravely born, and I remember her with as much admiration, affection and gratitude as ever. She might have agreed that it was about time her daughter had a book dedicated to her, which I do even if I am not quite sure what she thinks of its subject; although it would be a gross exaggeration to say that we have no secrets from each other in our married life, I am fairly confident that the dedicatee of this book has never voted for the party whose story it tells. Following an election last May, and its aftermath, which have done little to suggest that my title was wrong, it remains for other historians to relate, what, if anything, the future now holds for the Tories.

GEOFFREY WHEATCROFT
Bath
St James's Day, 2005

PROLOGUE

Magic Circle

As Thursday 17 October 1963 began, it looked like any other working day for the chairman of the Conservative party. The day ended with the knowledge that he would not be able to continue serving in the government. Three months later Iain Macleod described that Thursday in devastating detail, and in an account which held sway until it was challenged more than forty years later. What was for sure, though even he could not have known this as he wrote, was that one autumn day in 1963 would change the future of the Tory party and the history of the country. This episode would prove to be something like the fall of Parnell in Yeats's words, or the Jameson Raid in Churchill's, the moment from which so many later events – and so many later difficulties – would flow.

What was about to happen would be explained away in terms of party unity, when in fact it split the party: only temporarily as it seemed, but in reality for much longer. A kind of class war within the Conservative ranks would be brought into the open, and the party would be forced to reinvent itself, something it had often done before, but in this case for the last time. Two factions would engage, one of them upholding the old regime ideals of privilege through service and lineage and the virtues of an hereditary governing class, the other, of the contrary cause of the *carrière ouverte aux talentes* and of worth proved by ability rather than rank or connection. One faction would win, and go on to transform the country; thanks in part to that victory, the Tories would reach the end of the century in terminal decline.

At breakfast that morning Macleod had the first indication that the day was going to be unusual when his wife returned from a long telephone conversation with one of their oldest friends to announce that a decision would be made that afternoon. The information was third-hand but the links were strong, 'and the original source was the one man who would certainly know'. By that last sarcastic phrase, Macleod intended Harold Macmillan; what was to be decided was who would succeed Macmillan as prime minister, more than six years after he had arrived at Number Ten, and a week after his impending resignation had been melodramatically announced at the Tory party conference in Blackpool. Quite apart from their Hebridean names and roots, Macmillan and Macleod had a good deal in common. Macleod was a clever man, whose cleverness had not found academic expression. He was the son of a doctor, and had gone to Fettes (the Edinburgh public school where Tony Blair followed him forty years later) and Cambridge, where he wasted his time, though he might have argued that time spent at the bridge table was not really wasted: he was for a time a player of a very high standard, and it landed him his first job, at the printers De la Rue, thanks to a bridge friendship with its chairman. He was barely capable of doing his job in the office after sitting at the card table all night, but then again he was making ten times as much from high-stakes bridge as his £3 weekly salary.

He was one of a generation for whom the war was the making of them. Like his future political comrade in arms, Enoch Powell, Macleod enlisted as a private soldier in 1939, and he was then commissioned in the Duke of Wellington's Regiment. Serving with the British Expeditionary Force during the disastrous campaign in France, his leg was crushed by a German armoured vehicle crashing through a road block and ending his career in regimental soldiering, although he landed on D-Day as a staff officer. It was at the staff college that he had discovered his intellectual abilities and his capacity as a speaker: he would become one of the best parliamentary debaters of his day, and perhaps the best of all Tory conference speakers.

In the postwar years he met Powell while both were working for the Parliamentary Secretariat, which became the Conservative Research Department. He entered parliament in the famous Tory vintage of 1950, and was quite soon a minister, thanks to an episode which entered parliamentary legend when the House of Commons was still a living institution where argument was conducted, opinion was swayed, and reputations were made. Macleod had been planning to speak in a debate on a Health Service Bill in March 1952 when a change of order made him despondently throw away his notes. Then Aneurin Bevan spoke, the creator of the National Health Service, leader of the Labour left, and a spell-binding orator. When he sat down, and with Churchill conveniently on the Treasury Bench, Macleod caught the Speaker's eye and began: 'I want to deal closely and with relish with the vulgar, crude and intemperate speech to which the House of Commons has just listened', before making a good joke – a debate on the Health Service without Bevan would be like Hamlet without the First Gravedigger – and then demolishing him. Weeks later he was minister of health.

He joined the Cabinet in 1955 as minister of labour, and subscribed to the then prevailing Conservative view that almost all union action should be met with conciliation. His next office as Colonial Secretary was much more controversial – 'the worst job of all', according to Macmillan, who appointed him – and he left with some relief in 1961 to become party chairman. But he showed his ruthlessness in demanding that he should also become leader of the House, holding the two jobs *in commendam* with the honorific Chancellorship of the Duchy of Lancaster (Churchill had said of another grandiose office that the Lord Privy Seal was neither a lord nor a privy nor a seal, and Macleod's office had neither duchy nor chancery). It was ruthless because Macleod was a self-proclaimed adherent of R. A. Butler, who 'had always been particularly proud of being Leader of the House ... I had always known that Iain would like to follow me in my political career and so now I thought perhaps I had better be generous.' Those later words of Butler would take on a peculiar significance in October 1963.

Although Macmillan's departure had been long awaited, the October announcement threw his colleagues into confusion; and although the succession had been much discussed, it was no straight-forward matter. The unwritten English constitution allows for no equivalent of the American vice-president, who has few purposes in life except to succeed the president if needs be, and parties had and have various means of finding a new leader when one is needed. In democratic spirit, the Labour party had from the beginning chosen its parliamentary leader – and thus potential premier – by election among its MPs, an excellent system whose abandonment in the 1980s came at Labour's time of troubles. For many years Labour had only needed to choose a new leader when the party was in opposition, as when C. R. Attlee was elected in 1935, or when he was succeeded by Hugh Gaitskell in 1955, or again, earlier in that very year of 1963, when Harold Wilson succeeded Gaitskell. It was not until Wilson's abrupt resignation in 1976, more than half a century after the first Labour premier had taken office, that the procedure had to be put into effect to find a prime minister.

For the Tories, when the party was in power and its leader prime minister, the succession was in theory still a matter of Royal prerogative, with the Crown free to pick anyone who could form a government. In practice, there were certain conventions. The monarch might or might not consult the departing premier, who did not have to tender advice (Gladstone had not been asked for his advice in 1894, by which time he was barely on speaking terms with the queen: had he been he would have recommended Harcourt rather than Rosebery, who in the event was chosen); but if such advice was sought, it was expected to be followed. Since the Tories did not have a formal procedure for choosing a leader, this became more delicate when the succession was in any way controversial (as in 1923, when Stanley Baldwin rather than Lord Curzon was chosen to succeed Andrew Bonar Law, to the astonishment of Curzon at least, and as the result of what may at the least have been misunderstandings) than when there was an acknowledged crown prince. In 1902, A. J. Balfour had seamlessly inherited the premiership from Salisbury, as Neville Chamberlain had from Baldwin in 1937, and Eden had from Churchill in 1955. Then again, none of those was a very happy precedent. Balfour had been slung out by his own party after fewer than four years in office and six in opposition, Chamberlain had resigned after eight months of a war he had longed to prevent, while his less than three years in office was at any rate longer than Eden's twenty-one months.

When Eden left after the Suez fiasco damaged and deflated, some Tories supposed, or hoped, that R. A. Butler would take over, but Macmillan had 'emerged' ahead of 'Rab' Butler in somewhat dubious circumstances, by what the new prime minister would later call 'the customary processes of consultation'. In practice this had meant the veteran Lord Salisbury (the grandson of the prime minister) canvassing his colleagues with the question, 'Well, which is to be, Hawold or Wab?' Hawold it was, and Wab's chagrin was deep, and shared by others; the departing prime minister's wife wrote to him: 'Dear Rab, Just a line to say what a beastly profession I think politics are – and how greatly I admire your dignity and good humour. Yours ever, Clarissa.' For all the beastliness, the truth was that many of Butler's Cabinet colleagues had mixed feelings about him, and he would almost certainly have been defeated fair and square in a vote of Tory MPs, had there been one: John Morrison, the chief whip, told him, 'The chaps won't have you.' Butler became all the same a hero to younger Tories on what was loosely called the left of the party, and the representative of what they considered the modern party should be.

By October 1963 Macmillan was sixty-nine; the following year would see both his seventieth birthday and a general election. It had to be called by the autumn, five years after the last had been won more easily by Macmillan and the Tories than many had expected. Age by no means formally precluded him from leading the party into another election campaign. After all, Gladstone won the 1892 election at eighty-two and then resigned the premiership for the last time at eighty-four, while Churchill won the 1951 election at seventy-six and resigned at eighty (in both cases leaving the Commons more than sixty years after they had first entered it). Even in an era when retirement around sixty-five had become obligatory for many people, there was no vital reason for Macmillan to depart, although Macleod (as he said a little backhandedly) may have been, 'I think, at the end, the only member of Macmillan's Cabinet to hold steadily to the view that the Tory party would do better under Macmillan's leadership than under any of the possible alternatives.' In the event, the sudden decision to resign was precipitated by an operation, by more general medical worries, and by a needlessly pessimistic view of his prospects, less on the physician's part than on Macmillan's own, an echo of Eden's departure also. Both men, once so brave and calm as infantry officers, tended to panic in political crises, and in either case anxieties about health proved absurdly exaggerated in hindsight: each of them lived for more than twenty years after leaving Number Ten, Eden dying at seventy-nine and Macmillan at ninety-two.

If Macmillan were going, who would his successor be? As much to the point, how would the choice of successor portray the Tory party as it approached the last third of the twentieth century? There were several candidates, most obviously Butler still. Born in India, where his father was an eminent administrator, he came from that 'intellectual aristocracy' whose Debrett was Noël Annan. The Butlers had been a Cambridge dynasty since the eighteenth century, producing, *inter alios*, a master of Trinity and two headmasters of Harrow. Rab went to Marlborough after missing an Eton scholarship (a significant twist in the plot) and took a double first at Pembroke. He might have spent his life tending the groves of academe, but instead, fortified by marriage to a rich woman, he went into politics, winning in 1929 the safe seat at Saffron Walden he held for the best part of four decades. He was a natural 'ministry man' who became a parliamentary private secretary and then an under-secretary before he was thirty, early on incurring the dislike of the Tory ultras by sponsoring the mildly democratic India Bill of 1935.

He managed also to incur the dislike of the Tory 'glamour boys', loosely linked to Churchill and Eden, who opposed the policy of appeasement. His admiring friend Sir Henry Channon described him at the time. 'Chips' Channon was a very rich American by birth, a member of the Guinness clan by marriage, a homosexual amorist by inclination, an MP by inheritance, and a diarist of genius who left behind one of the best documents we have for London life and Tory politics from the 1920s to the 1950s. In his penetrating words, Butler had 'so little pleasure and complains constantly of the dullness of his life and his uninteresting background. But he has little social sense, no lightness of touch and he is unpunctual. But his charm lends colour to his high intelligence, and his capacity for work is immense; slowly he has become the PM's blue-eyed boy.'

Alas for Butler, 'the PM' was Neville Chamberlain. Butler strongly and sincerely supported the attempt to find a settlement with Hitler right up until the war began; he engaged in an intrigue with the Swedes the following summer which, had it been known, would have ended his career, if not led to his prosecution; he lamented 'the King over the water' when Chamberlain departed; and he called Churchill 'the greatest political adventurer of modern times'. Despite that (and the words were of course spoken in private), Churchill favoured and promoted Butler during the war, when he brought in the famous Education Act which bore his name, and after, both in opposition and in government.

In the 1951 Tory government, Rab was made Chancellor, and exercised that office in the spirit already adumbrated by him and his young men in the Conservative Research Department, Macleod and Powell among them. They had produced the famous 1947 'Industrial Charter'. The Tories had always had an uneasy relationship with the principle of the competitive market, spurning Free Trade in the early nineteenth century, adopting it in the 1840s, turning against it in the 1900s, abandoning it in the 1930s. The Prince of Wales's jocose saying that 'We are all socialists now-a-days' in 1895 might have applied to many Tories for much of the next century, and certainly few of them were what J. M. Keynes would have called true laissez-fairies. Rab's Charter was more Keynesian than Keynes, giving 'an assurance', as it said, 'that in the interests of efficiency, full employment, and social security, modern Conservatism would maintain strong central guidance over the operation of the economy'. Those were the watchwords of the party for more than thirty years, until an unlikely revolution captured the party; and in the 1950s the sheer proximity of the Tories to Labour in many essentials had been neatly caught by the name 'Butskellism', a politico-economic amalgam – or pantomime horse – combining Rab Butler and Hugh Gaitskell, the leader of the Labour party.

When Macmillan became prime minister he moved Butler to the Home Office, though his five years there from 1957 to 1962, liberal in principle and practice, only increased Rab's unpopularity with the right. Since the summer of 1962 he had been First Secretary of State, a hitherto unknown (and somewhat empty) office specially created for him. His devotees by now saw him more surely than ever as the obvious successor. In Macleod's words he was 'incomparably the best qualified of the contenders', who had but lately enormously strengthened his claim with 'a performance of matchless skill' in the closing stages of the Central African Federation, one of the more awkward episodes of late-imperial retreat, and one which had not endeared Butler (or Macleod either) to the right of the party.

His real problem was Macmillan. Early in 1964 a 'quickie' book on *The Fight for the Tory Leadership* was published by Randolph Churchill, Sir Winston's ne'er-do-well son. Alternately charming or intolerable, Randolph had been hanging loose on society and on the fringes of the Tory party all his life, noisily dissolute and altogether a grave embarrassment to the family. Between 1935 and 1951 he had six times stood unsuccessfully for parliament, and had become an MP from 1940 to 1945 only because of the wartime party truce. The great man's private secretary, Sir John Colville, was speaking for plenty of others when he called Randolph 'one of the most objectionable people I had ever met', and stories of his outrages abounded. As with one of P. G. Wodehouse's heroes, it would have been quite untrue to say that Randolph was never sober, since he was indeed frequently sober, sometimes for hours at a time. Unfortunately it was the rest of the time that he was most conspicuous. Those who watched television more than forty years ago may have happy memories of two men, Brendan Behan and Randolph Churchill, who had little in common except that they both appeared in live interviews when they were quite obviously drunk. Randolph had been in fine form when he turned up at the Blackpool conference boisterously handing out badges reading 'Q' for Quintin Hogg, Lord Hailsham, who had thrown his hat into the ring at the conference.

'It could be argued,' he said in his sorry little book, 'that Macmillan did all he could during his seven years as Prime Minister to advance the fortunes of Butler.' It was this which inspired Macleod's polemical reply, in which he derisively said that almost anything could be argued, but that anyone who had known the first thing about the government had been aware that, 'at all times, from the first day of his premiership to the last', Macmillan was determined that Butler should not succeed him. 'Once this is accepted, all Macmillan's actions become at any rate explicable', if not admirable or forgivable. In order to exclude Butler, Macmillan had for years been privately casting around for other potential successors. He had promoted three younger men, Reginald Maudling as Chancellor, Edward Heath as Lord Privy Seal – a nominal office but with the task, very much not a sinecure, of leading the first British bid to enter the Common Market – and Macleod himself, to see if one could make himself crown prince, but none had done so.

For a time Hailsham had enjoyed Macmillan's capricious favour, and he was popular with the right and with many party workers. He was clever, but his intellectual gifts were not matched by humility (at Oxford he stood with preposterous conceit for president of the Union in his first term), and his bumptious irascibility sometimes looked like buffoonery. His star had in fact fallen, partly because his bluster grated with colleagues, and partly because, as Macleod said to Nigel Lawson at the time, 'the sort of people who jumped on his bandwagon at Blackpool had clinched the matter'. There was another reason very few then knew. When Hailsham had been a British representative in the negotiations which led to the Test Ban Treaty that August, his erratic behaviour had so alarmed the Americans that they expressed their feelings to Sir David Ormsby Gore, the British ambassador in Washington, who relayed those misgivings to Macmillan.

And so, with all of those runners going out in the betting, it had begun to seem as if Butler deserved to be favourite after all, and on that morning, when Macleod and Maudling heard that a decision was imminent, they were pleased, since they assumed that this must mean it was Rab. Only when Maudling spoke on the telephone to Lord Dilhorne, the Lord Chancellor, shortly before lunch, and was told that while the 'collective views' of the party would be presented that afternoon, there was no question of the Cabinet meeting to discuss the succession, did he and Macleod begin to smell a rat. Formerly Sir Reginald Manningham-Buller, Dilhorne was a politician and barrister of the old kind, a third at Oxford (but almost a rowing Blue) with a modest career at the Bar before being returned an MP in an uncontested wartime election, and from 1951 he was a law officer, Solicitor-General and then Attorney-General, for more than ten years.

By immemorial custom now forgotten, the Attorney prosecuted in important trials such as treason and poisoning. But for all the nickname of 'Bullying-Manner' bestowed by Bernard Levin, Manningham-Buller was not the best of advocates and had conducted the prosecution of Dr Bodkin Adams in what seemed an open-and-shut poisoning case so ineptly that Adams was acquitted (allowing him to make a subsequent lucrative practice of suing newspapers which, in their astonishment, had forgotten the verdict and assumed he was dead). Despite this, Manningham-Buller was made Lord Chancellor in Macmillan's drastic 1962 reshuffle.[1]

In the autumn of the following year he played a central part in what was, in Macleod's view, a conspiracy. Dilhorne had been deputed ostensibly to sound out his Cabinet colleagues about the succession, but a decision had already been taken from which not only the public and the national party but some of the leading members of the Cabinet had been excluded, and it was about to be presented as a fait accompli. In mid-afternoon 'an important figure in Fleet Street' rang Macleod and said that the choice had been made – for the Earl of Home, Foreign Secretary for the past three years. Macleod could not believe this, but soon found that, if the stocks were not sold or the middle class quite prepared, the press had certainly been squared: soon all of Fleet Street seemed to know about the wholly unexpected choice; in Macleod's bitter words, 'news management can be carried too far.'

Until that moment Home had barely been mentioned as a successor. A few days after Blackpool, when another minister was trying unsuccessfully to have the Cabinet convened (the fact that it wasn't was an early sign that something was up), Macleod had given him 'splendidly ironical advice' in view of what was already afoot earlier. '"Try Alec," I said. "He's not a contender and he ought to be a king-maker."' As it happened, Home could only be considered at all because of a recent piece of legislation, which played an unforeseen but vital part in the story. In constitutional theory, members of either house of parliament, peers as much as MPs, could become prime minister. In practice, no one from the House of Lords had been prime minister since Salisbury resigned in 1902, and Curzon's failure to succeed Bonar Law in 1923 was widely (though not quite correctly) attributed to the growing sense that, in the twentieth century and an age of democracy, it was no longer realistic for a peer to head the government. Peerages had thus come to be seen as as much a burden

---

[1] When he took the title of Viscount Dilhorne he announced with characteristic pomposity that it should be pronounced 'Dil'n', at which the genially bucolic peer Lord Dillon let it be known that his own title should henceforth be pronounced 'Manningham-Buller'.

as a privilege, since inheriting one could actively hinder a political career. Towards the end of his extraordinary life, Churchill was the last Englishman ever to be offered a dukedom, an idea he took seriously enough to toy with the title of Duke of London, but was dissuaded in part by Randolph, who still nurtured fantasies of a renewed political career.

The existing reluctant peers were led by the Labour politician Anthony Wedgwood Benn, or Lord Stansgate as he had become in 1960 after inheriting his father's title. He stood again for parliament in defiance of the law and was elected but unseated. Then, thanks to his persistence, a Peerage Act was passed in 1963 making it possible for a peer to disclaim his title and become a commoner once more. Others followed him, such as Lord Altrincham, a Tory democrat who found the hereditary principle indefensible and who achieved much distinction as an historian under his resumed name of John Grigg. Home was not in such case, and it was only when his wife read an article by Anthony Howard pointing out that the Act, although intended for such 'reluctant peers', could be invoked for a period by any peer who wanted, that a gleam of ambition shone in his eye. The man who had been Lord Dunglass, as his family's courtesy title, and then succeeded his father as Lord Home, could turn himself into a commoner and emerge as Sir Alec Douglas-Home.[2]

That was exactly what was about to happen, once Macmillan had chosen him and then finessed this delicate operation. Although what had happened in 1957 had showed that, as Sam Goldwyn might have said, an unwritten constitution isn't worth the paper it's unwritten on, there was still that convention that a departing prime minister's advice must be followed, and Macmillan now prepared not only his own advice in favour of Home, but saw that the opinions of his Cabinet colleagues were collected and massaged in a way which was not so much tendentious as plain dishonest.

For the rest of the afternoon and evening of 17 October and well into the night, central London buzzed with telephone calls and hummed with meetings, as those members of the Cabinet who had been left outside the plot tried to stop Home's appointment. Macleod

[2] He had been made a Knight of the Thistle the year before.

had decided that, if he felt so strongly that Home should not be made prime minister, he could not serve under him, and this was apparently the position of several others, Powell, Maudling, Hailsham and Butler. Or was it? After a dinner 'where I made as gay and confident a speech as I could', Macleod went to Powell's house in South Eaton Place[3] and they both spoke to Home on the telephone. Macleod told him that, for all the affection and respect he felt for him, he had been given advice by people who had 'grossly underestimated the difficulties of presenting the situation in a convincing way to the modern Tory party'. Home was not a reluctant peer, and his appointment would be an admission that, after eleven years of Tory government, 'no one among the 363 members of the party in the House of Commons was acceptable as prime minister.' Powell said the same, and they were joined by Maudling and several other potential dissidents. This meeting was only one gathering of perplexed ministers, though it became famous because a journalist, Derek Marks, got wind of it and went to find out what was going on.

Despite everything, Macmillan would not be deterred. The following morning he sent his formal letter of resignation to the Palace, to which he appended a dossier of what purported to be the opinions of Cabinet ministers, MPs, peers and party workers, collected by Dilhorne, who had dealt with the Cabinet, and Martin Redmayne, the chief whip, who had dealt with the MPs; and, in the parlance of a later political generation, a distinctly dodgy dossier it was. Macleod and others had no difficulty in showing that the evidence had been gathered with an intention that it would provide the answer wanted, and even then manipulated. There was no limit to Macmillan's rhapsody; in one version of his memorandum to the queen, he praised Home in still more enthusiastic tones: 'Had he been of another generation, he would have been of the Grenadiers and the 1914 heroes.' In Macmillan's mind, there could be no higher praise.

Even now Home would have had grave difficulty forming a government if the dissidents had maintained a united front. It was not only Macleod and Powell, but Maudling and Hailsham too, who

---

[3] It was an interesting sign of the times, and a striking contrast with later years, that a politician with no independent means could afford to live in Belgravia.

disapproved of Home as premier and thought Butler the obvious choice. But a political compact is only as strong as its weakest link. In 1905, another cabal, of the Liberal politicians Asquith, Grey and Haldane, had tried to prevent Sir Henry Campbell-Bannerman taking office as prime minister in the Commons and to pack him off to the Lords instead, but Campbell-Bannerman had discerned the weakest link in the form of Asquith and offered him the Treasury. Asquith accepted, thus scuppering the plot.

Now it it all rested on Butler. As Powell later put it in lurid words, they had handed Butler 'a loaded revolver and told him that all he had to do was pull the trigger'. But he didn't. After some agonizing, Rab agreed to serve under Home, in the name of party unity. So did the others, apart from Macleod and Powell who stuck to their guns even if they could not themselves pull the triggers with effect. As consolation, Macleod was offered the editorship of the *Spectator* by his friend Ian Gilmour, and there published his now-it-can-be-told pasquinade. He would hold Cabinet office again only for a few weeks; Powell, never.

It was Macmillan's belief, as Macleod said, that Butler had not in him the steel needed for a prime minister or the inspiration to lead a party through a fierce general election, adding that, 'it is only honest to admit that many others shared this view'. What Macleod did not say was that Butler's very conduct that October in effect confirmed Macmillan's suspicion. Everyone would have thought that Galba had all the ability needed to reign, Tacitus wrote, if only he had never become emperor; Rab stood '*omnium consensus capax imperii nisi imperasset*' on its head: he showed his inadequacy to be a prime minister by the way in which he failed to become one.

Until then, Macleod and Macmillan had liked and admired each other, and had not been politically at odds. In any case, even if Macleod acidly said after Douglas-Home's succession that the party was being led from the right of centre for the first time since Bonar Law, to present the events of October 1963 in ideological terms would be misleading. Whatever the divisions within the party – from then, through the woes of the 1970s, the triumphs of the 1980s and the long decline into the next century – they were never simply a clash between left and right, progressive and reactionary, and individual issues as well as personalities cut across such lines. Certainly Butler had annoyed the right when he was Home Secretary and Macleod had incurred the wrath of Lord Salisbury when he was Colonial Secretary. It was the Attlee government which had taken the first decisive step in granting Indian independence in 1947, but it was Tory governments which had extended the process in Africa, beginning with Ghana in 1957. This new wave of freedom excited the most unlikely people; the Tory journalist Peregrine Worsthorne wanted to write a book, after de Tocqueville, on 'Democracy in Africa'. In view of what happened later in Ghana and elsewhere, it was as well that this was an abortive literary project.

Unlike West Africa, British colonies in the long plateau stretching from the Cape to the Horn of Africa, notably Kenya and Southern Rhodesia, had acquired substantial white populations (though proportionately still very small minorities). 'Bobbety' Salisbury was the fifth marquess, grandson of the great prime minister under whose aegis (although he was far from the most enthusiastic of imperialists) Rhodesia had been created by force and fraud, and its capital ingratiatingly named Salisbury. He had served under Churchill, Eden and, briefly, Macmillan as leader of the House of Lords, resigning in 1957 over the release from prison of Archbishop Makarios, the Cypriot nationalist leader, and also over the increasingly fraught matter of immigration to England. Bobbety had set himself up as standard-bearer for recovering imperialists, and thought that he had an hereditary duty to defend the white settlers in Africa. With Macmillan's encouragement, Macleod had accelerated the process towards independence in central and eastern Africa, and it was this that prompted in 1961 a savage attack on him from Salisbury in the Lords: Macleod had adopted 'to the white communities of Africa a most unhappy and entirely wrong approach. He has been too clever by half.'

Twisting the knife further, Salisbury had mentioned Macleod's reputation as a bridge player and said he understood that deception was sometimes admired at the card table, but not in politics. Macleod was stung, his friends thought unreasonably so, but he was right, and 'too clever by half' stuck. In private correspondence, Salisbury had already used the self-same phrase about Macmillan – his contemporary at Eton and in the Grenadiers – and the words said as much about Bobbety as about his foes. Macleod himself was uneasy about his reputation as a detached intellectual and liked to play the tough nut. When someone once used another well-worn phrase about not kicking a man when he's down, Macleod replied drily, 'That has always seemed to me the best possible time.' But this was bravado, and it was he who got the kicking that October.

He remained a model to some Tories – he always significantly preferred that word to the dull 'Conservative' – and his version of those events became the standard account. But Macleod should not be treated simply as a hero. Like plenty of party colleagues he tried to establish more serious credentials with a book, in his case a biography of Neville Chamberlain, but apart from the fact that it was mostly written by someone else (his assistant Peter Goldman), it was a poor thing, which added almost nothing to a previous and superior biography by Keith Feiling.

He was in any case an equivocal figure. He believed, he told the party conference in 1961, 'in the brotherhood of man – men of all races, of all colours, of all creeds. I think it is this that must be in the centre of our thinking.' That must have made Bobbety squirm, and it scarcely pleased all Tories. It was, after all, only a few years since Captain Waterhouse MP had addressed the conference, used the phrase 'nigger in the woodpile', added as an aside, 'Too many of them about anyway', and brought the house down. And yet it was Macleod and Butler who in 1961 had pushed through the first legislation to control immigration, to the rage of Gaitskell and part of the serious press.

Not that Salisbury was alone in thinking Macleod a political card-sharp, then or since. In 2004, there was a startling attempt to revise Macleod's account of that October. Nigel Lawson was a financial journalist who had left the *Sunday Telegraph* in 1963 to work as the prime minister's speechwriter, subsequently becoming editor of the *Spectator* in succession to Macleod, then an MP, and in the fullness of time a long-serving Chancellor of the Exchequer. Forty years on he claimed, following an earlier account in Alistair Horne's life of Macmillan, that 'Macleod had been somewhat economical with the truth' in his account. Dilhorne's notes on his soundings of the Cabinet had survived, showing a majority in favour of Home, and containing the bombshell that Macleod had been one of those. Butler had known of this towards the end of his life, Lawson said, and had not been surprised: 'Macleod was very shifty, much more than you think.' Macleod's real ambition was that he himself should succeed, said Lawson, who admitted that he would very likely have been an effective leader. Harold Wilson, the recently elected leader of the Labour party, had said privately a few months earlier that he saw 'Macmillan and (especially) Macleod as the most effective Tory leaders', while professing not to be worried by Butler or Maudling.

But there are several flaws in Lawson's story. It is true that Macleod was sometimes devious, that he contradicted himself, that Home did not emerge from nowhere but had been discussed as a dark horse at the party conference, and that Macleod himself may evidently then have said something to this effect. It is even possible for the sake of argument that his plan was 'to support Home in order not only to stop Hailsham but Butler as well, and then, when Home decided that he was not really prepared to take on the job after all, to allow his own name to go forward to break the deadlock', except that this hypothetical version has too many imponderables. Above all, if Lawson's version were true, then Macleod had been not only devious and treacherous but insanely reckless. His resignation, and especially his article, would have amounted to a gigantic bluff which could have been called, a hostage to fortune which could have been impounded. He had not only roundly abused Macmillan, Churchill and Home, but had directly impugned the honour of Dilhorne and Redmayne. Such bluffs had been carried off before, it is true. Disraeli told the House of Commons that he had never sought any favour of Sir Robert Peel, while Peel was sitting on the Treasury Bench with a letter from Disraeli, grovelling for office, in his pocket. Joseph Chamberlain told the Commons that he had had no foreknowledge of the Jameson Raid, as he most certainly had, and as some people knew he had. And yet if Lawson's 'bombshell' were true, why had it not been exploded under Macleod? If his entire account of the events of 17–18 October was false, why did nobody say so at the time? Why did those who had a note of his pledge for Home not reveal it? Any confidentiality on the part of his foes had plainly been absolved by his philippic. Home, Redmayne or Dilhorne might have been restrained by gentlemanly reticence from exposing Macleod – but Randolph?

All of this might have made those events seem luridly dramatic, yet no more than a shabby, ephemeral little intrigue. As it turned out, Home was prime minister for just under a year and Tory leader for less than two years. For Macleod there was much more to it. In some ways he was wrong. He might have been right in thinking that the Tories would have done better at the coming election under Macmillan than under any other leader (including Butler, as will be seen from Macleod's own assertion). It was remarkable enough that they nearly won under Home: in October 1964, the Tories were little more than 200,000 popular votes behind Labour in a poll of more than 27 million votes cast, or less than a percentage point, and ended with only thirteen seats fewer.[4] With the Liberals taking nine, Wilson was insecurely placed with a slender majority, until he called another election and won comfortably, before everything went wrong.

By refusing to serve under Home, Macleod had let himself in for a good deal of unpleasantness, both national and local, which became more unpleasant still after his *Spectator* article. Home himself was not merely upset but enraged by the way Macleod's resignation seemed to undermine the new prime minister's legitimacy and had removed the government's toughest jouster from the lists. At the subsequent election, on what proved his last night as prime minister, Home paced up and down at a colleague's flat, 'blaming the defeat on Macleod in language those who were present had not heard him use before'. No doubt there were also plenty of clubmen in St James's Street who agreed with Alan Clark's later verdict that his objection to Home's succession had 'derived from a feeling of social inferiority', but even among his friends his behaviour was considered rash. One of them was Nigel Birch, a clever, sardonic and rather unlovable

---

[4] Labour: 12.2 million votes, 44.1 per cent, 317 seats; Tories: 12 million, 43.4 per cent, 304 seats; Liberals: 3 million, 11.2 per cent, 9 seats.

MP,[5] who had resigned with Thorneycroft and Powell in 1958 in protest at Macmillan's inflationary policies and had turned savagely against Macmillan in the course of 1963. His verdict on Macleod's article was that 'He's cooked his goose and stuffed it with sour grapes.'

But Macleod would have replied that his mission was 'the modern Tory party', which overrode personal loyalty. It was astonishing enough that a member of the old guard was still leading the party in the 1960s. Could it really do so for much longer? Two of Macleod's passages entered the language of politics: 'It is some measure of the tightness of the magic circle on this occasion that neither the Chancellor of the Exchequer nor the Leader of the House of Commons had any inkling of what was happening.' That was a two-edged point – in his bitterness Macleod did not stop to think that this ignorance reflected poorly on the acuity of either man – but he was right in thinking that the way this magic circle had cast its spell was disreputable, and that the party could scarcely continue to be run by a small cabal. In the second passage he wrote:

The only interesting part of [Randolph] Churchill's book is the account of the advice Macmillan tendered; of how having first supported Hailsham in the decisive days, he switched to Home; of how he organized the collection of opinions by Lord Dilhorne, Lord St Aldwyn, Lord Poole, Mr John Morrison and Mr Martin Redmayne. Eight of the nine men mentioned in the last sentence went to Eton.

These words were a declaration of class war. And they would condition the Tory story for the next forty years. His angry phrase needs elucidating. By no means all of those Etonians were aristocrats. Morrison later became Lord Margadale and owned large estates in Wiltshire and Islay, but his money came from commerce; Macmillan was a publisher and, as he liked to boast, a Scotch crofter's grandson; Dilhorne was a barrister, as was Hailsham, whose family money had

---

[5] Though witty. In the heyday of literary competitions in the weekly papers, *Time & Tide*, later defunct, asked readers to write an *Observer* leading article on the subject of whether Lady Astor (mother of David, the paper's owner-editor) should be burnt at the stake. Birch won with a masterly parody of the *Observer*'s on-the-one-hand-on-the-other anguished liberalism, which concluded that Lady Astor should be gently singed.

come from the sugar trade. And, for that matter, although Randolph Churchill was the great-grandson of a duke and indeed educated at Eton and Christ Church, not many would have taken him as the beau ideal of the English gentleman.

Nor was Macleod a standard-bearer for proletarian revolution, or any kind of crypto-socialist. To the contrary, he had made his name as one of the cleverest and wittiest critics of socialism, a 'Tory democrat', but a Tory for sure. He did not believe in a centrally planned economy or high redistributive taxation, and although, like most of his contemporaries, he had accepted the principle of state welfare, he disliked the encroachments of the state. Well before 1900, the great historian F. W. Maitland had written that 'we have become a much governed country', and he didn't know the half of it. Since then it had become more governed with every generation, not least under Tory administrations. Ludwig von Mises, one of those exotic names who had kept alive the idea of traditional liberalism, said that once the principle was conceded that the state had a right to protect people from the consequences of their own folly there were no limits to what it could do, and Macleod said the same thing more pithily when he (in his *Spectator* guise of 'Quoodle') coined the phrase 'the nanny state'.

He believed in private property, and a property-owning democracy. He had no aversion to the traditional culture of the upper class, and loved White's Club in St James's Street. He did not even object to inheritance, any more than did Butler, who once occasioned a certain amount of radical derision when he defended class privilege as 'the richness of developed differences'. Macleod, for his part, ended his 'magic circle' essay by lamenting the way that Home's elevation had 'gravely weakened the House of Lords. Not only by the departure of the two outstanding Conservative ministers who were peers, but because the long-term effect of the use to which the Peerage Act was put can only be to diminish the importance, even the relevance, of the hereditary principle.' But he did believe still more in that career open to the talents, and that, in his own words, 'men should be equal to become unequal'.

In the events of October 1963, and still more their aftermath, were found the germs of the Tories' story for the next forty years. What was the party's purpose, who should lead it, and on behalf of whom?

It had reinvented itself and found new purposes before now; could it do so again? Related to that there was, in a concept as yet undreamt-of at the time Home became prime minister, the question of 'narrative'. Who would control the story? Toward the end of the twentieth century and in another context, the cruel and intractable struggle in the Holy Land, an Israeli conservative said something sour but telling. Historically the Arabs were the world's great warrior nation, while the Jews were the master of debate and dialectic; but in this conflict, 'the Arabs have lost every battle, and the Jews have lost every argument'. The Tories were destined to win many more political battles; whether they won the final argument was another matter.

I

Tory England

At the end of the twentieth century, the Conservative and Unionist party of Great Britain collapsed electorally: on either side of the new millennium the Tories suffered three disastrous defeats, raising the question of whether they would ever recover. And yet, if that collapse is striking enough, what might seem stranger still was the astonishingly long life of the England the party claimed to represent, and of the Tory tradition. A party calling itself Tory had existed for more than 300 years. From the early nineteenth century its members had been alternatively known as Conservatives, and for a time at the end of that century and in the early decades of the next as Unionists, but the name Tory had survived throughout. Under whatever label, this party had dominated the country politically for more than a century, the very period which had seen the United Kingdom become a full democracy and the masses enter the political life of the nation for the first time.

From their crushing victory in the 1874 election until their crushing defeat in 1997, the Conservative party was in office for 84 out of 123 years. Sometimes they held power alone, sometimes in coalition, though even that is misleading; the Tories dominated most of those coalitions, and they had a cannibalistic tendency to absorb parties which strayed too close, so that Peelites, Liberal Unionists, Coalition Liberals and National Liberals were first co-opted, then faded from view, and at last disappeared even as names.

What is more, and often overlooked, the Tories won a great majority of the elections of the twentieth century. Between 1900 and 1997, there were twenty-six general elections. Self-proclaimed Conservative governments were formed after eleven of them, but that underestimates the Tory achievement. The Coalition government which won in 1918 was Conservative in all but its own name and Lloyd George's, just as was the National government of 1931 in all but its name and MacDonald's, and in 1935 still more so; the elections in each of those years were in reality heavy Tory victories. Moreover, at five elections which the Tories 'lost' in the sense that they did not form the subsequent government – two in 1910, 1923, 1929 and February 1974 – they 'won' in terms of gaining more popular votes than any other party.[1] And so, apart from the outcome in terms of ministries formed, the Tories can be said to have won either practically or morally nineteen out of twenty-six elections.

It was an extraordinary achievement; and it was not meant to be so. This 'conservative century' confuted all Marxian notions of the inevitability of proletarian revolution, or the milk-and-water English version of socialism which took its name from the Roman general Fabius Maximus, the 'Cunctator' or Delayer, whose crafty procrastination had thwarted his foes. Like the Marxists, the Fabians believed in their inexorable final victory, though they called it 'the inevitability of gradualism'. As the Labour movement grew, as the franchise expanded, as the masses began to feel their weight, as the virtues of central planning and state ownership of the economy became obvious and unarguable, as rising taxes redistributed wealth, then the old order would be cast away for ever.

This sense of the inevitable was shared by many Conservatives themselves, from the nineteenth century onward. The name Conservative was, if not coined, given wide currency by Sir Robert Peel; and the other side of the coin of electoral success is that every Tory leader from Peel in the 1840s until Heath in the 1970s assumed that the future belonged with his progressive opponents. Their own task was to hold back this tide as best as they could, if not with good grace, to conduct the political equivalent of a fighting retreat. A Whig such as Macaulay sneered that the work of Conservatism was guarding the Whig achievements of the previous generation, and many Tories privately agreed; a Tory such as Disraeli (or his fictional character 'Taper') put it a little differently: 'a sound Conservative government'

---

[1] On one other occasion, in 1951, the Tories gained fewer votes than Labour, but this time it was they who profited from the vagaries of the electoral system and won a parliamentary majority.

meant in practice 'Tory men and Whig measures'. On either side of
the political divide it was very widely accepted – either hoped or feared
– that with the coming of universal suffrage parties of the left would
take more or less permanent power. The century which began with
the departure of Queen Victoria and Lord Salisbury was meant to be
what a progressive American, Vice-President Henry Wallace, hailed
in 1942 as the Century of the Common Man, in England as much as
anywhere else, and yet the common man quite failed to recognize his
political destiny.

To make the story stranger still, English Toryism is a highly distinctive growth, 'not a creed or a doctrine but a disposition', according
to the conservative philosopher Michael Oakeshott, who insisted still
more emphatically that 'There was nothing whatever in common
between British Conservatism and any of the categories of Continental
politics.' Its origins are appropriately remote and misty. The word
'Tory' is in fact Irish, and arrived in England, as 'Whig' did from
Scotland, during the turbulent seventeenth century, when the British
Isles were convulsed by a series of wars which were dynastic, national,
social and religious all at once. A *tóraidhe* was a 'pursuer' in Gaelic,
then a bandit killing English soldiers, 'a bog-trotter, a raparee', then
an Irish papist, and by extension a royalist. But just as the differences
described by 'left and right' predated the coining of that metaphor at
the time of the French Revolution, Toryism may have had a longer
lineage than its mere name.

In his *History of the Tory Party 1640–1714*, Sir Keith Feiling
(himself a Tory historian from Oxford, that spiritual home of Toryism, and lost causes) grandiosely claimed that 'the first germs of Whig
and Tory in England, like Florentine Guelfs and Ghibellines', dated
from a wedding: the marriage of Henry VIII to Anne Boleyn had led
to the great rupture which created the sovereign Protestant kingdom
of England and its scission from Catholic Europe.

Having then the same nativity with Queen Elizabeth, the embryo parties grew
in accord with the actions and reactions of the Elizabethan age, at the close
of which two twin schools of thought may be discerned, decisively opposed
to each other on the causes which most divide mankind – on religious
truth and political power. Here we are concerned only with the growth, the

flowering, and the decay of that Royalist party which boasted Falkland and George Herbert among its prophets, Strafford and Laud in its roll of martyrs; the party which in robust youth figured as the Cavaliers and walked after death with the Jacobites; which counts Hooker, Bacon, and Swift in its spiritual lineage, and was led successively by Clarendon, Danby, Harley, and Bolingbroke; that party, finally, which after living for three-quarters of a century crowded with heroism, passion, and suffering, disappeared with the last Stuart and vanished as though it had never been.

This splendid passage gave an imaginative and romanticized version, in which 'Tory England' might have been a numinous lost kingdom, as it were the shattered relic of medieval Burgundy or even Atlantis submerged by waves, never to be seen again. In Feiling's account, this golden age, this forgotten land, had disappeared like Richard II's mockery king of snow, to melt before the sun of the Protestant Succession once the first of the Georges placed his solid Teutonic bottom on the throne of England in 1714. Funnily enough, his doleful version was endorsed by A. J. P. Taylor from the left. When Feiling's later popular *History of England* was published in 1950, Taylor reviewed it part admiringly, part derisively, and wrote that 'True Toryism perished in 1688 or, at any rate, with the Hanoverian Succession. What sense had "Church and King" in an age of latitudinarian bishops and German princes?'

This was all of Taylor – clever, quotable, and yet obtuse, or simply wrong. And Feiling was wrong too with his melodramatic notion that the whole spiritual lineage of Toryism had vanished for ever with the arrival of the Hanoverians. It is true that some Tories felt this at the time and took this to its logical conclusion when they became Papists and Jacobites, but the Tory England which had existed under the Stuarts did not simply evaporate during the long Whig dominance under the first three Georges. Toryism remained the creed of thousands of albeit slow-witted country squires and albeit bigoted parsons. As much to the point, that was the age of Burke, whom Feiling hyperbolically called 'the largest mind ever given to politics in our island' and 'the inspiration of a second party of Tories'. And it was also the age of Hume, the greatest of English – or Scottish – philosophers, and of Gibbon, the greatest of English historians, who could both be accounted Tories and who in their different ways were certainly conservative realists.

Those causes of religious truth and political power would continue to divide mankind, from Glorious Revolution to French Revolution to October Revolution to Velvet Revolution. Samuel Johnson's own succinct definition of a Tory as 'One who adheres to the antient constitution of the state, and the apostolical hierarchy of the church of England' was of less and less use over the next two centuries: Wellington might have paid more than lip service to it, and Salisbury might have endorsed it more enthusiastically, but it would have meant little to Peel or Balfour, and nothing at all to Chamberlain or Heath. And yet there is a continuity of more than name.

A party which called itself Tory, harking back to the Cavaliers and those who fought the Exclusion Bill, may have been submerged during the long Whig supremacy of the Hanoverians, but the Tories then emerged to take power from 1784 to 1830. Fewer high-flown phrases about Church and King were heard now, although many Tories were devoted to a version of the ecclesiastical state and the Church of England's monopoly on office, which had very much survived Glorious Revolution and Hanoverian Succession, and opposed until the last moment any relaxation of the laws which made Dissenters second-class citizens and Roman Catholics third-class. The real story was the solidity of the conservative tradition, and still more its capacity for reinventing itself, not to say how protean the name and concept of Tory was. Just how adaptable is shown nomenclaturally by the way the word was paired over the ages. There were Tory Irish, Tory-Williamites (who adapted to the Glorious Revolution) and Jacobite Tories (who did not). Later came Tory Radicals, Tory Democrats, Tory Anarchists and even Tory Socialists. 'A sort of Tory-radical' appears in 1834, 'Tory radical' in 1868, the very idea having been bitterly denounced by Salisbury the year before, when 'the project of Tory democracy, which had been so long and so sedulously concealed, was at last given to the world'. Such Tories accepted the changes of the age and propounded a mixture of capital, social reform and patriotism (or 'an alliance of the City and the mob'). Churchill liked to claim that he was a Tory radical, although the flexibility of the term was seen when Macmillan applied it to Hailsham at a time when he was the darling of the right. 'Tory anarchist' was usually another way of saying Manchester-school laissez-fairy, and 'Tory socialist' was the name some Oxford men gave themselves in the early twentieth century to dissociate themselves from the acquisitive vulgarity of Edwardian Liberalism and the equally vulgar flag-waving imperialist Unionism of old Chamberlain and of young bounders like F. E. Smith.

Plainly the tradition of Laud, Cavaliers and Harley was not much in evidence in the age of political and industrial revolution. And yet under Pitt the Younger (himself the scion of a Whig family, who never called himself a Tory) the Tories found a new role as the bastion of order, especially once Rights of Man turned bloodily to Terror. Tories became above all the party of government. 'The ground whereupon government stands will not so easily be washed away,' the unfortunate Strafford had said, and it was still a good motto 150 years after his execution. The American literary critic Lionel Trilling, no conservative himself, put it with as much sympathy as he could, in saying that there was an authentic and in some ways admirable Tory tradition, embodied by Johnson, Coleridge and Scott; and that the defining characteristic of this tradition was that, where liberals believed in legislation, conservatives believed in administration. These revived Tories were not necessarily a party of black reaction, although they gave quite a good impression of one in the years after Waterloo, when absolutism abroad was encouraged and radicalism at home brutally suppressed. Beyond any devotion of the established Church or to the cause of property, the Tories believed simply that the king's government must be carried on. 'For forms of government let fools contest; / Whate'er is best administered is best': Pope was a true Tory when he wrote those lines.

They had instinctively found another reason for being. It was true then, in the 1820s, as it would be later in the 1930s or 1990s, that verbal violence between the parties exaggerated their real differences. Hazlitt said sarcastically that the Tories and Whigs were like two stage-coaches splashing each other with mud, but heading on the same road to the same destination. And yet profound differences remained about how life was viewed and understood. Whether Burke was a Whig or a Tory was less important than his expounding the organic nature of a community, whose living members have a kinship with, and a duty to, both their forebears in the past and their heirs in the future. More than that, in a great parliamentary speech in 1774 he had provided a touchstone for conservatism which would apply 200 years later. The previous Member[2] speaking in the Commons had asserted:

that retrospect is not wise; and the proper, the only proper subject of enquiry is, not how we got into this difficulty, but how we are to get out of it. In other words, we are, according to him, to consult our invention, and to reject our experience.

But this was 'diametrically opposed to every rule of reason, and every principle of good sense', Burke said. Far from ignoring whatever has caused our present difficulties,

we should take a strict review of those measures, in order to correct our errors if they should be corrigible; or at least to avoid a dull uniformity in mischief, and the unpitied calamity of being repeatedly caught in the same snare.

That was said 18 years before Robespierre's apotheosis, 145 before Lenin's. When Burke spoke, the concept of the left was unknown, the name of socialism was uncoined, Karl Marx was unborn. But he had perfectly summed up the spirit of intelligent conservatism, which would one day be forgotten by many supposed Conservatives (and still more by so-called neo-conservatives).

What the left ever after believed was precisely 'that retrospect is not wise'. We should never look back, only forward. We should never examine how anything had gone wrong, or how we had got into any difficulty, but only look ahead and wonder how we were to get out of another difficulty. If one revolution had led to bloodshed and tyranny, and then the next to more, we should ignore that and try again, always rejecting our experience and consulting our invention. No lessons should ever be drawn from past failure. It would be all right next time. If conservatism had no other purpose at all, it was to warn against that spirit.

[2] Charles Cornwall, whose duty to history was to provide Burke with a cue for this occasion.

A generation after Burke English politics were transformed by the rapid succession of Catholic Emancipation, Reform Bill and repeal of the Corn Laws, and in the process the old Tory party disintegrated. It was a form of suicide, and not an ignoble one. In the first and last of those cases, a precedent was set which would be followed many years later as far away as France and the United States by men as unlike Wellington as Charles de Gaulle and Richard Nixon: the 'wrong' leader or party taking a crucial and historically necessary step. In England, this took the form of a Tory government enacting Catholic Emancipation and then repeal of the Corn Laws, against the opposition of more obdurate Tories and with the help of the other side.[3] The pattern would be followed twenty years later with the second Reform Bill, and might have been followed twenty years after that with Home Rule for Ireland.

Out of the turmoil of the 1820s and then the 1840s, one more Toryism emerged, its form not so easy to descry at first, since this was still ostensibly the party of the parsonage and the 'gentlemen of England'. What sense had Church and King in an age of capitalistic agriculture and industrial revolution; of rapidly expanding population and migration from country to town; of scientific revolution and intellectual Enlightenment; of ever-expanding cities with a new indigent proletariat whose condition was unforgettably described by Engels, and also of a burgeoning new middle class? Maybe Cavalier Toryism did not have so much; but simple conservatism had a great deal of sense, and strength. Both Feiling, the Tory romantic, and Taylor, the mocking progressive, missed the point, and failed to understand the invaluable concepts of remaking and of invented tradition.

So far from vanishing as though it had never been, Toryism showed a rare gift for survival and for adapting itself to changed circum-

---

[3] Until the Napoleonic wars, England was still a confessional state with all privilege, not least the right to sit in parliament, reserved to communicant members of the established Church. Protectionist Corn Laws had been brought in to privilege, this time economically, the minority who produced food as against the ever larger majority who consumed it. The exclusion of Catholics from the constitution made the Union with Ireland grossly unjust and that country ungovernable. With Emancipation, Wellington in 1829, and with Repeal, Peel in 1846, implicitly recognized the essential new principles of government by consent and 'the greatest good of the greatest number'.

stances, for co-opting one social class after another, for quietly knowing when it was beaten and often – though not always – for following
the military maxim taught to generations of officer cadets in the British
army: never reinforce defeat. Changed circumstances inevitably meant
that Toryism itself changed almost beyond recognition over the course
of two and then three centuries, or indeed between Wellington and
Salisbury, but then even that is to say no more than that an English
country gentlemen in 1874 would have found his forebears of 1674
as outlandish in appearance and speech as Turks or Laplanders. In
the 1840s, the Tories, or many of them, voted with remarkable
selflessness to repeal the Corn Laws, which protected the landed
interest, and England, almost uniquely in Europe, stuck to Free Trade
from the 1870s, when cheap grain from America destroyed traditional
rural England with no resistance, and with no attempt to reintroduce
protection.

By then the party was led by Disraeli, who was, along with Margaret
Thatcher, the most startlingly unlikely leader the party has ever had.
Disraeli propounded his own romantic theory of Tory history. 'The
Tories have existed for more than a century and a half as an organised
political connexion,' he wrote in 1880, 'and having survived the loss
of the American colonies, the first Napoleon, and Lord Grey's Reform
Act, they must not be snuffed out.' Like almost all of Disraeli's history,
especially the idea of the 'Venetian oligarchy' which had supposedly
ruled under the Georges, this was ignorant piffle.

His legacy to his party would be very dubious, both politically and
intellectually, if that word can be used of his seductive vapourings.
Part genius and part charlatan, as he has been described (though he
was surely more of the latter than the former), he bequeathed an
ambiguous inheritance. Right up to the intestine battles of the 1980s
and later, there were people who described themselves as Disraelian
Conservatives, or One Nation Tories. That name was drawn from
Disraeli's trite observation that there were two nations, the rich and
the poor, as indeed there have been in almost every age and every
society; but then it was very much Disraeli's way to dress up statements
of the obvious as aphorisms.

More to the point was his political conduct, which demonstrated
his lack of principle. This was summed up in a devastating passage by

Lady Gwendolen Cecil in her life of her father, Lord Salisbury, itself one of the greatest of English political biographies:

And in all that is disreputable in Mr Disraeli's character . . . his lack of scruple as to the methods which he thought permissible is beyond question . . . He was always making use of convictions that he did not share, pursuing objects which he could not avow, manoeuvring his party into alliances which, though unobjectionable from his own standpoint, were discreditable and indefensible from theirs. It was an atmosphere of pervading falseness, which involved his party as well as himself.

With all his high-flown phrases, there was not only pervading falseness but humbug in Disraeli's position. 'One of the greatest of Romans,' he said, 'when asked what were his politics, replied *Imperium et Libertas*. That would not make a bad programme for a British Ministry.' And yet, although he blew the imperial trumpet, notably when to her great pleasure he made Victoria Empress of India, he knew very well that his own career owed more to earthier and more local concerns; it would have been truer to say that the Tories' programme was now Empire, Liberty and Drink. The party benefited immensely from the marriage between Liberalism and the chapels. For all that Dissent (or Nonconformity, as it was coming to be called) was such a powerful force between the early nineteenth century and its steady decline in the early twentieth, it was always a movement which repelled as much as it attracted, and its ethics, however virtuous, simply did not appeal to most people. This was something socialism later learned. Whether taking religious or secular form, Puritanism is a minority taste; most people want to build the just city less than they want their cakes and ale, particularly the ale.

While the chapels hated gambling and sexual impropriety (as Parnell learned the hard way at the time of his downfall), they hated drinking more than anything else. Once they had captured the Liberals for the cause of temperance, with licensing bills to restrict the number of pubs, and the almost undisguised final objective of prohibition, they presented the Tories with a huge gift. Bishop Magee of Peterborough, later Archbishop of York, nobly told the House of Lords that he would rather see England free than England sober, and at the 1874 election, the first real Tory victory in a generation,

Gladstone bemoaned: 'We have been borne down in a torrent of gin and beer.' He recognized that the chapel was fighting for him while the pub fought for Disraeli. What neither he nor many Liberals saw was that the pub would decisively outlive the chapel.

Against that, Disraeli made grave miscalculations in an equally cynical spirit. The most important legislation of his government carried to power by that torrent affected the budding trade unions, an episode in a complex story. An earlier generation of Tories had passed Combination Acts which made collective action unlawful, and imprisoned or transported those who transgressed them. Doctrinaire laissez-fairies disliked both unions and government intervention. A later Conservative leader, Stanley Baldwin, would say in his theatrically avuncular manner that unions would never have come into being if all employers had treated their men properly (in the way that, he liked to claim, workmen had always been treated at his family iron-works). Tory governments in the thirty years after 1945 would try to conciliate the unions. And finally, another Tory leader in the 1980s would deal with them brutally by reversing the work of Disraeli and R. A. Cross, his Home Secretary.

In 1875, the Employers and Workmen Act ended the provision of the Master and Servant Act which had made breaches of contract liable to criminal prosecution, and the Conspiracy and Protection of Property Act, despite its promising name, changed the law of conspiracy drastically in favour of the unions and legalized peaceful picketing. Disraeli's motives for this were far from high-minded. Dimly influenced by his unhistorical idea of an alliance of king and people against propertied oligarchs, he told his friend Lady Chesterfield that this legislation would 'gain and retain for the Conservatives the lasting affection of the working classes', not one of his happier prophecies.

But it was true that there was more to this than mere materialism, and to see the triumph of conservatism in merely material terms is to make just the mistake that the left so long made, by supposing that men would always follow economic ends and their 'objective class interests'. That had been disproved before the nineteenth century ended, and it would be falsified still more thoroughly in the new century. In 1900, the municipal elections in Vienna saw the working-class Social

Democrats worsted by clerical and nationalist parties, to the consternation of the left, though not of the Viennese writer Karl Kraus. He wrote that 'Adherents of the Marxist creed, which sees any victory of ideological factors over economic interest as anomalous, might learn from looking around European politics that such exceptions are practically the rule.' These were acutely prophetic words for anyone looking around British politics.

Between Disraeli and Macmillan three men dominate the story: Salisbury, Baldwin and Churchill. The third Marquess of Salisbury led the party for more than twenty years. Strictly speaking, from the death of Lord Beaconsfield (as Disraeli had become) in 1881 until Salisbury became prime minister for the first time in 1885, the leadership of the opposition was shared, as was then conventional, between Salisbury in the Lords and Stafford Northcote in the Commons, but it was clear well before the Tories returned to office who was the real leader. Salisbury's policy was to do as little as possible when in power and to frustrate the Liberals when he was in opposition by using the Lords to kill legislation. Less a conservative than a reactionary, Salisbury was a profound pessimist who shared the well-known belief that all change is change for the worse, even change for the better; a spiritual heir of Lord Liverpool, of whom it was said that if he had been present at the Creation, he would have begged the Almighty not to disturb Chaos. Salisbury had a baleful influence long after his death: a hundred years later, he became an idol to younger Tories of the fogey right. But for all the delight of his personality, his cosmic negativity was a strange example for anyone to emulate. He was a brilliant Foreign Secretary, though even then his inert fatalism could overcome him when dealing with imperial policy. As the Boer war began in October 1899, Salisbury complained to Lord Lansdowne, his war minister, that England was forced to act on a 'moral field' prepared by Milner, the unscrupulous and domineering proconsul in South Africa, 'and his jingo supporters. And therefore I see before us the necessity for considerable military effort – and all for people whom we despise, and for territory which will bring no profit and no power to England.' This would be affecting if written by a backbencher or a journalist, both of which Salisbury had been; from the man who was at the time prime minister and Foreign

Secretary of the greatest power on earth, it was almost ludicrous.

The other significance of Salisbury's period was that it saw the consolidation of class politics. Until the second half of the century, and despite the defection to the Tories of landowning aristocrats, many of whom had been Whigs, and of urban plutocrats, who had largely been Liberals, there were still Liberal noblemen. Most of the upper class who had not already joined the Tories finally abandoned the Liberals over Home Rule; Rosebery was the last aristocrat to lead the party, in the 1890s; and in the last Liberal government of 1905–15, two earls such as Lords Beauchamp and Spencer (kinsman of the future Princess of Wales) were decided oddities. What had happened was astutely perceived by another upper-class Liberal, the overbearing Sir William Harcourt, when he told Rosebery in 1894 that his desire to avoid a political 'cleavage of classes' was natural but too late: 'The horizontal division of parties was certain to come as a consequence of household suffrage. The thin edge of the wedge was inserted, and the cleavage is expanding day by day.' It would take rather less than a hundred years for that cleavage to be closed, by Margaret Thatcher to the Tories' immense benefit, and then by Tony Blair, to their ruin.

Just as events should have been going wrong for the Tories, they went right. Once again, the Tories did their best to tear themselves to pieces, this time over 'tariff reform' (or rather again, since it was the same question as the Corn Laws in a new form). Their relentless use of the Lords to sabotage a Liberal government with a huge Commons majority offended not only the nascent spirit of democracy but an elementary English sense of fair play; and their recklessness in inciting insurrection and mutiny over Ulster gravely discredited the party.

In all this they were saved from themselves and despite themselves. They had already made a most important discovery unconsciously. Over fewer than a hundred years, the franchise had been widened steadily and in the end dramatically, with almost every widening opposed by the Tories from the Great Reform Bill of 1832 to the second and third Reform Acts of 1867 and 1884. The first of these enlarged the tiny electorate of about a twentieth of the male citizenry, adding 217,000 voters to an electorate of 435,000, which meant that by the 1860s about a million men out of five million could vote; the next added 938,000 voters, and meant that many if not most urban seats had working-class voters in a majority; the last ended the franchise distinction between borough and county seats, redistributed constituencies on something like the equitable 'one vote, one value' of radical demand, and increased what was by then an electorate of three million to five million.

Needless to say, Salisbury fiercely opposed both the second and third Acts, appalled by the idea of democracy in principle, and of enfranchised working-men in particular. His successors on the patrician High Tory wing of the party then devoted their energies to opposing votes for women, with Curzon characteristically leading this resistance, and then characteristically surrendering. They did not realize that they had inadvertently stumbled upon the Conservatives' salvation. The Tories had managed on a patrician electorate, and they would more than manage with a plebeian electorate; they could not have survived with a merely middle-class electorate. And from the moment they were enfranchised, women voted predominantly Conservative: without them, the Tories would have won far fewer elections in the twentieth century than they did.

By his retirement in 1902, Salisbury was infirm and ailing, and he died not long after leaving office. His successor was his nephew Arthur James Balfour, whose career Robert Gascoyne-Cecil, Marquess of Salisbury, had encouraged in true nepotistic fashion (hence 'Bob's your uncle'). Balfour was a clever, fastidious bachelor, given to phrasemaking. He had shown a gift for plain language on one occasion when he told Major Wingfield, an acquaintance who had just invented a new game and patented it under the name 'Sphairistike', that 'lawn tennis' might be catchier. Other Balfourisms still sparkle: 'I would sooner take advice from my valet than from a Conservative conference', 'I never forgive but always forget', and – perhaps best of all as an expression of laid-back Toryism – 'Nothing matters very much and most things don't matter at all.'

But he forgot that last when he led the party into a series of bitter conflicts. The final crisis over the Lords saw the Tories in an hysterical spasm, and there was something altogether unbalanced about the party in this period, with its wild schemes and its fantastically exaggerated language. In the fight over Lloyd George's 'people's budget' of

1909, immensely rich dukes claimed that they and all their tenantry and dependants would be ruined by an increase in income tax from 1s. to 1s. 2d. (5p to 6p) in the pound. One of the contentious measures which could only be passed when the Lords' veto was broken was Home Rule, in opposing which Andrew Bonar Law, Balfour's successor as Tory leader, well-nigh began a civil war. Another was the disestablishment of the Church of England in Wales (which principality had for generations been lost to Protestant Dissent, so that in many parishes the squire and parson were the only resident churchmen), a measure which, according to the clever and unscrupulous young Tory F. E. Smith, 'shocked the conscience of Christian Europe'.[4] The extreme High Tories in the Commons, led by Salisbury's son, Lord Hugh Cecil, and known as the Hughligans, surpassed the Irish MPs a quarter-century earlier in shouting down the prime minister. Lord Hugh himself gave a fine example of the temper of the time when a measure was introduced to make it legal for a man whose wife had died to marry her sister; any such marriage of a deceased wife's sister, Lord Hugh said, was 'a case of sexual vice'.

'Then all at once the quarrel sank', as Philip Larkin put it in another context. In 1911 came the final showdown. After the Lords tried, quite against constitutional precedent, to block Lloyd George's (by later standards none too radical) 'people's budget', the Parliament Act was passed. The Lords' veto was thereby ended – and the Tories were to benefit from this far more than the Liberals. They were liberated from an incubus which would have made it impossible for them to fare so successfully for the rest of the century. It was the Liberals who found that they no longer had the excuse provided by the recalcitrant Upper House, and maybe it was not by accident that they never won another election after the passing of the Act. Keeping the resentful Irish in the Union by force had, as Gladstone had perceived, come to poison the body politic, which was surgically cleansed by the departure of southern Ireland in 1922. The Anglican Church in Wales, if not the Welsh Conservative party, was generally held very much to have profited by disestablishment. And if allowing men to marry their

---

[4] The preposterous phrase in turn prompted G. K. Chesterton's brilliant squib, 'Chuck it, Smith.'

deceased wives' sisters had no very profound effect on the course of politics, it now seems an unlikely cause to have fought against in the last ditch. Even within the party, passions abated. 'It is not a principle of the Conservative party to stab its leaders in the back,' Balfour said in 1922, 'but I must admit that it often appears to be a practice.' He was speaking from sarcastic experience after his own ousting, but he was also speaking at what would prove on the whole a more tranquil period for the party.

No contrast could have been greater than that between that earlier phase of hysterical anger and the course the Conservatives took under Baldwin's leadership from 1923 to 1937, for most of which time the Tories held or shared power, and for seven years of which he was prime minister. Many of his contemporaries found Baldwin intolerable in his sentimentality and ineffectuality, a mere 'hole in the air' to Orwell, but that was greatly to underestimate him as a political operator. In the 1920s he subtly reshaped the political culture of the country, calming the passions of his more aggressive colleagues, notably Churchill during the general strike of 1926, and trying not to treat the strikers – there were after all many millions of them – as an alien or unpatriotic force. Even at the harshest sector of the industrial class war, in the mines, some Tories were unenthusiastic about fighting to the end on behalf of the 'stupid and discourteous' mine owners, in Baldwin's phrase.

This was a more important development than it seemed at the time, when the healthy games-playing middle classes of England were enlisted as strike-breakers in a bruising defeat for the proletariat. Baldwin knew that the Tories could only prosper if they ruled as a coalition in spirit rather than a sect, and if they at least pretended to stand above mere class war. He hoped for a further reshaping of politics, with a moderate Labour party and a moderate Conservative party complementing one another, but that hope was dashed by the financial crisis of 1931, the collapse of the second Labour government amid charges of betrayal, and the consequent radicalization of the Labour rump. There was no little hypocrisy in Baldwin's position, or in any form of Tory paternalism, but then again, no Tory party led by Churchill in his 1926 guise, when he was the most pugnacious enemy of the strikers, was ever going to win many elections or form many stable governments.

Without question, Neville Chamberlain was the outstanding minister in British domestic politics in the years from 1918 to 1939, and a genuinely tragic figure. As health minister in Baldwin's 1924–9 government, he not only (for better or worse) hugely increased the building of council houses, and carried in all twenty-one Bills in the space of four years, but almost single-handedly devised the 1929 Local Government Act, with its 115 clauses and twelve schedules, a far better system of local government than its replacement devised by another Tory government forty-four years later. All this was one of the better-kept secrets of British political history. If the foundations of the welfare state had been laid by the Liberals before 1914, and it was topped out by Labour after 1945, a great deal of the solid structure was the work of Tories between the two wars, with Chamberlain responsible for more than any other man.

From the crisis of 1931 to victory in 1945, the government was ostensibly 'National' but in practice Tory: in a House of Commons of 615 Members, the Conservatives won 473 seats in 1931, 432 in 1935. This government finally abandoned the old talismans of Free Trade and the gold standard, while it continued to introduce modest social and welfare reforms, and rescued the country from 'the Slump', but could not avoid war in 1939, nor what, in Tory terms, had long seemed the still more alarming arrival of Churchill as prime minister in May 1940.

In many ways Churchill belongs to the history of England, or of mankind, rather than of any Tory party. Even before he died, and still more after, critics did everything they could to denigrate him, but it never quite worked. 'Things and actions are what they are,' said Bishop Butler, and one such thing was Winston Churchill's absolutely crucial personal role in saving his country, and civilization. And yet for all his stature in world history, Churchill played a most ambiguous part in the story of the Tory party. Near the end of his life he told his constituents that he stood before them as what he had always been, 'a Tory Democrat and Free Trader' like his father before him. That had to be said almost tongue in cheek. His career was one of breathtaking changes of course, of reckless gambling, and of shameless opportunism as well as of high courage. He began political life as a Unionist, was elected in 1900, but adroitly crossed the floor in 1904 not long before the Liberal landslide. One result was that, with a few short interludes, he was a well-paid minister for almost the whole quarter-century 1905–29, an impressive feat for any professional politician.

His 'wilderness years' when he was out of office from 1929 to 1939 became part of the Churchillian legend, the prophet without honour warning his country of impending shame and disaster. That was not how it seemed at the time. Even Churchill the Immortal required some retouching of the historical canvas. For much of his life he was a highly controversial and even disreputable figure. His private financial life would not survive examination by today's intrusive media and by later standards (though that is true also of Disraeli, Gladstone and Salisbury). Churchill was kept afloat by some of his very dubious plutocratic associates, as well as by his hugely lucrative career as a journalist and author. At the same time, his diatribes against Hitler and appeasement, though vindicated by posterity, were not popular at the time, and he did everything he could to keep himself out of the political mainstream, from his stubborn opposition to any self-rule for India to his quixotic championing of the cause of King Edward VIII at the time of the abdication crisis. There were respectable people who would not have Churchill in their houses in the 1930s, and there were old-fashioned Tories who agreed with Guy Crouchback's assessment of Churchill, even when he reached the highest place at last: 'Guy knew of Mr Churchill only as a professional politician, a master of sham-Augustan prose, a Zionist, an advocate of the Popular Front in Europe, an associate of the press-lords and of Lloyd George.'

Although he became prime minister, and national saviour, in May 1940, Churchill did not become leader of the Conservative party until the following October. His great coalition government initially saw him, by implication a man above mere party politics, presiding over the leaders of the three parties, Attlee of Labour, the Liberal Sinclair – and Chamberlain, who self-abnegatingly remained as a member of the War Cabinet but also as leader of the Tory party, until he was stricken with cancer in the autumn. Tory MPs on the benches behind the new prime minister heard him in near silence for most of the heroic summer of 1940; it was only when Churchill announced his astonishing *coup de Jarnac*, the sinking of the French fleet at Mers el

Kebir, that the Tories applauded to the echo this slaughter of their recent allies; and even then Churchill's relationship with the Tories remained ambivalent. One of the more teasing 'ifs' of history is what would have happened if Chamberlain had still been alive and willing to lead the Conservatives into the election at the end of the war.

As Simon Ball says, no middle-aged Tory politician had made career decisions before the war on the basis that Churchill would become prime minister. 'As a result, very few had a well-defined relationship with him. No serious prewar politician was a Churchillian. Churchill's praetorian guard was therefore a rag-tag and bobtail of outsiders and amateurs' – not to say, as some might have done, of chancers, mountebanks and plain crooks. There was another side to that coin. Not only did Churchill's stature by 1940 put him above party, but he was also outside the conventional class system. As usual, Orwell saw this: Churchill may have been the grandson of a duke, an Old Harrovian, and a hussar officer, but he wasn't a gentleman.

'While there's death there's hope', went the cheerful saying in the Labour party, and it was Chamberlain's death which handed Churchill the leadership of a party with which he had had uneasy relations for so long, and which he would now lead for almost fifteen years, though for more than six years in opposition when the Labour landslide of 1945 came as a devastating surprise to him (and scarcely less of a surprise to Attlee). The election used to be seen as belated revenge by the British people on the Tories for the Hungry Thirties, the dull dishonest decade of unemployment and appeasement, although this was exploded by Taylor: most British people were distinctly better off at the end of the 1930s, most had not wanted war, and in any case Labour was no better equipped to manage the economy and no more bellicose than the Conservatives. A more plausible explanation for 1945 was that it was largely a personal vote against Churchill by an electorate tired of dreams of glory. His rhetoric, so inspiring in 1940, was exhausted by 1945. The writer Kenneth Rose was commanding a troop of Welsh Guards tanks that spring in the final offensive into Germany when they drew up to listen to Churchill's final oration: 'Advance, Britannia!' After a pause, the troop sergeant said, 'Sounds as if the old bugger's pissed.'

The old bugger's party leadership in opposition was one of lordly negligence. Churchill took the very sensible view that the country wanted to come to terms with its new government and did not want to hear about the Tories for the time being. He organized the parliamentary opposition with a light hand and wisely: instead of a formal shadow cabinet (a somewhat absurd phrase, from the French *cabinet fantôme*, and a somewhat absurd concept, causing more problems than it solved), he held a weekly dinner for privy councillors which decided on whipping arrangements and on who would speak to which motions. Even if he sometimes called his clever young men the 'pink pansies', he left them to get on with their plans (although when he heard, after Indian independence in 1947, that one of the plans being made in the research department by a classical scholar and former intelligence brigadier called J. Enoch Powell was for reconquering India, even the old imperialist was taken aback). In any case, Churchill was, while leader of the opposition, at best a part-time politician, who devoted most of his attention with magnificent insolence to writing or supervising the writing by others of his lucrative and sinuously misleading war memoirs (making use of a great haul of official documents which were driven away from Downing Street by the van-load when he left in 1945) while playing his part on the world stage. Churchill said with engaging cheek that he knew history would judge him well, since 'I will write the history.' There was a lesson here for the party. The Tories might yet take political power again, but it was another matter whether they would also take permanent control of the historical narrative.

2

Winds of Change

Acutely dramatic as they were, the events of October 1963 had been a miniature performance played by a handful of people in or about Westminster at the heart of 'high politics' (with a low aspect). And yet the drama was acted out on a vaster stage, against a backdrop of social change, and in a peculiarly significant year. It came at the end of a long period in which the Tories both had and had not reshaped themselves, in opposition for six years and then in office for what proved a total of thirteen. Macmillan's own premiership lasted more than six years, an uninterrupted span longer than any twentieth-century predecessors, apart from Asquith and Attlee. They were years of rapidly increasing prosperity. Within months of becoming prime minister, Macmillan had told a Tory rally, 'Let us be frank about it, most of our people have never had it so good', words which were condemned as vulgar but which were perfectly true. How far this was his own government's achievement was another matter, and Macmillan more than most premiers swayed from planned failure to unplanned success, his benign inactivity often more fruitful than his wilful interventions. There was an unmistakably louche flavour to his years in office. He did not pretend that politics had a high ethical purpose, and used to say that if people wanted moral guidance, they should get it from their bishops. The bishops replied by condemning such innovations as the introduction of premium bonds, a government security dressed up as a lottery or vice versa.

His knack for political prestidigitation earned Macmillan the soubriquet 'Supermac' from the cartoonist Vicky, who portrayed him flying upwards like a transformed Clark Kent; the same pen drew him less flatteringly as the Entertainer of John Osborne's play, the seedy song-and-dance man Archie Rice. In either role he was giving one more display of Tory reinvention, from the earnest, humourless, rather dull young man he had once been. In later life he was widely seen as both a patrician and a great wit, playing up the role of cabaret entertainer in club and common room, and at Chatsworth, his in-laws' country house, he became veritably the Dowager Duke of Devonshire.

But that was not how it had earlier seemed. Several episodes had marked him. His staid family of publishers had sent him to Eton, though as a scholar. To coach him for Oxford entrance, the family hired a young don, the Reverend Ronald Knox of Trinity. Knox was a leader of the extreme ritualist or Romanizing movement within the Church of England, and he introduced his young charge to these exotic doctrines, to the rage of the low-church Macmillans. Then came the war, when Macmillan joined the Grenadier Guards. Another of Knox's protégés, Guy Lawrence, joined up and was killed, but before that he 'poped' or converted to Roman Catholicism. Macmillan very nearly followed him, but held back at the last moment. When Knox too became a Catholic in 1917, he wrote *A Spiritual Aeneid*, a memoir in which he referred to Lawrence and Macmillan as 'B' and 'C', which designations were followed by Evelyn Waugh in his biography of Knox. It was published while Macmillan was prime minister and Malcolm Muggeridge identified 'C' as Macmillan, to Waugh's rage.

And yet, although Waugh was on civil terms with Macmillan, he privately described what he thought was his flaw: 'he saw the light & rejected it. If he had made his submission to the Church in 1916 when he momentarily decided to, he would not be prime minister nor married to a Cavendish but he would have been a happy and virtuous publisher.' Novelist and politician had met in North Africa in 1944 when the news came that Churchill and Roosevelt had abandoned Catholic Lithuania to Stalin. Waugh recorded Macmillan's obvious satisfaction – 'Well, that's one problem the less' – and added shrewdly, 'I think he has grown a carapace of cynicism to protect a tender conscience.' Shortly after they met, all that cynicism was needed when Macmillan played a leading part in one of the most shameful episodes in modern English history, the forcible repatriation of Russian and Yugoslav prisoners to imprisonment and death.

A carapace was needed to protect him against other humiliations also. As a young officer, he had been notably valorous. He was very badly wounded, spending much of the war in hospital, and it was no more than the bad luck of the draw that he was not decorated. When he was standing for parliament soon after the war, his agent incorrectly claimed among the biographical details on his election address that he had won the Military Cross, which looked as though it was Macmillan's deliberate mistake, and a most embarrassing one.

Whatever Lady Dorothy Cavendish, daughter of the ninth Duke of Devonshire, may have first thought of him when they married in 1920, she was to blight his life by falling in love with Robert Boothby, a younger Tory MP, a bisexual, a charlatan and nearly a scoundrel: their decades-long liaison was known to 'everybody' (in the days when that meant it was unknown to almost the entire British public), and was the cause of much grief to Macmillan, who retreated into business and politics, and whose heart was hardened: that sarcastic manner had private as much as public causes. In the 1930s he had advocated a Middle Way between socialism and free-market capitalism, with an earnestness for which he and his progressive colleagues were known in the Commons as the Young Men's Christian Association.

Sometimes brave soldiers display less courage and chivalry elsewhere in life. Macmillan reached the premiership by unappealing means. In Churchill's peacetime government he had first made his mark by promising to build 300,000 new houses a year, subsequently succeeded his great rival Butler as Chancellor, and then effectively helped to bring down Eden over Suez. Macmillan became notorious for 'first in, first out', in Harold Wilson's gibe, strong for the attack on Egypt and then stronger for withdrawal when things went wrong. He completely misunderstood Eisenhower and supposed that the Americans would accept the Anglo-French operation, which he enthusiastically supported until American resentment and opposition became clear. For all that, it was he rather than Butler who succeeded Eden (who liked neither man and made no recommendation).

There was indeed a complacent if not boastful side to Macmillan. He enjoyed, in more than one sense, that miraculous prosperity of his time, without paying much attention to its causes. The year after he succeeded Eden, his Treasury ministers, the Chancellor Peter Thorneycroft and his lieutenants Nigel Birch and Enoch Powell, warned him that the economy was overheating dangerously and that inflation would soon spiral out of control. He ignored their warnings; they resigned; he dismissed the resignations almost contemptuously as 'these little local difficulties' before he set off to explore 'the wider vision of the Commonwealth'. Throughout his premiership he much preferred cutting a dash upon the world stage to the mundane local difficulties of the economy. At home, he wrote plaintive memos asking who the middle classes were and what they wanted, or arranged what Macleod called somewhat pointless weekend meetings of ministers to discuss 'the modernization of Britain', but these were activities which soon palled. Abroad, on the other hand, he could play the world-historical figure at summits with Khruschev, or tell the South African parliament about the wind of change blowing through the continent, or chat cosily with the glamorous young President John Kennedy (to whom he was indirectly related: Kennedy's elder sister had married Billy Hartington, Lady Dorothy's nephew).

He drifted towards the 1959 election with a confidence that seemed nonchalant, though it also proved justified. Labour was bitterly divided by a feud between Gaitskell and Bevan and then, when that was ostensibly healed, by the question of unilateral nuclear disarmament. Macmillan led the party into the election on the Baldwinesque slogan: 'Life's better under the Conservatives. Don't let Labour ruin it', and the electorate responded as in 1931 or 1992, not with any deep enthusiasm for the Tories so much as a wary sense that Labour were not fit to govern. The verdict was convincing: the Tories gained votes and seats, Labour lost them. As in 1955, the Tories very nearly won half the popular vote.[1] As usual since the female franchise which so many Tories had so fiercely resisted, a clear majority of women voted Tory, and so did a large part of the upper working class, whose new prosperity (many of them now owning cars, washing machines and other 'consumer durables') so disconcerted those on the left who wanted the proletariat to remain proletarian. When Macmillan said

[1] 1955: Tories: 13.3 million votes, 49.7 per cent, 344 seats; Labour: 12.4 million, 46.4 per cent, 277 seats; Liberals: 0.7 million, 2.7 per cent, 6 seats. 1959: Tories: 13.7 million, 49.4 per cent, 365 seats; Labour; Liberals: 1.6 million, 5.9 per cent, 6 seats. 12.2 million, 43.8 per cent, 258 seats.

after that election, 'The class war is over', he was boasting again, but he had a point; and he might have added, 'We won it.'

Still, the Tories had other problems. One which would not go away was the prospect of a Liberal revival. Within less than half a century of its historic high water mark in 1906, the Liberal party had almost vanished, at least in terms of parliamentary seats, thanks mainly to the cruel electoral system so inimical to third parties: in 1945 the Liberals still won 9 per cent of the popular vote, but no more than twelve seats in the Commons, and then three fewer in 1950 with a slightly larger vote. They came at last to a collapse in support in the 1950s, as though it seemed finally pointless to vote for the shade of that which once was great. In 1951 and 1955, the Liberal popular vote fell below 3 per cent, and a sad little rump of six Liberal MPs huddled together below the opposition gangway.

Unable to forget the great heritage of Gladstone and Asquith and the 1906 election, the Liberals were prone to delusion and *folie de grandeur*. In 1958, an international crisis nearly led to what might have been an appalling war when two small islands which lay off the coast of China and had remained in the hands of Chiang Kai-shek's Nationalists were bombarded by the Communists from the mainland. The chairman of the Liberal Assembly that year was Sir Arthur Comyns Carr, a jurist and public man of the old school, grave of mien and stentorian of speech. Addressing this gathering of a party whose handful of MPs represented a sliver of the electorate, Sir Arthur intoned gravely, 'And I pray that nothing I say here today will in any way exacerbate the situation in Quemoy and Matsu.'

But then came a surprise, a genuine revival, marked first of all by victories in by-elections. These were themselves once an important and admirable feature of political life. Individual elections in parliamentary seats occasioned by the death, resignation, or occasionally imprisonment of an MP acted as an invaluable barometer of the national weather, until towards the end of the century when, barely noticed, the by-election all but disappeared. During the parliament of 1918-22 there were 108 by-elections, in 1931-5 there were sixty-two, in 1992-7 there were seventeen and in 2001-5 there have been six, which is to say the number has plummeted from a yearly average of twenty-seven, to fifteen, to three, to one and a half. By-elections dwindled because of a variety of factors. MPs lived longer and were not so prone to die abruptly in middle age. But, just as important, politics had now become a full-time trade attracting a new class of professional practitioner who was in the job for money and prestige, and would never relinquish his seat and its attendant income in the light-hearted way earlier MPs had.

One bright moment, but a false dawn as it proved, came in March 1958 when Mark Bonham Carter narrowly won Torrington for the Liberals from the Tories. This seemed to presage a larger revival, and indeed at the 1959 election the Liberal vote more than doubled. And yet still the party won no more than the same number of seats as four years before, while Tories attending a fashionable election-night party in London jeered and cheered when Bonham Carter lost his seat. In 1962, the Liberals won another by-election, at Orpington on the south-east edge of London, which put the wind up Macmillan and put heart into the Liberals. Too much so: addressing the assembly in 1963, the party leader Jo Grimond caused further derision by saying, 'I intend to march my troops towards the sound of gunfire.' All the same, the Tories should have been worried, had they been able to see beyond the horizon. There would be successive false hopes for the Liberals, until at last three-partying politics finally returned, at first greatly benefiting the Tories and then contributing to their downfall.

By 1962 events were beginning to slip out of Macmillan's control. The previous year he had begun the first British application to join the Common Market, with an eloquent speech to the Commons explaining this decision. He had feared a substantial rebellion from what would later be called Eurosceptics or Europhobic Tories, but in the event only one MP voted against, the obstreperous right-winger Anthony Fell, and only thirty abstained. For more than a year tortuous negotiations were conducted, with considerable skill on the British side by Edward Heath, whom Macmillan characteristically patronized in private as a dull fellow, 'first-class staff officer, but no army commander'. It was not the antipathetic Tories who thwarted this bid, but Charles de Gaulle, acutely aware ever since the war of the dangers from *les anglo-saxons*, of American rivalry, and of the likelihood that Great Britain would be a disruptive force within the new Europe.

In the summer of 1962 Macmillan's loss of nerve became painfully apparent when a Cabinet reshuffle turned into a massacre, with a third of his ministers disposed of. They included Lord Kilmuir, the Lord Chancellor, an ironical comment on the one saying for which he would be remembered, that 'Loyalty is the Tories' secret weapon.' This was the most extensive reconstruction of a Cabinet by a prime minister since MacDonald formed the National Government in 1931, but it did not provide the same political benefit. Macmillan had been dismayed when unemployment rose from 500,000 to about 800,000, a figure which, though trivial by both earlier and later standards, called into question the Tories' claim to be the party of prosperity. Both the larger public and many of his colleagues took the sackings not as a sign of strength but of panic.

Then in 1963, sorrows came for Macmillan not in single spies but in battalions, although there were enough spies as well. He had already been buffeted by the case of John Vassall, a homosexual Admiralty clerk whose conviction as a Soviet agent sent out ripples of suspicion towards Tory ministers and embittered relations with the press when two journalists were imprisoned for not revealing their sources. De Gaulle finally vetoed the British application to join the Common Market, and Hugh Gaitskell died, to be succeeded as Labour leader by Harold Wilson. Far from the desiccated calculating machine of Aneurin Bevan's phrase, Gaitskell was a convivial man who enjoyed a lengthy liaison with the hostess Ann Fleming. But he had never set the Thames on fire, he had been hemmed in by Labour's internal sectarian disputes, he was a Wykehamist without much populist flair, and he had compromised himself by his opposition to British entry into Europe. Wilson was a much cannier operator, notably free from principle and calculatedly plebeian in his appeal, albeit in a manner that was hammy and not entirely convincing (Nicholas Tomalin pointed out that whereas some men – doubtless including himself – smoked a homely pipe in private but more dashing cigars in public, Wilson did the opposite).

More to the point, in a famous speech he invoked the 'white heat' of the scientific revolution. Orwell had once described the new caste of technocrats, living in suburbs and estates, working in chemicals or radio engineering, risen free from the culture as well as the indigence of the proletariat without in any way acquiring the culture of the older educated classes, and had shrewdly said that they were ripe for Labour. Many of them had indeed voted for Attlee in 1945, but Wilson was one of their own. Here was another *Kulturkampf* the Tories were destined eventually to lose.

Then in March, John Profumo made a statement in the Commons. He was War Secretary, though not a member of the Cabinet, a man who had himself had a good war, as the Tories liked to say, which included one dramatic moment at Westminster. The twenty-five-year-old Profumo won a by-election and entered the House only a month before the historic Norway debate in May 1940, which he attended as Member for Kettering and subaltern in the Northamptonshire Yeomanry and in which he was one of the young Tories who voted against Chamberlain, precipitating his resignation and saving civilization. For his pains, Profumo was hauled before the chief whip, the magnifico Captain David Margesson, who subjected his recalcitrant recruit to a torrent of abuse, which concluded: 'And I can tell you this, you utterly contemptible little shit. On every morning that you wake up for the rest of your life, you will be ashamed of what you did last night.'

Having begun with one confrontation with the whips, poor Profumo's parliamentary career ended twenty-three years later with another when he was placed in an impossible position by being asked to confirm or deny his connection with a woman, and he acted as many other perfectly honourable men might have done by at first denying it. What became known as the Profumo affair began to break after a shooting incident and a court case brought to light the lurid doings of Stephen Ward, an osteopath and part-time procurer (and the son of a clergyman), and two demi-mondaines he had enlisted, Christine Keeler and Mandy Rice-Davies. Profumo had had a liaison with Keeler, who was, as it happened, sharing her favours with a Russian military attaché. When Profumo was summoned in the middle of the night by Redmayne and other colleagues and asked about the girl, he might have thought of Johnson's saying that a man is not obliged honestly to answer a question which should not properly be put. He denied the rumours and was then told he must repeat the denial in the Commons, where on 22 March he said that there was 'no impropriety whatever'. The story ballooned all the same, and Profumo resigned ten weeks later after remorsefully admitting that he had not told the full truth. When a salacious film was made about the story many years later, it was foolishly touted as the story of a scandal 'which brought down a government'. Nothing of the kind happened. Macmillan found a replacement for Profumo, and was himself succeeded in October by a prime minister who remained in office until the general election which the Tories nearly won. All the same, something had changed. The affair knocked more of the stuffing out of Macmillan: at the end of June there was an opposition censure motion on the largely spurious question of security, with the prime minister mumbling that 'I acted honourably', and coming close to tears when nearly thirty Tory MPs abstained.

In a more general sense the events of that summer were very damaging for the Tories, because they bruised the prestige of the traditional ruling class – a phrase which it was still possible to use then, though not for much longer – and because they suggested that the party was on a different moral and emotional wavelength from the British people. Ward took his own life, claiming that he was a fall-guy for 'the establishment'. This was a potent word at the time, borrowed from ecclesiastical history and at any rate popularized (the original authorship was claimed by A. J. P. Taylor) by Henry Fairlie. In 1959 a collection of essays called *The Establishment* was edited by Hugh Thomas, in 1961 a satirical revue club called (with somewhat leaden irony) 'The Establishment' was opened by Peter Cook. Although the establishment in Fairlie's concept went beyond party politics, the very name implied derisive hostility to the Tories, and however much the new sceptics looked derisively at Labour politicians also, Tory England was unquestionably the loser in this new mood.

A certain plausibility was given to Ward's claim when his rich friends like Lord Astor, at whose Cliveden swimming pool Profumo and Miss Keeler had met, deserted him with remarkable alacrity. And Macmillan made a bad job worse when he appointed the famous judge Lord Denning to investigate and report on the affair. Denning's own reputation, whether for fair-mindedness or for lucid and elegant prose, was one of the puzzles of the age. His report published in September was a shabby piece of writing, which combined censoriousness with lip-smacking prurience, and stern stricture with antique obsequiousness. He had been obliged to investigate the doings of 'people of much eminence', Denning wrote, not to say 'some of the most distinguished and respected names in the land'. Everyone speculated – and were encouraged to by Denning – on the identity of a masked but naked man in a lewd photograph whose relevance to Ward's death was obscure. There may have been no real causal connection between Denning's report and Macmillan's resignation a fortnight later, but it looked as if there was.

And although there was no direct connection of cause and effect between the Tories' tribulations and the spirit of the age, they were related. Among his beautiful and touching poems, Philip Larkin wrote two with opening lines which entered the language, were hackneyed by repetition, and came to haunt him.[2] 'Annus Mirabilis' opens with the words:

> Sexual intercourse began
> In nineteen sixty-three
> (Which was rather late for me) –
> Between the end of the *Chatterley* ban
> And the Beatles' first LP

and for all Larkin's delicate irony, something did happen at that time.

Maybe 'the sixties' had begun earlier, in 1956, the years of Suez and *Look Back in Anger*. The Campaign for Nuclear Disarmament was one fashionable expression of the new mood, and so was the larger campaign to end capital punishment. In theory, social and penal questions did not correspond directly to party differences or to left and right, and in the century of the Moscow Trials and the Gulag it was quaint to suppose that 'the left' was gentler and more tolerant than the right. All the same, in the 1950s and 1960s the Tories were invariably seen as less humane and tougher on crime. Under the 1951–64 governments murderers were still hanged, abortion was still illegal, homosexual men were still imprisoned, and miscreants were still birched. Or rather, that last was one of the few older punishments which were ended under the Tories, to the regret of those who became known as the hanging and flogging brigade at party conferences, and

---

[2] The other was 'This Be the Verse', whose first line, 'They fuck you up, your mum and dad', he fully expected one day, as he told a friend, 'to hear recited by a thousand Girl Guides'.

of some MPs. One young Member who voted to retain the birch against the party line ('the whip' would be an intolerable pun here) was the Member for Finchley since 1959, Margaret Thatcher. The Commons also voted to suspend capital punishment, but this was thrown out by the Lords.

Many Tories gloried in this penal ferocity and opinion polls usually suggested that they had the public on their side, but that was not the end of the matter. A populace which professed to approve the death penalty in theory would be shocked by its application in practice. Several executions during those Tory years were taken up by campaigners who claimed them to be wrongful convictions, notably those of Timothy Evans and James Hanratty (the former but not the latter subsequently being given a posthumous pardon, for what that was worth). And two other cases in the 1950s etched themselves into the nation's consciousness.

In 1953 the eighteen-year-old Derek Bentley was hanged after the murder of a policeman during a robbery, although he had already been arrested when the shot was fired by his accomplice; the jury recommended mercy, and so did a House of Commons motion supported by 200 MPs. And in 1955 Ruth Ellis was hanged for shooting her errant lover outside a pub. In both cases the strict letter of the law had been applied, but both left a bitter taste, and that damaged the Conservatives. It was quite true that some Labour politicians were as keen on punishment as any Tory. Lord Jowitt, Lord Chancellor in the Attlee government, had told Lord Goddard, the Lord Chief Justice, that he hoped the judges would not be too lenient to armed 'bandits' who shot the police: 'I take the view, which I think you share, that we have got rather soft and woolly in dealing with really serious crime.' Goddard certainly shared it, as he showed when he tried Bentley in a manner many years later condemned by the Court of Appeal as 'highly rhetorical and strongly worded', directing the jury in language that was 'not that of a judge but of an advocate'.

In both cases it was a Tory Home Secretary who refused a reprieve. MPs gleefully congratulated Sir David Maxwell Fyfe for his decision that Bentley should hang, and Major Gwilym Lloyd-George[3] took a

[3] Of all people, son of the prime minister and originally a National Liberal.

similarly stern line with Ellis. Along with other reflections of Tory toughness, it left the party increasingly out of joint with the times.

Maybe Larkin wasn't entirely wrong. For one thing, the summer of 1963 was more important in English sexual history than he, or for that matter Denning, can have realized: two weeks after Profumo resigned, the contraceptive pill became available, ending for ever the connection between sexual intercourse and procreation and greatly accelerating a revolution in sexual behaviour which was burgeoning for years past. So was a kind of cultural revolution, before that phrase had been made so unhappy by murderous persecution in China. It was expressed in pop music and television and in what became known as the satire boom. *Beyond the Fringe* was a stage revue, for long a popular form at the time in West End theatre, but completely new in content. It played for months in London in 1961, with four clever Oxford and Cambridge men performing their own sketches. One of them was Peter Cook, who, the following year, bailed out a scandal sheet which another group of mostly Oxford men had begun called *Private Eye*. And they were followed by the television programme *That Was the Week That Was*.

In retrospect (or even at the time) these were not all of a piece, despite their overlapping personnel, or equal in merit. *Beyond the Fringe* was very funny, *Private Eye* was intermittently funny, and for the most part *TW3* wasn't funny at all. Later on it also became clear that there was no radical agenda uniting them, and that *Private Eye* – which is still going more than forty years later – was, if anything at all, Tory anarchist in tendency. The clever and witty, though posturing and foolish, theatre critic Kenneth Tynan, the embodiment of radical chic *avant la phrase*, befriended the *Eye* gang and berated them for not having a point of view, though not having one was the magazine's whole purpose.

And yet, the tendency of this satire had been subversive of tradition and authority, and of the Tories. Macmillan was a special butt, sneered at in *Private Eye*, cruelly lampooned – most cruelly of all when he was himself in the audience – by Cook in *Beyond the Fringe*. Once Macmillan had departed, the mockers found his successor almost beyond satire. In truth Home was not a hopeless booby, but a better than average Foreign Secretary who, unknown at the time, had been keener than some African rulers to eject white-supremacist South Africa from the Commonwealth. But his manner and even appearance made him seem a relic by the time of the Beatles' first LP. He had been described in 1938 by his Eton contemporary Cyril Connolly in his curious book *Enemies of Promise* as

a votary of the esoteric Eton religion, the kind of graceful tolerant sleepy boy who is showered with favours and crowned with all the laurels, who is liked by the masters and admired by the boys without any apparent exertion on his part, without experiencing the ill effect of success himself or arousing the pangs of envy in others. In the eighteenth century he would have become Prime Minister before he was thirty; as it was he appeared honourably ineligible for the struggle of life.

When Home became prime minister just after he was sixty, that passage was given a fresh lease of life. And the votary took 'Floreat Etona' to heart: his Cabinet, formed without Macleod and Powell, actually contained eleven old Etonians, more than any other of the twentieth century. The question now was whether the Conservative and Unionist party was itself eligible for the struggle of life.

3

Officers and Gentlemen

Among the reasons for his aversion to Butler, Macmillan said that Rab was *embusqué* and *munichois*, two of his greatest terms of contempt. 'Municher' Butler had surely been, a strong supporter of appeasement, but *embusqué*, the French soldiers' word for a skrimshanker or draft-dodger, was cheap when used of a man physically incapacitated from service. At the same time, so keen to promote Home as his successor was Macmillan that he granted him honorary membership of his own generation of Grenadiers. Without quite knowing it, Macmillan was here touching on a subject which would play a large part in the Tories' fate.

One reason that the twentieth century became 'the conservative century' was that so many of the premisses of socialism were simply falsified. The proletariat were not immiserated and driven inexorably toward revolution, the masses did not even follow their objective interests so far as to vote regularly for their class party, and the Fabians' 'inevitability of gradualism' proved no more inevitable than revolution, the classless society, and the withering away of the state. But there were other reasons for this conservative hegemony, and for the survival into the ages of totalitarianism, nuclear weapons and cyberspace of what could still call itself a Tory party, harking back to the Cavaliers and Young England, the romantic reactionaries of the 1830s who invoked the (real or imaginary) traditions of the Middle Ages. One was also unforeseen: the experience of war, which first brought much discredit to the Tories, then benefited them immeasurably, and finally ceased to help them at all.

Between Waterloo and the Marne there was a golden century, which has been called the age of capital and of empire; but what made it more remarkable still was that it was an age of peace. Europe exported violence through imperial conquest, and the continent was not free of wars, but they were intermittent, small and, by later standards, remarkably unsanguinary. Even if Balaclava in the Crimea created a new image of military incompetence, even if the sufferings of the wounded at Solferino led to the creation of the Red Cross, even if plenty of French lives were extinguished at Sedan along with Napoleon III's sham empire, in that golden age Europe knew little of the horrors of the Thirty Years War and the Napoleonic wars, or of the far greater horrors which the vast wars of the twentieth century would bring.

For the British in particular, the age was astonishingly pacific. England fought a long line of colonial wars as the empire expanded across the world, and stationed troops in India and the colonies. And yet between 1815 and 1914 the British army only once fought on the European continent, and then on its remotest periphery in the Crimea. By contemporary European standards that army was tiny even during the Napoleonic wars, let alone after, and at the beginning of the twentieth century England was still the only European great power which did not have compulsory military service. When war began in 1914, the Kaiser sneeringly told his generals that they should direct 'all your skill and all the valour of my soldiers to exterminate first the English, and to walk over General French's contemptible little army'. With a fine touch of native irony, the British Expeditionary Force cheerfully took up his phrase: having fought with astonishing courage 'in the days when heaven was falling', they were known ever after as the Old Contemptibles. The Kaiser's words could scarcely be extenuated, but they may have been misunderstood. Since German makes the same word do duty for both adjective and adverb, he no doubt intended 'contemptibly small', which the BEF indeed was, next to its enemies or allies: the British army was no more than 160,000 strong compared with the huge conscript armies of Germany, who had 850,000 men in the front line with a reserve of four million ready to be called up in four days, or of France with more than a million, or even of Belgium, with 350,000 men.

Although British military policy reflected foreign policy, an unspoken determination during most of the nineteenth century to keep out of European wars, it also reflected political and commercial supremacy. A great navy and an 'army of mercenaries', in the words of A. E. Housman's haunting poem, were very expensive. Those shilling-a-day mercenaries were poor beside the well-to-do of their own country, or even beside the respectable working class, but they were highly paid beside the peasant conscripts of Europe. And the British could afford it.

When George Orwell wrote about the 'extreme gentleness' of the English he was exaggerating, as quite often (in hindsight it was unfortunate that the example of this gentleness that he liked to cite was the restrained and kindly demeanour of football crowds). It is effortless to say that the gentleness of the English had not always been obvious to Indians and Africans, or to the indigenous peoples of North America and Australia, or before that to the Irish. And yet Orwell was quite right to say that England was unmilitary to a startling degree compared with other European countries.

That contemptibly small army was recruited from the poorest of the poor and officered by a cross-section of the landed gentry and part of the middle class. By continental standards, those officers were very few in number – at the end of the nineteenth century no more than 5,000 infantry officers and fewer than 1,000 cavalry officers – and there was indeed really no 'officer corps' in a Prussian sense. 'What English people of nearly all classes loathe from the bottom of their hearts,' Orwell wrote accurately, 'is the swaggering officer type, the jingle of spurs and the crash of boots', and it was very significant that in the peacetime British army officers wore civilian plain clothes off-duty. Before 1914, common soldiers were likely to be jeered at in the street and turned out of pubs: 'It's Tommy this, an' Tommy that, an' "Chuck him out, the brute!"' (until, as Kipling just as memorably added, 'it's "Saviour of 'is country" when the guns begin to shoot').

No doubt this English hatred of war seemed hypocritical to foreigners, almost more conscious than the English themselves of the British empire, but it was not just hypocrisy. A country with a tiny army and an unarmed police force under civilian control – Peel's priceless legacy – cannot easily succumb to Bonapartism, and although the Royal Navy was the greatest on earth, and helped to control the commerce of the globe as well as to build the empire, it was not a threat to domestic liberties. Infantry divisions never pay 'friendly visits to other countries as warships do', and Orwell again observed that 'there is no such thing as a naval dictatorship'.

If England was the most pacific of the great powers in the context of European politics, as was undoubtedly the case, there were several objective reasons for that. In the game of nations played out during that century after Napoleon, she was the only power that could not in any imaginable circumstances make any territorial gains in Europe. The Angevin empire in France was long gone, Calais was engraved on Mary Tudor's heart and, apart from Gibraltar, the nearest thing to European possessions Great Britain enjoyed in the nineteenth century were offshore islands picked up in the post-Napoleonic settlement: Corfu and the Ionian islands, where the one unlikely heritage of the brief British protectorate was cricket, and Heligoland outside the Elbe estuary, swapped for Zanzibar in 1890.[1] Then again, England was the greatest making and trading power of the age, and war is bad for trade. 'Buy to the sound of cannon, sell to the sound of violins', was the first Rothschild's maxim for commercial success, and the English wanted to sell. Finally there was a reason which grievously confused Anglo-German relations in the generation before the Great War: in England, the class which exercised political power was the class which paid taxes, unlike Germany, where the ruling class, the Junkers and their allies, were in the fullest sense irresponsible, above all when it came to waging war.

That English suspicion of militarism had important political conse-quences. In very broad terms, war and the military meant the right; peace and civilian life meant the left. That equation was made flesh in the middle years of the nineteenth century by the middle-class radicals Cobden and Bright, with their campaign for Free Trade and for non-interventionism, which meant against the landed interest and against an active foreign policy which had become 'a gigantic system of outdoor-relief for the aristocracy'. Until well into the second half of the nineteenth century the army was indeed aristocratic in leadership,

[1] Though not before the obscure poetaster Heinrich Hoffmann von Fallersleben visited the island and by an odd irony wrote the nationalist ode *'Deutschland über Alles'* there, upon British territory.

unreconstructed, gallant and all too often downright incompetent.

Between them, Cobden and Bright gave magnificent voice to a policy of avoiding foreign entanglements. 'It is not my business to make my country the knight-errant of the human race', 'The maximum of intercourse among nations, the minimum of connection between governments', or simply 'No foreign politics.' These were not inherently anti-Tory sentiments. Traditional Toryism, with its deep roots in the English shires, had always been uneasy at best about European wars and imperial expansion. Nevertheless, the army was almost as much the Tory party in uniform as the Church of England was the Tory party at prayer. With a few eccentric exceptions its officers were solidly Tory, and the military disasters of the Crimea reflected indirect discredit on Toryism, along with Lords Raglan and Cardigan.

From the 1870s, serious attempts were made to reform the army, which was indeed remodelled, with a new regimental system which was a fine example of invented tradition, and with the purchase of commissions replaced by some modest degree of promotion on merit. But if anyone thought that gross military incompetence was a thing of the past, the Boer war, with the catastrophes of its first months culminating in the successive disasters of 'Black Week' in December 1899, and its larger display of ineptitude, provided 'no end of a lesson'. And although the vast resources of the British empire inevitably ground down a few score thousand simple settlers, even the way that was done brought further discredit to the army, to its officers, and to the Tory government of Salisbury, for all his own world-weary lack of enthusiasm for the war in the first place.

As the new century began, the repute of the military class was thus very low among many of the British people, and was about to fall lower still. The Ulster crisis of 1912–14 is an important episode in the history of Ireland (see Chapter 7), but not less important in the history of Toryism. It saw the Tories, or Unionists, ostensibly the party of Crown and Constitution, come closer to open treason than any British democratic party of the left has done. Andrew Bonar Law, the Unionist leader, fomented rebellion in Ulster. Tory diehards in the House of Lords proposed, with what one historian called breathtakingly unpatriotic recklessness, to block the Army Annual Act and effectively disarm the government months before a great war broke out. And in March 1914, most of the officers of the 3rd Cavalry Brigade at the Curragh in County Kildare said that they would resign their commissions if ordered north to deal with the incipient rebellion in Ulster.

When the government caved in to the Curragh mutineers, there was intense popular resentment of their action, of Unionist subversion, and of officers as a class. Fifteen years earlier the Dreyfus affair had sundered France and drawn up the ranks of the left on the side of the falsely convicted captain, but the immediate reaction to Dreyfus's conviction by Jean Jaurès, the great socialist leader, had been to complain of the class justice by which an officer was merely sent to Devil's Island when a common soldier would have been shot for the same offence. A comparable sense of outrage inflamed the British Labour movement, vehemently expressed in early 1914 by J. H. Thomas of the railwaymen's union, and popular feeling might well have led to a purge of the old officer caste and, along with it, a further discrediting of Tory Unionism and everything from public schools to fox-hunting.

But for the guns of August. Then everything changed. War against Germany was declared by the last Liberal Cabinet England would ever know, and it spelt the death of Liberal England. Death sentence was pronounced partly by the intrigues of wartime politics, which saw a coalition government formed in May 1915 with Asquith still as prime minister but with Tories in prominent or even predominant positions, but almost more importantly by the final abandonment of Liberal principles, of Free Trade (over the esoteric but emblematic question of the disposal of enemy property in Africa) and, just as important, of free enlistment to the armed forces. Under pressure from Tories and the high command of the army, conscription was introduced in 1916, though no conscripts reached the front line until late that year. If the BEF which held the line at the Marne had been an army of mercenaries, the force which fought, bled and died on the Somme two summers later was the greatest citizen army in history. The 21,000 British soldiers killed on 1 July 1916, every one a volunteer, constituted a peculiarly sombre landmark in their country's history.

In one way the war made no distinctions of class or party, rich or poor. One of Kipling's bleak epitaphs for that war (in which his own only son was killed) is an exchange called 'Equality of Sacrifice':

'I was a "have".'
'I was a "have-not".'
Together: 'What hast thou given which I gave not?'

That sounds convenient, coming from an aggressive supporter of the war and of the existing social order, but it was true. By the end of the war, three-quarters of a million British soldiers had died (as well as another quarter-million from the empire). They included great numbers who had voted and worked for the young Labour party, as well as very many Liberals. Asquith's own eldest son Raymond was killed, so was Gladstone's eldest grandson William, aged twenty-nine but already Lord Lieutenant of Flintshire and an MP when he fell, and so were some other younger Liberal MPs such as Captain the Honourable T. C. R. Agar-Robartes.[2]

And yet in another way it was a Tory war, to both the detriment and the credit of Toryism. The upper classes were expected to make a supreme sacrifice, and they did. That was all the more true, to a degree unknown in any other war before or since, because of what soon became clear as the new nature of fighting. For four years, the two sides were locked into a terrible war of attrition in trenches stretching south from the coast of Flanders and which, between the early German incursion in the summer of 1914 and the Allied breakthrough in the summer of 1918, and despite vast offensives and unimaginable casualties, scarcely moved. Those offensives acquired an ill repute for senseless slaughter, which no later historical revisionism has been able to shift. Hundreds of thousands of men came out of their trenches to march towards the enemy trenches and be cut down.

And it was the officers who were killed above all. Those officers, and the classes from which they came, were not better or braver than the masses, but they were meant to show leadership and perform a duty. In the only half-ironical phrase, they were there to go ahead

---

[2] Who had sponsored the narrowly and regrettably unsuccessful amendment to the Home Rule Bill in 1912, which would have excluded four Ulster counties, and spared very much later trouble.

and get shot first, which they duly did. Casualties among regimental officers were three times as heavy in proportion as among other ranks. The toll was especially heavy for the aristocracy, and for the Tory ruling caste: five of Salisbury's grandsons were killed, including three of the four sons of Lord William Cecil, Bishop of Exeter.

Ghastly as was the total of those killed in the war, it is smaller details which burn in the mind. The poet Robert Graves joined up straight from his public school and later wrote a classic memoir of the war, *Goodbye to All That*. He describes matter-of-factly one day's fighting at Loos in 1915, and the battalions on either side of his own Royal Welch Fusiliers: 'The Argyll and Sutherland had seven hundred casualties, including fourteen officers killed out of the sixteen who went over; the Middlesex, five hundred and fifty casualties, including eleven officers killed.' Or again, seven boys at Eton in 1906 started a magazine, as schoolboys will (with the curiously modern title of the *Outsider*), whose cover was a facetious group photograph of the editors. All of them went up to Oxford together; two later took Holy Orders; and they were the only two who lived to see their thirtieth birthdays. The others – five out of seven – were killed in the war. One of the survivors was Ronald Knox, who had tutored and befriended the young Harold Macmillan. All of Knox's close friends were killed, as were all but two of the scholars and exhibitioners in Macmillan's year at Balliol. Plenty of old landed families came to an abrupt end, as their sons were killed before begetting their own heirs.

All of this wrought a great change in consciousness. If the hundred years before 1914 had been an age of peace, the next thirty years saw war on a scale the British had never before imagined, and greater than any known before. Within four years of the outbreak of the Great War, the army had grown more than twenty-fold in numbers to more than four million, and those killed in little more than four years outnumbered all the Englishmen who had died in battle for the previous 1,000 years. More than 200,000 officers were commissioned, and some 50,000 were killed. Something similar happened in 1939–45, though without the same terrible level of mortality. For the first time ever, most British men of a certain generation had worn uniform, an experience which did not end with the second victory over Germany. National Service, the fine euphemism for military con-scription or 'call-up', continued for another fifteen years after 1945.

The social and political implications of this were enormous. Orwell pointed out that the only popular poems about battle in English told tales of disaster and defeat, and he dwelt rightly on the humorous and mock-defeatist songs the Tommies sang in the Great War, which are among their lasting memorials: 'When this bleeding war is over, Oh how happy I shall be' (to the tune of 'What a friend we have in Jesus'), or 'We are Fred Karno's army, the ragtime infantry, / We cannot fight, we cannot shoot, no bloody use are we.' It was those useless infantrymen who fought with a grim fatalistic courage no army had ever shown before.

Not only had the bulk of the respectable working class been ignorant of and hostile to military life, so had much of the educated classes been, something illustrated by the startling fact that in all the revolutionary and Napoleonic wars fought by England from 1793 to 1815, only two men educated at Oxford or Cambridge had died. After 1918, the chapel of every college at the universities and every public school and grammar school erected huge monuments to their fallen.

Immediately after the Great War there was a lull. The country was gripped first by a mood of intense mourning and a consciousness of sacrifice, although also by a kind of wilful and very telling hedonism, until ten years after the Armistice. Then a flood of memoirs, novels and plays all appeared by unplanned coincidence in 1928–9, all telling the same story of terrible suffering and useless heroism, and of military folly. The stupid old men had sent the flower of the nation to needless death: stupid Tory politicians and stupider Tory generals. By the early 1930s, fashionable pacifism had permeated down from the Oxford Union, which voted that it would not fight for King and Country (a resolution which passed into myth, notably the myth that Hitler took any notice of what a few undergraduates had said or done), to the larger populace, many of whom supported a 'peace ballot'. The Tories themselves were infected by the same mood. In October 1933, there was a dramatic Labour victory in the East Fulham by-election, which was widely interpreted as a vote against rearmament and war, although it was in fact almost certainly decided, like most by-elections, on domestic or even local issues.

Since by-election upsets are often transient, it has been foolishly argued that they don't matter at all. This quite misses the point. Maitland profoundly said that events now far in the past were once in the future: the objective outcome of events is less important than how men subjectively see them at the time. In this case, Baldwin was badly shaken and nervous about his ability to rearm the country, as he later told the Commons, prompting Churchill's malicious index entry in his history of the world war, in which he cited Baldwin as admitting 'putting party before country' when he told the Commons about the difficulties of opposing the dictators. Even Baldwin's authorized biographer G. M. Young said that 'I always felt that the nerve, injured in October 1933, the East Fulham nerve, never quite healed.'

Even then, and even though those 'anti-war' books may have told of the suffering and futility of war, they did not necessarily disparage the officer class. Graves expressed his admiration for regimental officers of the regular army (rather than generals and staff officers), who might not have been the brightest and most original of spirits, but who were loyal, decent and brave. Wartime could even inspire a larger admiration for ruling castes, with their darker and their finer sides. Before the Great War, a disproportionate number of those regular officers had been Ascendancy Irish, from the Protestant squire-archy of the 'garrison', in the tradition of frontier gentry throughout Europe, such as the Junkers, or the Croats who were likewise dispro-portionately represented as officers of the armies of the Habsburg empire. Such Herrenvolk, of whom the Boers were another example, have two faces: one brutal, toward those they rule over, one noble, when fighting to the end. Macaulay captured this in a fine passage about those Irish Protestants in earlier centuries:

The character, thus formed, has two aspects. Seen on one side, it must be regarded by every well-constituted mind with disapprobation. Seen on the other, it irresistibly extorts applause. The Spartan, smiting and spurning the wretched Helot, moves our disgust. But the same Spartan, calmly dressing his hair, and uttering his concise jests, on what he well knows to be his last day, in the pass of Thermopylae, is not to be contemplated without admiration.

Just so, the bigoted Unionist officers, taking the country to the brink of civil war rather than concede Home Rule, were widely viewed with disgust. But the same officers, calmly facing what for so many of them was their last day, at Ypres or Passchendaele, were not to be contemplated without admiration.

Just as the English seemed to be turning from a nation which knew little of war, as they had been before 1914, to a nation which knew all too much and wanted to study war no more, the mood changed again. Mussolini's posturing militarism could be laughed off even when he invaded Abyssinia in 1935, and when the Hoare–Laval plan to placate him caused a huge outcry, but Hitler was not funny at all. And in 1936 the pacifism of the left suffered another blow with the Spanish civil war. Suddenly radicals rediscovered the military virtues, the hollowness of the slogan 'against fascism and war' was exposed, and Kipling's wisdom was revealed. For nearly twenty years the left had been engaged in 'making mock of uniforms that guard you while you sleep'. No more. Orwell saw the change of mood. During the Spanish war, those who had jeered at the idea of glorious war, at patriotism, even at physical courage, were now parroting stuff that could have come from the *Daily Mail* in 1918 with only the names changed.

The same people who in 1933 sniggered pityingly if you said that in certain circumstances you would fight for your country, in 1937 were denouncing you as a Trotsky–Fascist if you suggested that stories in *New Masses* about freshly wounded men clamouring to get back into the fighting might be exaggerated.

Few Tories joined in the enthusiasm for Republican Spain, and few wanted another war against Germany (if anyone sane ever actually wants a war), but it was significant that the Conservatives who were strongest for appeasement were mostly of middle-class, non-military and not least non-Anglican background: Chamberlain, Hoare, Simon. Churchill, who spoke against Munich, had served as a cavalry officer in the 1890s and as a battalion commander in 1915; Eden, who resigned in protest at appeasing Italy, had won an MC in the Great War. And on the other side, the beloved but baffled pacifist George Lansbury was succeeded as Labour leader by Major Attlee, another wartime infantryman, who would become one of the two British prime ministers (Macmillan, the other) to have been wounded in action.

In 1939, part of the left forgot its new-found zeal for war, or at least those on the left who sympathized with Soviet Russia so much that they supported the Molotov–Ribbentrop pact, and some simply remembered the better part of valour by absenting themselves from the fray. Compare two writers from the left and two from the right. Christopher Isherwood and W. H. Auden were to be the butt of Evelyn Waugh's satirical sneers against 'Parsnip and Pimpernel' (and of the American poet E. E. Cummings as 'Flotsam and Jetsam'), the two English writers who have run away to America in 1939 in *Put Out More Flags*, and the target of Anthony Powell's abuse (Auden was a 'shit' even at the time of his death). On their side, Powell and Waugh were both apolitical and idiosyncratic conservatives who disdained the fashionable contemporary causes and the 'stage army of the good'. Auden and Isherwood epitomized the fashionable left, angrily – though verbally – attacking fascism for years. When the war came, Powell joined the army and Waugh the marines, while 'at the first squeak of an air-raid siren the gang dispersed', in Waugh's cruel phrase, Auden and Isherwood spending the war on the other side of the Atlantic.

That ugly display was disposed of with superbly concise eloquence in the *New Statesman* on 14 October 1939, in one of the finest 'letters to the editor' of the century:

Sir, The intelligentsia of the Left were the loudest in demanding that the Nazi aggression should be resisted at all costs. When it comes to a showdown, scarce four weeks have passed before they remember that they are pacifists and write defeatist letters to your columns, leaving the defence of freedom and of civilisation to Colonel Blimp and the Old School Tie, for whom Three Cheers.

J. M. Keynes
King's College, Cambridge

Rather than rushing to enlist in the 1914 spirit, 'Now God be thanked that has matched us to this hour', another generation of young Englishmen were now conscripted and served with grim determination and a sense of a job to be done. They too learned that war is hell, but also necessary, and that those who wage it can be admirable men; like Graves before him, Kingsley Amis would recall the regular officers he encountered as slow-witted and unimaginative, but brave and honourable. All of this redounded to the indirect credit of the Conservatives again, or certainly to the credit of tradition, and of the old governing class and its institutions. A most vivid example is found in Frank Thompson, Wykehamist, classicist, Communist, who joined the army from Oxford and served in North Africa before he transferred to Special Operations Executive, was attached to the Bulgarian partisans, and in 1944 was captured by the local pro-Axis forces and executed. His poignant and bitter story was much later told by his brother, the Marxist historian E. P. Thompson. At one droll moment Frank wrote home from active service in the Western desert to his younger brother and fellow Bolshevik: 'There's no getting away from the fact that the regiments whose officers are the most blue-blooded – the Guards, old cavalry regiments – have proved themselves the best fighting regiments in the British Army.' Sure enough, Edward took the point, and when his own time came he joined the 17th/21st Lancers, than which they did not come much more blue-blooded.

In the postwar decades the Tories enjoyed this indirect lustre, and capitalized on the military virtues as blatantly as they dared. Apart from Attlee, there were members of his Cabinet, such as Hugh Dalton, who had served in the Great War, and younger socialists had served in the subsequent war: Tony Crosland had been a Parachute Regiment officer and was unlucky not to win the MC. But many had not, and by the 1950s there was a subterranean accusation that Labour was a party of *embusqués*, men who had avoided service when of an age for it. It was quite true that Hugh Gaitskell, who succeeded Attlee as Labour leader, and his fellow-Wykehamists Richard Crossman and Douglas Jay, had been wartime civilians. As Auberon Waugh maliciously put it in a review of Jay's memoirs, when the war came 'he desperately wanted to be where the action was – by his own reckoning, in the Ministry of Supply.' Macmillan said just as maliciously about the gathering at the Cenotaph on Armistice Day that 'Poor Mr Gaitskell always seems a little conscious on these occasions that he has no medals. However, he supported the war from Dr Dalton's side, in the Ministry of Economic Warfare.'

Not only did Macmillan most unfairly direct the same contempt toward Butler, whose arm was crippled by a childhood riding accident so he could not have served, but with an astonishing double standard he absolved Home from the charges of *embusqué* or *munichois* when they applied just as much to him. He was an undisguised appeaser in 1938, who did not join up when the war began, although a later attempt at enlistment was thwarted by ill-health. Home was younger than Butler and in September 1939 had been thirty-six, exactly the age at which Raymond Asquith had joined the Grenadiers in 1914.

With his spite and evasion, Macmillan still personified a fascinating historical episode. No prime minister from 1830 to 1940, between Wellington and Churchill, had ever worn uniform in the armed forces. By contrast, all four prime ministers between 1940 and 1963 had served in the Great War, and had held high political office in the world war of 1939–45. There were subsequently two prime ministers who had served in that war, Heath and Callaghan, and it was sometimes muttered that Wilson was another malingerer who had managed to avoid service. The last premier of the wartime generation was Mrs Thatcher, who was much given to invoking Churchillian glory, although she was eighteen in 1943 and could perfectly well have joined the Wrens or the ATS rather than going straight to Oxford.

If that period of national grandeur conferred credit on the military, on the class from which officers came, and in effect on the Tories, then it was likely that the lustre would dim when the memories of war faded. The traditional ruling class which Macmillan was happy to salute would lose its own reputation once the big wars that make ambition virtue were no more. 'An officer and a gentleman' was the resonant phrase in military regulations; if the officer came to be discredited, so would the gentleman.

As a word, 'gentleman' dates from the Middle Ages, meaning someone who was not noble but not base. England never acquired an aristocracy on the continental pattern, a legally privileged landowning caste (a quite large class in many countries and very large in some: in the old kingdom of Hungary, the nobility was a tenth of the population). In England the peerage was no more than a few hundred in number, and birth conferred no permanent status; an English nobleman was a member of the House of Lords, but his sons – even his eldest sons – were legally commoners and could sit in the House of Commons. The idea of gentle birth was a potent one, but it was quite flexible, 'For he today that sheds his blood with me / Shall be my brother; be he ne'er so vile / This day shall gentle his condition', and at no time was there ever a pure or exclusive aristocracy which no one could enter.

Then something else happened. The idea of 'the English gentleman' was born, his birth plausibly dated to the middle years of the eighteenth century. In the golden age of the first Tory party, Toryism had been the creed of the Cavaliers and their church. By the time of the next Tory ascendancy under Liverpool, England had changed from a society based on rank to one based on class. Before that, the virtues of the middle class had been celebrated by writers like Defoe and Oliver Goldsmith, who thought that 'in this middle order of mankind are generally to be found all the arts, wisdom and virtues of society', and at the same time social barriers in England were famously more easily surmounted than almost anywhere in Europe. Thanks to this process, in the age of industrial revolution, and doubtless connected with it, a new breed was born. This might be called the making of the English upper middle class, and it was hugely important for the survival of the Tories. Gentlemen were admired, gentlemen were the natural governing class; and yet at the same time anyone could become a gentleman, or at least have children who became gentlemen, a process the great expansion of public schools in the nineteenth century encouraged.

This idea was eloquently expressed by Palmerston in his famous 'Don Pacifico' speech of 1850 (with its peroration promising that 'a British subject, in whatever land he may be, shall feel confident that the watchful eye of England will protect him from injustice and wrong'). He told the Commons that 'We have shown the example of a nation, in which every class in society accepts with cheerfulness the lot which Providence has assigned to it.' And he went on: 'at the same time every individual of each class is constantly striving to raise himself in the social scale.'

As long as traditional values were esteemed, and flattered by emulation, they helped the Tories. But how long would that be? The thrall of the governing class and its martial virtues lasted very much until the 1939 war began, the more so since that war was universally held to be noble. But even as it was fought, such values were becoming suspect. The very phrase *Officers and Gentlemen* was given (with no little irony) by Evelyn Waugh to the second novel in his great trilogy about the war, in which the hero Guy Crouchback trains in Scotland with a unit of commandos whose officers have been recruited, as happened in real life, from 'the most blue-blooded' regiments. They are visited by Ian Kilbannock, a peer himself and fine specimen of the upper-class rotter on the make, now a public relations officer in the RAF looking for copy. He does not like what he sees, and warns Crouchback not to expect any favourable publicity for his unit.

'Heroes are in strong demand to boost civilian morale. You'll see pages about the Commandos in the papers soon. But not about your racket, Guy. They just won't do. Delightful fellow, heroes too, I daresay, but the Wrong Period. Last-war stuff, Guy. Went out with Rupert Brooke.'

'You find us poetic?'

'No,' said Ian, stopping in his path and turning to face Guy in the darkness. 'Perhaps not poetic, exactly, but upper class. Hopelessly upper class. You're the "Fine Flower of the Nation". You can't deny it and it *won't do*.'

In the various stages of inebriation, facetiously itemised for centuries, the category 'prophetically drunk' deserves a place.

'This is a People's war,' said Ian prophetically, 'and the People won't have poetry and they won't have flowers. Flowers stink. The upper classes are on the secret list. We want heroes of the People, to or for the People, by with and from the People.'

It took years for Kilbannock's prophecy to come to full fruition, but when it did – when the memory of sacrifice in two great wars faded, of the 'heroes of 1914' and of the fine flower of the nation – the effect would be grave for the Tories. In 1963, Macmillan could still assume that the Household Brigade embodied the highest values, and commend someone who was 'clearly a man who represents the old governing class at its best and those who take a reasonably impartial view of English history know how good that can be'. Nor did the electorate obviously think that the class from which the fourteenth

Earl of Home, as Wilson derisively called him, was so bad. Home led that Cabinet of his schoolfellows into the election a year after the magic circle chose him, and he very nearly won.

And yet even as Macmillan dictated those words, the outlook they expressed was already suspect. No one had foreseen as the twentieth century began the great wars which made ambition virtue for the Tories, which conferred an unexpected prestige on those who fought and died for their country, indirectly on the ideal of gentlemanliness, and on 'the old governing class' which Macmillan had praised in his valediction. All this had quite without any plan conferred in turn a benefit on the Tories. And in turn again, as the memory of those days of glory faded, of the heroism of the Somme and Alamein, so the military virtues would fall into discredit, the very idea of the English gentleman would become suspect, and 'the old governing class' would disappear from politics.

4

Unacceptable Faces

Between the 1959 and 1964 elections, Labour had involuntarily changed leaders, and gone on to win. Between the 1964 and 1966 elections, the Tories voluntarily changed leaders, and went on to lose. That was despite the most dramatic shift of personal emphasis at the head of the party since Disraeli reached the top of the greasy pole in 1868, more even than Bonar Law's replacing Balfour in 1911.

For Macleod, Alec Home's appointment had said the wrong thing about the modern Tory party, made worse by the way it was said, through the arcane medium of the magic circle. In his pasquinade, Macleod insisted that 'contradiction and misrepresentation' lay at the heart of the way Home's succession had been engineered, and added, 'I do not think it is a precedent which will be followed.' And, for all the anger and detraction aroused by Macleod, nor was it. Influenced to whatever degree by him, the party at last decided to elect its leaders.

Even before the events of October 1963, the way the party chose its leader had been described by Humphry Berkeley as 'more appropriate for the enstoolment of an Africa tribal chief' than for a political party in a great democracy. A clever, cocky, young Tory MP, more than a little camp, Berkeley was the son of the playwright Reginald Berkeley, once famous for pieces like *French Leave*. He certainly did not lack self-confidence, as he had shown when, while a Cambridge undergraduate, he had posed as H. Rochester Sneath, an imaginary headmaster who wrote to numerous important personages soliciting advice and stimulating ludicrous responses. In the new year of 1964, after Home's accession, he wrote, under his real name, to the prime minister. He had been convinced even before recent events, Berkeley said, that a new method of choosing a leader was needed and that, since then, 'many talks with our colleagues in the House' had confirmed a widespread view that the existing system should not be used again, adding with almost sarcastic ingratiation that this did not imply 'any criticism of your leadership'. He suggested that the party should set up a small committee to examine the question, to which Home replied, not quite as guilelessly as those taken in by Sneath, that nothing should be done before the next election. But after it came, he followed Berkeley's advice.

First there was a sombre reminder of past glories when Churchill was taken gravely ill in the early days of 1965, at the age of ninety. His death agony over ten days, followed by his magnificent and moving funeral, put into perspective the petty squabbles of Westminster, and maybe made the Tory party seem diminished. Then, just as the party might have been regrouping after the election, it suffered another vexing by-election defeat at Roxburgh, Selkirk and Peebles, at the time a Tory seat. The Conservative candidate was Robin McEwen, a local grandee, heir to a baronetcy, an Etonian, a brilliant academic lawyer, a drinker of international stature who could polish off a bottle of kümmel before luncheon. He was also a man of much charm, which was not seen to best effect during the campaign. A pack of reporters led by George Gale decided to relieve the boredom of the Borders by making a butt of McEwen. Having learnt about an obscure though apparently controversial agricultural subsidy called winter keep, they asked him again and again where he stood on winter keep, until he lost his temper and told them what they could do with their keep, before going on to tell the whole press corps that he disliked and despised the lot of them. If news management can sometimes be carried too far, in Macleod's words, then sometimes a little can help, and that kind of aristocratic *goût de déplaire* was by now going out of fashion. When McEwen lost the seat to the young Liberal David Steel, the Tories were sunk in renewed despondency.

Once again a by-election played an oblique part in political history, and once again the Tory leadership was affected by a newspaper column. Home had been excited by the possibility of becoming leader when Anthony Howard's article observed that the Peerage Act might apply to him; now William Rees-Mogg in the *Sunday Times* wrote elegiacally that Home had 'played the sort of captain's innings one used to see in county cricket before the war' from the kind of amateur who, leading his side because he was a gentleman rather than from pure playing ability, could nevertheless 'by dint of concentration and a well-coached forward prod survive to maybe twenty runs or so and see their side past the follow-on'. For all that, it was now, as the headline said, the 'Right Moment to Change'. Home took the hint, maybe also silently agreeing with those much-quoted words of Cyril Connolly. He was besides cast down by an opinion poll which showed that Wilson was regarded as more honest and sincere than himself, an astonishing verdict given that Wilson was as devious as he was clever and, with all his undoubted skills, by any standards one of the least sincere or honest men ever to be prime minister. Perhaps the poll was more of an indictment of Home's class and generation, and that itself posed a problem for Tories. At any rate, in July Home told the 1922 Committee[1] that he wished to resign.

Devastating as his attack on the magic circle had been, it proved something of a suicide mission for Macleod. It changed the way the Tories chose their leader, and the kind of leader they chose, but it also increased his personal unpopularity. Recognizing that he had no chance of the leadership, he did not even stand in this historic first election. The runners were the other two whom Macmillan had brought forward as *papabile*, Maudling and Heath, and the other dissident of October 1963, Powell. Butler had left politics for a peerage and the Mastership of Trinity, Cambridge (a characteristically nice gesture by Wilson, in whose gift it was), and Hogg knew that his time – and the day of what he represented – had come and gone. Altogether a mark of the defeat of the old guard was that there was no 'White's candidate': the famous aristocratic Tory club in St James's Street was baffled, unable to find one of its own to run; Macmillan's old governing class was losing its nerve, or its will to win. And the party collectively seemed to have learned its lesson almost too well. In a violent mood swing, the Tories had gone from the heart of the aristocracy to three men not at all aristocratic, two of them, Heath and Powell, frankly lower class.

[1] The formal association of the parliamentary party, taking its name from the year of its creation in the wake of Lloyd George's departure.

In Macleod's notorious phrase, eight of the nine conspirators had been to Eton. Less than two years later, none of the three candidates was remotely Etonian. Maudling was an affable, gifted man, a clever undergraduate at Oxford where had taken a First in Greats, a barrister, a wartime 'wingless wonder', who had served in RAF intelligence and the civil service and who had then worked after the war in the Conservative Research Department with Macleod and his Oxford contemporary, Heath. For the public, Maudling was favourite, easily ahead of Heath in opinion polls. In the eyes of conventional opinion he was seen then and even later as the 'right' candidate, one of a succession of such men who should have been chosen as leader but who were not. He would very likely have succeeded Home if the Tories had won in 1964, but he had been a somewhat spendthrift Chancellor for two years before the election, and after it he was blamed for misleading the public while at the Treasury. There were other marks against him. For all his intelligence and geniality, he had already acquired an air of indolence and carelessness. Well before then, civil servants had been concerned about his lack of judgement in business matters – an understatement, as events would prove – and hints of that must have filtered through to the parliamentary party. At any rate, his hopes were soon dashed.

The electoral mechanism which had been devised was not simple plurality or progressive elimination, as Labour practised; refinements had been built in, so that the winner had to gain an absolute majority and a 'surcharge' of 15 per cent more than the next candidate. This might have been a better idea if Tory MPs had been capable of understanding modestly complex arithmetic, but successive leadership elections suggested that they were not. Since MPs were unused to this newfangled election and did not know how to handle it, the choice of Heath might even in some measure have been a mistake: they may have thought that they were administering a playful shock, without actually wanting to elect him. At any rate, in the first ballot Heath won 150 votes, Maudling 133 and Powell a derisory 15; the latter two withdrew and, to satisfy the surcharge requirement, a formal second ballot was held returning Heath *nem. con.* As his friend Sir Edward Boyle well remembered, Maudling was utterly cast down by the vote, which soured him against politics generally, and turned his mind to making money. Powell turned his own mind to the meaning of nationhood and to the threat from immigration. Soon he would return explosively to the forefront of the political stage and would have an enormous, and disastrous, effect on the Conservative story, but he would never again hold office.

In a trite phrase not then current, the Tories had made a statement, almost more surprising and dramatic than Macleod could have wished for, even if it was not immediately clear what the statement was. The election was not decided on ideological grounds, where there was in any case little to choose. Maudling and Powell had been colleagues in the late 1940s, and in the early 1950s had belonged to the One Nation group (taking its name from Disraeli's phrase about the division between two nations), which was a more or less high-minded and mildly romantic faction of young backbench MPs, including Heath and Macleod. The group was devoted to revitalizing the party but could not be categorized in terms of left and right: its members were not free-marketeers or premature monetarists, but neither were they mere Keynesian interventionists and social paternalists, as was often later supposed. They accepted a welfare state but wanted to 'set the people free' economically.

The party had long been far from purely aristocratic in leadership, let alone rank and file: Disraeli, Bonar Law and Chamberlain showed that. But Heath was more obviously plebeian than any of those. It was even more surprising that he had risen as far as he did, from Broadstairs to Oxford, where he was president of the Union, then through the army, the Commons, and the whips' office, without acquiring any social graces or displaying any recognizable personal charm. He had ended a creditable war as a major in the Gunners, after one grim episode: late in the campaign in north-western Europe, he had commanded a firing squad which executed a young Polish soldier convicted of rape. When he revealed this in his memoirs more than half a century later, Auberon Waugh wondered why he had never mentioned it before, if only to win the feminist vote. As much to the point is what effect it might have had on his undoubtedly harsh and joyless personality. Marriage might have smoothed some of the edges, but he remained a bachelor with, as far as anyone knew, no amorous interests; it was an ironical reflection on the sexual revolution and the permissive society, Bernard Levin wrote at the time, that the end of the swinging sixties saw the first prime minister in British history who was a virgin.[2]

He had been made a junior whip as soon as Churchill won the 1951 election, having become an opposition whip shortly before, thanks to the abrupt departure of Sir Walter Bromley-Davenport, a Grenadier, a boxing enthusiast and all in all a Tory of the old school. One evening as a division approached with a three-line whip, Bromley-Davenport had descried a well-dressed man leaving the Palace of Westminster, whom he did not recognize but took to be a recalcitrant Tory wilfully ignoring the vote. Bromley-Davenport tried to make him stop and, since he did not, kicked him downstairs. When the miscreant turned out to be not a Tory MP but the Belgian ambassador, Bromley-Davenport's career as a whip ended and his place was quickly taken by Heath.

If the Tories hoped that by changing the languid Home for the coarser Heath they would transform their electoral fortunes they were disappointed. After a tricky eighteen months, with a slender majority and harried by refractory elements in his own party, Wilson called another election in 1966. A curious but persistent myth took hold that he was influenced by the timing of the football World Cup, or that the result of the election was itself affected by the England team's lucky victory in that competition. The fact was that England won the Cup at Wembley on 30 July, after Labour had won the election on 31 March, and no amount of Wilsonian prestidigitation could show any connection between those, unless perhaps Bobby Moore's side was inspired by political events.

This time there was no problem with the majority. Like Baldwin before him, Wilson in effect asked for a doctor's mandate, and the public gave him one. He won 100 more seats than the Tories, and an absolute majority of 98 seats.[3] It was Labour's one unassailably clear victory in the half-century between 1945 and 1997. Not least, Wilson did what only Attlee before and then Blair later of Labour leaders achieved, winning a majority of English seats and not having to rely

[2] Though was this so? Pitt the Younger and Balfour were bachelors.
[3] Labour: 13 million votes, 47.9 per cent, 363 seats; Tories: 11.4 million, 41.9 per cent, 253 seats; Liberals: 2.3 million, 8.5 per cent, 12 seats.

on Labour's rotten boroughs in the Celtic fringe. Even in 1966 the Tories won easily in southern England, London included, by 140 to Labour's 103. This was a significant sign that the Tories were on their way to becoming an English national party or even a regional party, though one which represented the most important and prosperous part of Great Britain, an ironical reflection on any contrived attempt to invoke the phrase 'One Nation'.

Not often have the sweets of victory turned so sour so soon. In May the government was 'blown off course', in Wilson's self-exculpatory words, by a seamen's strike, to which he reacted as if it were part of a vast conspiracy, a notion which always came naturally to his suspicious mind. Within two months, crisis had engulfed the government, as inflation began to run out of control for the first time in living memory and Wilson invoked what had become the accepted remedy, a freeze on prices, wages and dividends. The country recovered before long, more or less, but Wilson's reputation never did, and the damage went further.

Now the longest-serving of London political columnists, Alan Watkins was writing in 1966 for the *Spectator*, whither he had been lured by Macleod and whence he would depart for the *New Statesman*. He always maintained that those 'July measures' had dealt a mortal blow not to one Labour government alone but to the whole prestige of Fabian managerialism. Not insignificantly, the *New Statesman*, which embodied that Fabian tradition, reached its highest circulation at this time (more than 94,000, under the editorship of Paul Johnson) and then began a steady decline, which later became rapid. Such managerialism had been the central intellectual inspiration of Labour since Sidney Webb wrote its constitution in 1918. It meant the Webbs' own belief that all ills would be cured by the efficient compilation and application of statistics; it meant Douglas Jay's claim, stated with commendable honesty in 1947, that 'the gentleman in Whitehall really does know better what is good for the people than the people know themselves'; it meant Aneurin Bevan's conviction – the more striking because held until his death in 1960 by a genuine democratic socialist who disliked the Communist terror state – that Soviet Russia was bound inexorably to overtake the west economically, since it was axiomatic that a centrally planned command economy must be more efficient and productive than ramshackle competitive market economies.

The Conservatives themselves had supped from the same draught, and the *dégringolade* of 1966 affected them as well as Labour. Butler's Industrial Charter, the One Nation group's 'social Conservatism', Butskellism, the inflationary interventionism of Heathcoat Amory and Maudling at the Treasury, all assumed likewise that the gentleman in Whitehall knew best how to manage the economy. If he did not after all, then there might be something to be learned again from the almost forgotten traditions of the market and strict money supply. The seeds of what became Thatcherism were planted in July 1966.

For the next four years there was little for the Tories to do but sit back and wait. They had a few turmoils of their own. Like Macleod, Powell returned to the opposition front bench, as shadow defence minister, and in 1966 he warned the Tories emphatically that Great Britain should on no account get involved in the American war in Vietnam, advice which would have considerable resonance in the early twenty-first century. Then in April 1968 he made the most famous speech of his life and one of the most significant in postwar British history. At a Conservative meeting in Birmingham, he warned of the dangers brought about by mass immigration from the 'New Commonwealth', which meant the Indian subcontinent and the West Indies, which in turn meant (in an old-fashioned but accurate phrase) people of colour. He spoke of fears that within a generation the black man would have 'the whip hand' over the white man, and rubbed it in with lurid tales of white districts overrun by 'piccaninnies' and persecuted by means of packets of excrement pushed through their letter boxes.

Some of Powell's cleverer disciples on the fogey right would expend a certain amount of nervous energy over the years trying to deny that he, or this speech, was racist. Had he not as a wartime army officer in India taken a keen interest in Indian culture and befriended Indian brother-officers? He had indeed, but to acquit Powell of racism in this way was either disingenuous or wilfully ignorant. Richard Wagner was surrounded by doting Jewish admirers, which scarcely made him a philosemite, on the evidence of his published writings or his private *obiter dicta*; and when Dr Karl Lueger, the leader of the antisemitic Christian Social party and mayor of Vienna in the 1890s, was reproached by a more doctrinaire colleague for dining with rich Jews, he replied, 'Wer e' Jüd' is, döss bestimm' i'' ('I decide who's a Yid'). Powell evidently thought he could decide who was 'coloured'. In a celebrated passage from his speech he said that he was filled with foreboding: 'Like the Roman, I seem to see "the River Tiber foaming with much blood"', by which he intended Virgil and the passage in the *Aeneid*, 'Thybrim multo spumantem sanguine cerno'. After the storm had broken Powell said he was sorry that he had not left this in the original. But then what is the Latin for 'piccaninny'?

Without hesitation, Heath sacked his old friend Powell from the shadow cabinet, and the friendship between Powell and Macleod was clouded. His run-in with Salisbury had only strengthened Macleod's dislike of late-imperial racism, and he was one of a handful of Tory MPs who voted against the Wilson government's timorous and demagogic legislation to keep out East African Asians. Macleod was respectful of Powell's abilities, less so of his judgement: 'I take Enoch's train part of the way but get off before it hits the buffers,' he said, and on another occasion, 'Poor Enoch, driven mad by the relentlessness of his own logic.' But it was to be Powell who cast much the longer shadow over the Tories for the next thirty years and more.

If the Wilson government had been blown off course by the seamen's strike, still harsher winds blew in 1969. In Ulster, simmering conflict erupted into full-scale violence which the Unionist government of Northern Ireland was quite incapable of dealing with. The government was torn apart over the plans for union reform known as 'In Place of Strife', and divided over Europe. Not many members of the first Wilson government emerged with credit, although two who did were on the revisionist right of the party. Denis Healey as Defence Secretary was the only man apart from Wilson to hold the same office throughout 1964–70, and he managed the job more capably than many Tories had done or would do. He had been a rival of Roy Jenkins since Oxford three decades earlier when Healey was a keen young Communist and Jenkins had led the opposing democratic socialists. By now they were almost indistinguishable politically, but personal antipathy held them apart, and weakened their cause.

In his two years at the Home Office Jenkins managed to make himself, as he would remain until his death, as much a *bête noire* as Powell was a hero to the noisy Tory right, who thereby demonstrated their political ignorance and their incomprehension. He was portrayed as the only begetter of the 'permissive society' thanks to legislation which decriminalized adult homosexuality, permitted abortion in limited circumstances and made divorce easier. He had already as a backbencher sponsored the law which granted a defence of literary merit in obscenity cases, and he warmly supported the abolition of capital punishment which had followed the Labour victory in 1964.

Later the Jenkins reforms would be held up by the fogey right as symptoms of moral decay. Certainly the times they were a-changing, as a gruesome Bob Dylan song put it, and sexual morality had changed more than most things. But this had very little to do with party politics or left and right. Jenkins's detractors quite forgot, if they ever knew, the background to all these developments. At the end of the 1950s there was universal agreement that the law on obscenity was in a state of complete disarray. The Jenkins Act was intended to clarify the position and make life easier and fairer for writers and publishers. As much to the point, it was supported inside parliament by paladins of romantic High Toryism such as Hugh Fraser and Lord Lambton, and outside by Sir A. P. Herbert, the whimsical humorist, who threatened to stand at a by-election to the Tories' disadvantage if parliamentary time were not made available, and Herbert, if not a conventional Conservative, was no radical.[4]

That law apart, none of the liberal Home Office reforms was Jenkins's own work or a government measure – they were all private bills, the abortion bill being sponsored by Steel, the victor of Roxburgh, Selkirk and Peebles – and he merely took a friendly view of them by granting them parliamentary time. They were all endorsed as well as opposed across the political spectrum. The divorce, homosexuality and abortion reforms were supported not only by a liberal Tory such as Ian Gilmour but by Ronald Bell, often described as belonging to the hard right of the party but an authentic libertarian. For that matter, Powell was among other things an opponent of capital

[4]He had defeated the official Conservative candidate for Oxford University when it still had its own MPs, and then himself had brought in an earlier law to ease divorce.

punishment throughout his parliamentary career, a stain on his record forgotten by his more vehement admirers.[5]

For the last two-and-a-half years of the Wilson government Jenkins was Chancellor, when the future biographer of the GOM exercised a truly Gladstonian rectitude in his custodianship of the public purse. So much so that he was blamed for losing the 1970 election by refusing to cut taxes and inflate the economy as electoral sops, though he was also admired for his honesty by Margaret Thatcher, among others. Whatever his responsibility, the fact was that from 1966 to 1979, three successive governments ended in defeat – Labour, Conservative and Labour again: not merely electoral but administrative and moral defeat, which raised the question, much discussed at this time, of whether the country was governable. For all Jenkins's sensible budgets, the Wilson government had quite failed to resolve the besetting problems of low economic growth and trade union power, the last after a capitulation engineered by Callaghan. The uncured 'British disease' remained a commonplace of gloomy analysis.

Although the Wilson ministry was petering out, Heath had no clear or distinctive programme, and his opponents flattered him when they said otherwise. In January 1970, a matter of months before the election, the shadow cabinet met at Selsdon Park, an inelegant businessman's hotel near Croydon. There was no deep discussion of strategy, only some idle chatter about legislative priorities, little more than a working lunch writ large. But when asked what they had been up to, Heath blurted something about discussing law and order, which gave Wilson an opening. Always tactically clever at exploiting his enemies' weaknesses, he sneered that 'Selsdon Man is not just a lurch to the Right, it is an atavistic desire to reverse the course of twenty-five years of social revolution. What they are planning is a wanton, calculated and deliberate return to inequality.' What they were planning was nothing of the kind, or nothing at all, and Wilson may have done Heath a favour by making him more popular than he had intended and attributing to him a programme more coherent than he possessed.

Or than Macleod did. In June 1970 Wilson went to the polls in

[5] At a *Spectator* party in 1979, when there was a debate on restoring the death penalty, I asked if he was going to vote and he said in his baleful way, 'Do you think you know how I shall be voting?', as of course I did.

confident mood, only to be astonished by the result. It was a two-horse race: this was the last election of the twentieth century at which the third party won less than 10 per cent of the vote; and it was the last at which the Tories won more than 45 per cent of the popular vote.[6] Macleod returned to sit on the Treasury Bench as Chancellor, for all of five weeks. Barely had he begun his new work than he died of a sudden heart attack, at the age of fifty-six. It was a peculiarly bitter blow for the Tories, and provided a kind of grim finality as the sixties closed. Macleod was never going to become prime minister, as he knew very well, but he might have influenced the direction the party took, and he would almost certainly have made a better fist of running the Treasury than his successor. His death was a poignant might-have-been.

In the interpretation of history which would later be formulated by an increasingly influential academic-journalistic right, Heath was an utterly hopeless prime minister and his government an unmitigated disaster. That was silly, but no one could honestly call the government a success. Heath did achieve the one goal on which he had set his heart, entry into what was then the Common Market, although even there he left himself open to the charge of contradiction and misrepresentation (to borrow Macleod's words), by maintaining that the European enterprise was essentially an economic project, when he knew very well that it had long had a goal of political union, and that no essential sovereignty was being surrendered, when he knew that it was.

In their management of the economy, the Tories fared no better in 1970–74 than the previous government, and in some ways they fared worse. Attempts to control the unions through legislation and industrial courts came to little more than 'In Place of Strife' had done, and the miners, led by the militant Arthur Scargill, scored a great victory over the government in 1972 through the use of flying pickets. Scargill became a hero to the left, both industrial and intellectual. He was reverentially interviewed in the *New Left Review*, the organ of English neo-Marxism, whose expensively educated ideologues sat at his feet

[6] Tories: 13.1 million votes, 46.4 per cent, 330 seats; Labour: 12.2 million, 43 per cent, 287 seats; Liberals: 2.5 million, 7.5 per cent, 6 seats.

absorbing his wisdom to produce a general effect rather as though the Jehovah's Witnesses had been granted an exclusive interview after the Second Coming.

Buffeted and baffled, Heath and his Chancellor, Anthony Barber, flirted with new-found monetarist doctrines but in 1972 made a complete volte-face. They not only unleashed what proved rampant inflation, they intervened in the everyday running of industry in defiance of all free-market principles. One of Heath's first appointments was John Davies, an outsider whose tenure as Trade and Industry Secretary proved embarrassing and short-lived, not least because he was a hopeless performer in the Commons. Although it was truly said that when Enoch made a joke it was no laughing matter, Powell was capable of a kind of sarcastic humour, as in his stage aside during one of Davies's first appearances on the Treasury Bench, 'We've got a right one here.' One very brief mark in parliamentary rhetoric was made by Davies when he said in the November after taking office that 'the essential need of the country is to gear its policy to the great majority of the people, who are not lame ducks.'[7] But before long the Heath government had filled a whole pond with lame ducks.

Before his time was up, in a worse departure from free-market principles, in contradiction of previous assurances, and as a mark of sheer despair, Heath even embarked on a statutory incomes policy. All experience had shown that such state control of wages and prices could not work without voluntary restraint, which would make state control unnecessary in the first place, or without a near-totalitarian control of the political economy. The degree to which Heath was ill at ease with the unrestrained free market was revealed more vividly still when a scandal around the colourful Lonrho company erupted in 1973, and he condemned 'the unpleasant and unacceptable face of capitalism'. It was another member of the Cabinet, Peter Walker, who coined his own unintentionally memorable phrase when he said that the government was suffering from 'problems of success'; that was far from the case then, though it would later be more apt.

But it was other unacceptable faces which stared at Heath, in Ulster,

[7] In reply to an opposition demand for safeguards 'against the support of lame ducks' voiced by of all people Anthony Wedgwood Benn.

where violence worsened until the Stormont parliament was suspended in 1972, and still more among the unions invigorated by their successes. In the end Heath himself gambled for high stakes. He was encouraged in this by Lord Carrington. A prime specimen of the Tory old guard, patriotic and brave, a wartime Grenadier and MC, Carrington's political career had been a long line of accidents whose consequences he had nimbly avoided. He had been a junior agriculture minister as far back as the early fifties and had been involved in the Crichel Down affair which forced the resignation of his chief, Sir Thomas Dugdale; he had been First Lord of the Admiralty at the time of the Vassall scandal; and now, after serving as Defence Secretary, he was moved to Energy as the government faced its great crisis. The latest Arab–Israeli war had led to the quadrupling of the price of oil. The government responded with power cuts and a three-day week, and then at the beginning of 1974, urged on by Carrington, Heath called an election on the challenge 'Who governs Britain?'

Young barristers are taught that the first rule of examination-in-chief is never to ask a question to which you don't know the answer. This would not be a bad rule for politicians either. In answer to his question, Heath was told by the electorate: Not you. The result was inconclusive. Labour won four more seats than the Tories but not an absolute majority while the Tories had a slim lead in the popular vote.[8] Rather than resign, Heath began bargaining to stay in office. This was portrayed as wrongful and unconstitutional – in the words of Marcia Williams, later Lady Falkender, Wilson's formidable secretary, it was 'as if the referee had blown the whistle and one side had refused to leave the field' – but it was not so. It is a quite recent idea that the general election itself must immediately change the government, with a concession in the small hours on the morrow of polling day, immediately followed by furniture vans at Downing Street.

Under parliamentary government the prime minister is he who at any moment can command a majority in the primary or lower house of the legislature, or at least command a parliamentary grouping not so far defeated in the Commons, but the rules of the game had

[8] Labour: 11.6 million votes, 37.1 per cent, 301 seats; Tories: 11.8 million, 37.9 per cent, 297 seats; Liberals: 6 million, 19.3 per cent, 14 seats; Others (mainly Celtic fringes) 23 seats.

long been more elaborate than that bald summary suggests. A prime minister could at any time ask for a dissolution, which the sovereign would certainly grant. Or a prime minister could at any time resign, whereupon the sovereign might try to find someone else to form a government. Sometimes this was a ruse, as when Gladstone resigned in 1873: Disraeli was too wily to accept the invitation and Gladstone had to continue in office. In December 1905, the Unionist government still had some time to run and still had a clear majority, but Balfour chose to resign, and this time Campbell-Bannerman picked up the gauntlet, asking for his own dissolution as soon as he took office. Even after elections with a clear result, it had once been the custom for the government to remain in office until parliament met and the ministry was defeated. So Heath was within his rights, in a limited way.

And yet his attempt to hold on to power seemed pigheaded; if not unconstitutional, it was characteristically clumsy and grace-less. Nor did he recognize how much the political landscape had changed. When he entered parliament in 1950, there had only been nine Liberals and three 'others' out of 625 MPs, and the Conservative ranks had included, as they did for most of half a century from 1922, up to a dozen 'UUs', Ulster Unionists, who voted tamely with the Conservatives. Now the Union was beginning to fracture, and those twenty-three Others comprised Scottish and Welsh Nationalists, and 'Unionists' most of whom were in reality now Ulster nationalists and had fled the Tory fold. Heath may have tried to lure some of them back; he certainly held long conversations with Jeremy Thorpe, the Liberal leader. The full story of this only emerged from the official archives in 2005. When Heath and Thorpe met secretly, the prime minister proposed a centre-right coalition, arguing that Tories and Liberals were united in support of the Common Market and of a statutory incomes policy. Thorpe went even further, suggesting a 'grand alliance' of all three parties on the model of the 1931 National government, but he made it clear that any such coalition would have to be led by someone other than Heath, presumably Whitelaw. On top of the inevitable stumbling block of electoral reform, Heath's displeasure at the idea of giving way killed the negotiations, although Thorpe expressed sympathy: 'This is obviously hell – a nightmare on stilts for you.'

One way or another, a nightmare was certainly unfolding for Heath. His attempt to hang on ended in a way which made him seem even more incompetent, and drove one more nail in his coffin as party leader. Having formed a government in February, Wilson asked for another dissolution within months, as he was entitled and almost obliged to do. Labour very slightly increased its vote and seats at the October 1974 election, to leave Wilson with one more seat than an absolute majority.[9] He was in for a bumpy ride. But not as bumpy as Heath, who had now fought four elections as party leader and lost three. In increasing the Labour seats by eighteen, that second election within eight months might not have been a resounding vote of confidence in Wilson; in decreasing the number of Tory seats by twenty it was clearly a vote of no confidence in Heath by the British people, soon to be echoed by his parliamentary colleagues.

Like nations or like families, political parties have an unconscious instinct, and change their course without knowing why, or even knowing quite what has happened. The Tory party repeatedly did this over forty years, often to the astonishment of observers. In the conventional wisdom of the moment, Tories had each time made the wrong choice of leader: Home instead of Butler in 1963, Heath instead of Maudling in 1965, Thatcher instead of Whitelaw in 1975, Major instead of Heseltine in 1990, Hague instead of Clarke in 1997. Each of these choices was a surprise at the time, and yet the evidence does not necessarily suggest that each choice was so wrong.

For all Macleod's admiration, Butler had shown his lack of steel by the very way he failed to seize the leadership. Maudling's financial waywardness might easily have brought disgrace on the party as well as himself if he had been leader. Whitelaw was at best an amiable old buffer of a type whose demise the Tories later had some cause to regret, but at worst an ineffectual booby (for whose abilities Thatcher expressed little admiration in private), whom it is very hard to imagine winning three elections. And either Heseltine or Clarke, for all their ability, might have torn the party to pieces even quicker than happened in any case.

[9] Labour: 11.4 million votes, 39.2 per cent, 319 seats; Tories: 10.5 million, 35.8 per cent, 277 seats; Liberals: 5.3 million, 18.3 per cent, 13 seats; Others: 26 seats.

Still, by whatever standards, the events of 1975 were astonishing at the time, and scarcely less so in retrospect. Not many people saw Margaret Thatcher coming, and when she arrived the British didn't quite know what had hit them. After the failures of the Heath government, after the humiliating sequence of events in 1973–4, Heath's stock in his own party was low; once he was defeated in October 1974 his days were numbered. A Tory leader in power as prime minister who loses the support of the Cabinet cannot survive, as Mrs Thatcher would one day learn; a Tory leader in opposition who loses the support of the executive of the 1922 Committee cannot survive either, and that was the case by the autumn of 1974. Nor was Heath helped by personal factors, the way he had antagonized so many colleagues, and in particular the fact that he had sacked Edward Du Cann from the chairmanship of the party in 1967. Thus the whirligig of time brings in its revenges: seven years later found Du Cann chairman of the 1922.

One of the more fascinating bit players in the Tory drama, Du Cann had been known as 'the Duke' to his close-knit, and in hindsight remarkable, circle of Oxford friends, the bibulous group at St John's led by Kingsley Amis and Philip Larkin. He had risen fairly high, but not very high, in politics, and he aroused a suspicion which could not be quite pinned down. Alan Watkins memorably said that conversation with Du Cann was disconcerting, like walking down a flight of stairs and missing the last step. He even played up to this evasive reputation: when a colleague asked him the time, he replied, 'What time would you like it to be?' Yet another Tory with a chiaroscuro financial life, he had been a director of Lonrho, the very company which inspired Heath's phrase about the unacceptable face of capitalism. He had a score to settle.

Despite its halting attempts to democratize itself, the Conservative party still had only the recognized means for choosing a new leader when the last one had gone quietly, or at least gone: a 'sit. vac.' had to be created before it was advertised, and there was no mechanism for mounting a challenge to an incumbent who refused to budge. That would now change. By December 1974, a committee under Home had looked into the matter and recommended that in future an election could take place annually, so long only as a challenger could find a proposer and seconder, an innovation which came to be known as 'Alec's revenge'. Home also advised that the existing rule, that to be elected someone should need not just a majority of votes but a 'surcharge' of 15 per cent, should apply as a percentage of all eligible MPs, rather than, as before, of votes cast. That would one day have fateful results, although it was in any case clear from the beginning that the electoral system was simply beyond the intellectual capacity of many MPs. In 1965, there had been an element of perversity, of MPs wanting to cock a snook at the establishment and put the wind up the grandees, without necessarily changing the order of things; that was truer still in 1975, when the MPs again made a choice they may not fully have intended.

If anything it was surprising that Heath had lasted as long as he had, given not only his political failures but how unfailingly graceless or downright rude he was to everyone he dealt with. His awkwardness and gruffness were notorious throughout Westminster, as well as his lack of any form of pleasing manner, or even of basic good manners. He would greet such a well-known – and influential – journalist as Peter Jenkins with the words, 'So *you*'re here, are you?' Or, when Airey Neave, as a junior minister, suffered a heart attack, Heath's response was, 'So that's the end of your political career, then.' When Heath's position became precarious, not only was Du Cann crucially placed, but Neave led Mrs Thatcher's campaign for the leadership.

The end of Heath's own political career on the front bench was approaching faster than he knew. This was one of the subterranean revolutions the Tories specialized in, and there was at first no obvious doctrinal as opposed to personal basis for the challenge, although one man was undergoing his own conversion to a new politics. Sir Keith Joseph was the scion of a prominent Anglo-Jewish family with a fortune from the building trade, a very clever as well as – in a strangulatedly neurotic way – charming man, a Fellow of All Souls with a good wartime record in the Gunners. When he entered parliament at a by-election in 1956, there were dozens of Jewish MPs on the Labour benches, but he was then one of only two Jews on the Tory side, something which would one day change dramatically.

With all the bigotry Disraeli had himself encountered, and which could still be found in the party well into the second half of the twentieth century, he had made one of his more astute observations when he said that 'The persecution of the Jewish race has deprived European society of an important conservative element and added to the destructive party an influential ally.' From the 1960s, a group of American savants who had begun life on the left, often the far left, began to desert the Democrats and move steadily rightwards as 'neo-conservatives'. Most of them were Jewish, and the proximate cause of their disenchantment was the question of Israel, once loved but then spurned by the liberal left. That question mercifully never played the same part in British politics, but British Jews also began to move away from a reflexive identification with the 'destructive party' of the left.

As a junior minister in the Macmillan government Joseph had followed Macmillan's own lead in building ever more dwellings with Soviet zeal, many of a new type, tower blocks of flats. Plenty of mistakes were made by politicians and planners in the thirty years after 1945, but none quite as unforgivable as this. In the name of slum clearance, vast numbers of the poor had already – before the war, mostly under Tory administrations – been decanted into huge, dreary, one-class housing estates, of which Orwell had said that they were better than the insanitary back-to-back houses in mean streets, but not much better. Now hideous towers sprang up on the edge of almost every city in the country, into which more of the working classes could be poured, a policy begun by the Tories and then continued by Labour politicians such as Dick Crossman.

Nowhere was this worse than in Scotland. Those of us covering the 1978 by-election in Garscadden – when the seat was retained for Labour by the young lawyer Donald Dewar – found a terrifying spectacle. Garscadden held the national record at the time for the constituency with the highest proportion of its inhabitants who were housed in municipal dwellings: 96 per cent. And what dwellings! An outer suburb of Glasgow had become a forest of vile cheaply built concrete towers. It might have been Magnitogorsk. This was what the left's vision – shared by many Tories – had come to.

In truth, Labour had always been driven by dreams of human liberation, but also by more mundane objects. Sidney Webb wrote the party's socialist constitution of 1918, Clause Four and all; and it was he who had once said: 'The perfect and fitting development of each individual is not necessarily the utmost and highest cultivation of his own personality, but the filling, in the best possible way, of his humble function in the great social machine.' Even in the 1970s there were still plenty on the left who hated the idea of a prosperity which would remove the workers from the class into which they were born; now the Tories could find a new mission of their own in liberating the individual from the great social machine.

By the 1970s, Joseph had begun to see the error of his statist and collectivist ways. Intense and highly strung, he would sometimes literally beat his breast, gesticulating and writhing with anguish as he contemplated his past folly. More calmly, he began to study anew the great tradition of economic and social liberalism, which had been almost submerged by the high tide of socialism in mid-century but had been kept afloat by writers such as F. A. von Hayek and Ludwig von Mises, with their belief that the competitive free market was ultimately the most humane as well as the most productive of all systems. And Joseph began, with the joy of the convert, to use language rarely heard before from Tories: 'I want to put to you the moral and ethical case for capitalism.'

He was now seen as the first likely challenger to Heath. Maybe Joseph was never entirely plausible as a potential premier, even before he managed, with an endearing mixture of candour and ineptitude, to put himself out of contention with a speech in which he discussed the fact that the lower socio-economic sectors of the population – the lumpenproletariat, the poor – had more children than the educated classes and were doomed to permanent welfare dependency as a self-perpetuating underclass. The American journalist Michael Kinsley once observed that what we call a 'political gaffe' is whenever a politician tells the truth: not the absolute or objective truth, whatever that might be, but just what he honestly thinks at the time. Joseph's speech was a gaffe and a half. He was touching on a perfectly serious subject, but in his holy-fool innocence he allowed himself to be represented as a rich baronet complaining that the lower classes bred like rabbits, or, still worse, as a Jew who seemed to be echoing National Socialist rhetoric about 'racial hygiene' or 'life unworthy of life'. All that was unfair, no doubt, but the episode did raise the question of whether Joseph was fit to lead a great party, or even fit to be out on his own.

His real importance was in the influence he had on another Tory, whose ascent had gone almost unnoticed. Just after the second 1974 election, an MP introduced herself to two journalists as 'Sir Keith's campaign manager for the leadership'. Most people at Westminster realized that, once the new procedure for a leadership election had been set in motion, Heath's fate was sealed, but very few guessed that this woman would be his nemesis. Almost the only journalist who did predict the ascent of Margaret Hilda Thatcher was the fascinating, doomed figure of Patrick Cosgrave, a clever, cocksure, dissolute Dubliner who had come to Cambridge and then to London where he saw himself as the Burke *de ses jours* and attached himself to sundry causes and persons, from Israel to Mrs Thatcher. She regarded him and his excesses with the mildly sarcastic tolerance she showed towards many of the eccentrics who gravitated into her orbit, unflappable even on the occasion when Cosgrave harangued her pausing in his oration only briefly to be sick. He later drifted away, and died before his time, but his role as Mrs Thatcher's John the Baptist, or at least Sancho Panza, deserves to be recorded.

Even when Mrs Thatcher announced her intention to stand, it was assumed by almost every lobby correspondent and columnist that she would act as a stalking horse (an image beloved of commentators who had no experience of field sports and no idea what such a horse did), and that if she shook Heath from his perch she would open the way for William Whitelaw, one of the remaining old guard, a Wykehamist, a Guardsman, an MC, a Cabinet minister under Heath, and – what he surely regarded as the greatest honour of all – a sometime Captain of the R & A at St Andrews. 'Willie' was a master of the mildly surreal malapropism, as when he accused Labour of 'Going around stirring up apathy', or averred that 'The Archbishop of Canterbury is a very religious man.' He was a loyalist through and through, who could never have been the first to challenge Heath, but waited on events.

They did not wait on him. Once more with an air of devilment, the Tory MPs voted on 4 February 1975. Again there was no White's candidate. Sir Christopher Soames, Etonian, Coldstreamer,

Churchill's son-in-law, had been an MP before losing his seat, and was then made ambassador in Paris and vice-president of the European Commission. There was some talk of his returning to politics and even being a potential successor to Heath, but nothing came of it. A friend once told Macleod he had heard that behind Soames's bluff exterior there was a keen mind, to which Macleod replied, 'Believe you me, behind that bluff exterior there lurks a remarkably bluff interior', and the Tories silently decided that his bluffness was not what they now needed. The one representative of unideological traditional High Toryism who did stand was Hugh Fraser, a most engaging, melancholy man, who won 16 votes. Heath won 119, and Thatcher 130. Accepting inevitable defeat, Heath withdrew with angry ill grace and began to sulk, for thirty years as it proved. Now Whitelaw stood, as well as three others, Geoffrey Howe, James Prior and John Peyton, who respectively won 19, 19 and 11 votes in the second ballot. It had been widely supposed that Whitelaw would come into his inheritance, but the Tory MPs on this occasion followed the logic of their position – as they did not fifteen years later – and chose the one who had showed the courage to strike the blow. Whitelaw won 79 votes, and Thatcher an absolute victory with 146.

Thus began one of the most extraordinary episodes in British political history, and thus ended a strange and unhappy passage in the evolution of the Tory party. Within less than twelve years the patrician magic circle so derided by Macleod had faded away but the party had not quite decided what to put in its place. Likewise the collectivist and consensual policies pursued from Baldwin until Heath had been discredited by failure. Intellectually and ideologically as well as socially, and almost without any collective conscious knowledge of what it was doing, the Conservative party had chosen to take a quite new direction. 'Is it a revolt?' Louis XVI had asked about the commotion in the streets of Paris in July 1789, to be told, 'No, sire, it is a revolution.' Whether the Tories realized it or not, that was just what they had embarked on.

5

Rejoice!

When Mrs Thatcher became leader of the opposition, the Labour government still had more than four years to run, and dismal years they were. Scarcely any government from the 1950s to the 1980s could be accounted a complete success by any measure, but the Labour government of 1974–9 was in a class of its own, with few positive achievements to its credit except a grim struggle to survive. That did not mean that Mrs Thatcher and the Tories lorded it over the government; to the contrary, her opposition years were nothing like as confident as later hagiographers would like to pretend. She was feeling her way towards one more reinvention of Toryism, and did not launch her attack, political, personal or ideological, until well after she became prime minister. Nor did she have any kind of easy ride in parliament or with the public at first.

Events ran her way all the same, as the government staggered from one crisis to another, and as the Labour party grew ever more fractious. Rather more than a year after Mrs Thatcher deposed Heath, Harold Wilson resigned. She had not cut an impressive figure against him during that interval. He had been sharpening his skill in repartee on one side of the despatch box or the other, as opposition leader or prime minister, for many years, and he was more than a match for a woman who, with all her courage, was still unsure of herself, and he more often than not crushed and demoralized her at question time. His departure was one of her early strokes of luck.

Worldly-wise observers have maintained that there was no mystery about Wilson's resignation in March 1976: he had been saying privately that he wanted to depart for some time past, and he may well have been conscious of imminently declining powers, the first hints of the senile dementia which enveloped him in later years.[1] But an episode is surprising if it comes as a surprise, which Wilson's announcement certainly did, the atmosphere heightened by every kind of lurid rumour and then by a resignation honours list some of whose names were plucked from among his weird entourage of 'entrepreneurs' and plain crooks.

He left behind a government and party in disarray. In 1974 Wilson had promised a referendum on continued membership of the Common Market once he had somewhat speciously renegotiated terms. This was an election stunt, and a way of holding his party together, although togetherness was not quite the word. When the referendum came, it was decided quite absurdly that his Cabinet could agree to differ on this, the most important question of the age, some campaigning for and some against. The opposition by contrast – and still more of a contrast to the spectacle the Tories would present twenty years later – appeared to be less bitterly divided, although there were seeds of disaster already sown. Enoch Powell had finally left the party in disgust and in protest at adherence to the Common Market, more than hinting that his followers should vote Labour in the first 1974 election. At the second election that year he returned as a Unionist Member for a seat in Northern Ireland, in Hailsham's words having found another cause to betray. That may not have been fair, but he certainly continued to infect the Tories from outside with an ideological virus which would produce pathological symptoms for decades to come.

For Powell and the 'Powellites', as some of them were happy to call themselves, the crucial word was sovereignty. England, or the United Kingdom, or 'Britain' (a solecistic and highly ambiguous term for all its universal currency), was a sovereign state and that was that. Its sovereignty was impossibly compromised by membership of the Common Market, although not many of Powell's disciples followed his own logic and supposed that it was equally compromised by the American alliance. The same word was flourished in the context of

[1] When this flawed but amiable man would push a trolley round his local supermarket and stop people to tell them that he used to be prime minister. The decline may have been accelerated by his consumption, unknown to the public or even many colleagues, of a bottle of brandy a day during his years in office.

Ulster, and in both cases the ideological right was acquiring a tendency to make good cases badly. The obsession with sovereignty showed a lack of historical understanding which Samuel Johnson had exposed two centuries earlier (in the matter of 'Falkland's islands'); in Europe and in Ulster, the real question was democracy and not sovereignty.

After Wilson, Labour MPs might have chosen either Roy Jenkins or Denis Healey on the social democratic right of the party or Michael Foot on the romantic or Little England left. However, rather as, when the zealous followers of Austen Chamberlain and Walter Long could not stomach each other in 1911, the Tories compromised on Bonar Law, James Callaghan won as the least unwanted man. The atmosphere inside the Labour leadership was warmer and more loyal than ever. Barbara Castle was desperate to exclude Callaghan because of their fight over 'In Place of Strife', the proposed union reforms of 1968–9, while other candidates fought sharp little personal battles. Healey was routed, while Anthony Wedgwood Benn, the former Lord Stansgate, a patrician who had followed the tradition of the Roman republic and assumed plebeian status in the guise of 'Tony' Benn, won a few votes, as did C. A. R. Crosland, more admired by chattering highbrow society than by his colleagues. Roy Hattersley was ostensibly a friend and supporter of Tony Crosland. When Hattersley turned up at his office and asked if he wanted to know why he wasn't voting for him, Crosland replied, 'No. Fuck off.' This was a good party to be opposing.

And it turned out to be a good time to be leading the Tories for other reasons besides. Although it was not yet entirely obvious, the whole social-democratic managerialist tradition, and indeed the consensual corporatist tradition of Heath and Maudling, was now imploding faster than ever, ten years after the 1966 crisis. That version of social democracy had been given its last most eloquent expression in 1956 by Crosland in *The Future of Socialism*. In Roy Jenkins's words, 'It assumed the triumph of Keynesianism, and with it a future of broadening abundance and the withering of the Marxist class struggle . . . [There was] no conflict which could not be resolved by the flowing tide of continuing economic growth' and the only problem was how the state should distribute this larger and larger cake. On the other hand, Crosland had at least tried to break free of the Webbs' joyless and jejune vision, and had suggested that there might be more to life than 'total abstinence and a good filing system'.

Less than a year after his woefully unsuccessful bid for the leadership, Crosland died suddenly. In the previous few years he had begun to rethink his own legacy, perceiving that the welfare state had become largely a racket run in favour of the middle classes, and recognizing that profligate spending by local government could not continue: as he said in 1975, 'the party's over'. He would have been insulted by the idea that he was an indirect apostle of Thatcherism, but there was a link between his recognition of the failures of statism and the limits of government action, as well as his understanding of the simple desire of ordinary men and women to have a good time, and the tenor of Mrs Thatcher's government.

More generally the party was over for the government. Although most people were still in work and better off than before (as they had been during the 'hungry thirties', for that matter), every economic indicator went more and more awry in the little more than three years of Callaghan's premiership, until 1979 when, by most unhappy statistical coincidence, inflation and interest rates both reached 17 per cent. This took the form of 'stagflation', as economic growth slowed down to half a percentage point, or effectively nil. Callaghan returned from an international summit meeting in the West Indies in January 1979 and said breezily that most people elsewhere in the world would not 'share the view that there is mounting chaos', which the *Sun* paraphrased as 'Crisis? What crisis?'

Most people in the prime minister's own country had no difficulty discerning crisis and chaos, with the 'winter of discontent' at its darkest and coldest. A lorry drivers' strike demanding a 25 per cent pay rise was followed by strikes of public sector workers, a million and a half of them by the end of January. Hospitals took only emergency patients (as defined by the unions), rubbish piled up in the streets, and the dead lay unburied. During the course of the year, one industrial dispute closed ITV for twelve weeks and another closed *The Times* for eleven months.

One of the bitterest verdicts was given by Sir Nicholas Henderson, the British ambassador to Paris. In the summer of 1979, shortly after the election, he described in a despatch home how his country was viewed in Europe. British GDP per head had fallen to 46 per cent below the German level and 41 per cent below the French. 'Our economic decline in relation to our European partners has been so marked that today we are not only no longer a world power, but we are not in the first rank even as a European one.'

From the second 1974 election Labour had enjoyed the barest of parliamentary majorities which then dwindled away, and Callaghan was reduced to cutting patently cynical deals with the Liberals and with the Ulster Unionists. The latter were granted an increase in the number of Northern Ireland seats in the Commons, which was a corrupt sop, even if abstract justice commended it. Likewise plans for devolved government in Scotland and Wales were brought in by the government for reasons of calculation rather than conviction, but this proved Callaghan's undoing. When the Lib–Lab alliance was formed in the spring of 1977 Mrs Thatcher moved a motion of no confidence without success; it was a trial run.

As though she remembered the saying that governments lose elections rather than oppositions win them, Mrs Thatcher approached the 1979 election with considerable caution; there was as yet no sign that she would follow radical policies or purge the party. She had disposed of one or two colleagues while in opposition, notably Maudling, who was very angry indeed to be kicked off the front bench while further financial disgrace enveloped him, but the party was in many ways little changed from Heath's days or even Home's. Its benches contained more than a sprinkling of MPs very much redolent of another age, some of them still found in the whips' office, such as Spencer le Marchant, an Etonian of antique intellect and drinking habits.[2] And in

[2] When he ordered 'a pint' in one of the innumerable bars which fill the Palace of Westminster, he intended a pint tankard of champagne, though that was far from his only tipple. One day at eleven in the morning he summoned his young colleague Cecil Parkinson to discuss whipping matters in 'the Kremlin' (one of those many bars, so-called because it was formerly frequented for their own intrigues by the left-wing Tribune group), where he ordered two large Bloody Marys. When they were drunk, Parkinson ordered his round. As he could foresee yet another round being bought by le Marchant, and as it was still well before noon, with a long day ahead, Parkinson thought of a tactful excuse, and said he wouldn't have another, as he found too much tomato juice acidic at that time of day. Le Marchant pondered this deeply, then said, 'Quite right', and turned to the barman to order 'Two large Bloody Marys without the tomato juice.'

general the parliamentary Tories were much as they had been a decade earlier, a mixture of the upper-class old guard, hard-faced men who had done well out of the unacceptable face of capitalism, and professional politicians on the make.

In theory, the fact that he can call for a dissolution when he wants gives a prime minister a great electoral advantage, but in practice this advantage can be difficult to realize. Callaghan dithered through 1978, when the omens seemed good for him, or not so bad, and when the conventional political wisdom (as was forgotten later) held that a party led by a woman would be severely handicapped in the eyes of the electorate. By the spring his position had collapsed. On top of union anarchy, the government's cynical and self-serving proposals for devolved government in Scotland and Wales were defeated in referendums (in the Scottish case, not meeting a threshold which a Labour backbencher had set). At the end of March Mrs Thatcher moved another no confidence motion. Amid high drama, with MPs being dragged from their sickbeds, Irish nationalists being plied with plentiful whiskey by Labour whips, and one of those Fenians refusing all inducements to vote but nevertheless turning up at Westminster 'to abstain in person', the government was defeated by one vote. It was only the second time in the twentieth century that a government had fallen on a Commons vote, following the demise of the first, minority Labour government in 1924.

Even as the election was called, not many foresaw the outcome. The electorate had increased by a million since the last election, but two million more voted, with an increase in turnout from 72.8 to 76 per cent. The Labour vote remained almost exactly what it had been, but the Tory vote increased by more than three million and shot up by eight percentage points.[3] The Tories had won 339 seats to Labour's 269, and Mrs Thatcher was entitled to regard it as a personal triumph. She arrived at Number Ten and quoted lines from St Francis: 'Where there is discord may we bring harmony.' Even at the time Callaghan said that this was humbug, and it was certainly no guide to her future conduct. Much apter were the next lines: 'Where there is error, may

[3] Tories 13.7 million votes, 43.9 per cent, 339 seats; Labour: 11.5 million, 36.9 per cent, 269 seats; Liberals: 4.3 million, 13.8 per cent, 11 seats; Others: 16 seats.

we bring truth. Where there is doubt, may we bring faith.' That was more like it.

Doing his best to be more gracious in defeat, Callaghan said that it was good to see a woman as prime minister; she preferred to take a different credit, as the first scientist to reach Number Ten. So she was, and unique in other respects also. The Tories had shown their originality before, by choosing men from outside the traditional governing class of Macmillan's phrase, from Disraeli to Bonar Law to Chamberlain to Heath, but Margaret Thatcher was the most extraordinary choice ever. She was a woman, she was from the lower middle class, daughter of a shopkeeper in Grantham, she was a Methodist by upbringing. When she became an MP at the 1959 election, the Tories were still in thrall to patrician and military values, a chaps' party echoing the mores and language of Eton, 'the Brigade' and Clubland. By definition Mrs Thatcher had not gone to Eton, served in the Guards or joined White's (though she was later made an honorary member of the Carlton), and being an outsider was both a weakness and a strength.

She was not stupid – to suppose so was one of the mistakes her enemies made – but nor was she in any way learned or cultivated. Denis Healey liked to extol politicians with a hinterland, meaning broader cultural interests, which many prime ministers had truly had. Disraeli wrote novels which are still readable, Gladstone wrote enormous theological and critical essays besides reading 20,000 books in six languages in the course of his life, Salisbury was a visual philistine but a devoted reader from the classics to Jane Austen, Churchill wrote prolifically and entertainingly, Eden was an aesthete who broke the ice with the clever French-Jewish socialist Léon Blum when they discovered their common love of Proust, Macmillan was a middlebrow but at least read Trollope, and even Heath was interested in music.

His successor had no artistic taste at all. Margaret Hilda Roberts had gone to Oxford to study science, and had later read for the Bar before becoming an industrial chemist working for a food company; one of her lesser-known and perhaps less happy achievements was inventing the 'whippy' ice-cream which squirts from a nozzle. Her marriage to Denis Thatcher, a rugby-loving (and refereeing) business-man, had provided her with the independence to pursue a political career, and her ability had shown as a junior minister in 1961–4. All of this had hardened an already formidable and naturally bossy or aggressive personality. In her first years as a backbencher we have seen her disobeying the party line only once, to vote for retaining the birch: her colleagues would come to know the kiss of her whip all too well. Merely to survive in the Tory party meant that she had to grow several extra skins: she sensed that the old guard looked down on her as a capable and industrious woman though unsophisticated and frankly rather plebeian; not for the first time in history, such patronage would lead to violent revenge.

In the Heath government Mrs Thatcher had served as Education Secretary, for no very good reason except that she had been shadowing the department and it was a 'woman's job': only one woman had previously sat in a Tory Cabinet, Florence Horsburgh as minister of education in Churchill's peacetime government. At Education Thatcher showed her mettle, resisting the complacent pieties of the department and for the first time entering the demonology of the left as 'Mrs Thatcher, milk snatcher' when she cut back the automatic entitlement to free milk at primary schools. Nevertheless she also (as some of her acolytes would later rather forget) pursued the same policy of turning grammar schools into comprehensives that Crosland and Shirley Williams had begun under Labour.

As the years went by she became not less but more abrasive, in public, in parliament, and in Cabinet. Her sycophants liked to say that she was more open-minded than generally believed, and that she enjoyed an argument (the most extreme manifestation of such sycophancy was the claim that she really had a good sense of humour, when it was quite clear that she had none whatever). It was true that she allowed more discussion in Cabinet than had Heath, and Malcolm Rifkind has recorded that toward the end of her premiership she even accepted decisions against her own inclination, if not quite with good grace. But there was nothing imaginary about her bullying manner, which anyone could encounter. At a somewhat gloomy dinner given by one of her admirers to discuss policy I once attempted to make a courteous and reasoned point about agricultural policy, which she answered with a basilisk glare and the words 'Are *you* a farmer?' It was this side of her which prompted Carrington's reply, when the question of her succession was being discussed, in the conventional form of what would happen if Margaret were run over by a bus: 'It wouldn't dare.' There was beside that a real human personality, and a feminine personality. One of her ministers, not inexperienced in the field of female companionship, used to say that 'She's a sexy blonde', and François Mitterrand later agreed with that in his phrase about 'the eyes of Caligula and the mouth of Marilyn Monroe'.[4] Women are famously brave, and even those who disagreed with and disliked her were sometimes obliged to admire her courage. Altogether, she was someone who had to be accepted with all her faults. Maybe she really was the one person who could carry out an historically essential mission, in which case the Viennese saying applied: If you want the meat you have to pay for the bones.

But even if she was entitled to take personal credit for the election, it was not merely, or mostly, her personality which had unseated Callaghan. That was caused by general revulsion from the Labour government and disgust at the unions' behaviour, but also by a *longue durée*, deeper currents which were sweeping away the dominance of the labour movement and state socialism. Not only on the right was this perceived: the veteran Marxist historian E. J. Hobsbawm had descried 'Labour's long march ended', as the supposedly ineluctable assumption of power by the masses had obviously faltered, for the good reason that 'the masses' had changed out of all recognition, or even for the large part disappeared.

Nowhere was this more marked than in the matter of income tax, which more than anything else decided Mrs Thatcher's first election victory. This was sometimes cited as a crucial Tory issue, as it was, but not merely in terms of the levels of taxation. Under the Callaghan government these had indeed reached heights never known before: a standard rate of 33 per cent (compared with 4s. 6d. in the pound before 1939, and almost exactly the same, 22 per cent, which it would be again from 1987) and top marginal rates of 83 per cent on earned income, 98 per cent on 'unearned' or investment income. But the really vital figures were not how much tax was paid but by how many; and if a single explanation were required for Mrs Thatcher's victory it

---

[4] Adding less genially that she had 'l'air d'une femme mal baisée'.

was that in 1939 fewer than four million British people paid income tax, and that by 1979 nearly 26 million did. What that meant was that the whole shape of society had changed. It had been a pyramid, and was now a lozenge. Instead of a vast mass of 'the poor', who had once unmistakably been the great majority of the populace, tapering upwards all the way through the middling orders to the rich at the pinnacle, there were very rich and very poor at either end swelling out in the middle, which now encompassed the bulk of the populace.

Even then, she was careful and almost hesitant at first. There were a few hints of the later Thatcher in the months following her victory. A small but significant one was her decision to name Anthony Blunt as a former Soviet agent, despite the deal he had done years before with the intelligence services, avoiding prosecution in return for a full but secret confession. Her provincial Dissenting sense of right and wrong was offended by this: treason was treason, not less so when committed by a refined art historian who had once served the queen. And she swung the handbag with which satirists already identified her at another target during her first European summit in Dublin at the end of the year, when her vehemence in asking for a rebate on British contributions – 'I was not prepared to settle for a third of a loaf' – startled those of us from London covering the meeting, let alone the other European heads of government who had a full taste of her for the first time. Much more important was the ending of exchange controls by the new Chancellor, Sir Geoffrey Howe. These were a relic of the wartime command economy, not to say of a financial police state, and had been imposed with ferocious rigidity. For years after 1945 an Englishman could not even spend abroad what he earned abroad, and the great explosion in foreign holidays was impossible until the first easing of controls. Their final abolition in 1979 was an heroic first step in what would be a financial revolution.

On the other hand there were plenty of compromises in the first two years. Within months of taking office, her government had broked a deal in Rhodesia which meant abandoning Bishop Muzorewa, who had been favoured as a moderate, abandoning Ian Smith and the white Rhodesians, and, as it proved, abandoning the whole population to the tyrannical care of Robert Mugabe. Without her having perhaps quite noticed, this was the Thatcherite equivalent of de Gaulle's 'Je vous ai compris' to the white Algerians, meaning that he had understood what they wanted, he couldn't help them, and was about to desert them in the name of the sacred national egoism. Bobbety Salisbury had died in 1972, and must now have been turning in his grave at this new 'unhappy and entirely wrong approach' to the white community; he would not have been so wrong if he had said that Thatcher and Lord Soames (as Sir Christopher had become), in charge of the negotiations, had been too clever by half, as far as the peoples of Zimbabwe were concerned. For the British people, and the Tories, it was one more tiresome incubus which had been shed, and an early intimation of the lady's sheer ruthlessness.

In domestic politics, Mrs Thatcher likewise trod carefully. She kept her distance from a steel strike in early 1980, and even encouraged sundry forms of state interference in the economy by ministers as various as Michael Heseltine at Environment, a recognized interventionist, who set up new enterprise zones to encourage urban regeneration, with considerable success, and to Keith Joseph at Industry, who was meant to be a laissez-fairy, but who proved to be too tender-hearted to put many lame ducks out of their misery.

Before long political parlance had been enriched by the language of 'wet and dry' Tories. The 'dries' were born-again free-marketeers who disliked managerialist government in the economy. They longed to get rid of state-controlled industries. They believed, like Milton Friedman and his British disciples, that inflation was the consequence of increased money supply (the purest such monetarists always held that, whatever many people had thought of the experience of the 1970s, the unions were entirely blameless in the case of rising prices: they might cause unemployment, but never inflation).

In truth, the distinction between wet and dry, or those who could and could not be counted 'one of us', in a phrase later attributed to Mrs Thatcher, was largely illusory at this stage. James Prior, an interventionist sceptic inside the Cabinet as Employment Secretary, wrote later that those like him 'grossly underestimated her absolute determination, along with Geoffrey and Keith, to push through the new right-wing policies', but those policies were actually still in embryonic form, and the battle lines inside Toryism not yet drawn up. Earlier in the century, when Prohibition was the burning issue in

American politics, dividing those called wet and dry in a more obvious sense of the words, a man running for governor of a southern state was asked at a meeting where he stood on whiskey. He replied:

If by whiskey you mean that scourge and curse which rots men's health and enfeebles their minds, sapping the will to work and ruining families, then I am first among the Dries. If by whiskey you mean that gentle balm which relaxes the body, eases the spirits and brings men into harmony with one another, then count me in the front rank of the Wets.

In 1980, Mrs Thatcher gave an 'If by whiskey . . .' answer on the economy, or her government did. There was to be sure a group of ministers who were formulating an economic strategy – John Nott, Joseph, and the Treasury team of Geoffrey Howe as Chancellor, John Biffen as Chief Secretary and Nigel Lawson as Financial Secretary – but neither dry nor right-wing was an adequate description of them. The latter trio have been called the most economically literate group at the Treasury since the ill-fated Thorneycroft, Birch and Powell in 1957; it was an unforeseen irony that Thatcher and Lawson would later reprise the inflationary role of Macmillan and Heathcoat Amory when that team resigned.

All in all, not only was the 'Thatcher revolution' slow in reaching its Bastille or Winter Palace, its Girondins or Mensheviks played an important part in the first years of her government. Patrick Jenkin was her first Health and Social Security Secretary and was more successful in curbing welfare spending than many later and ostensibly more right-wing ministers (including Tony Blair's) were able to do, and Prior himself played a crucial role, not less so for being stealthy, in reducing the powers of the unions. Peter Walker, the most obvious wet holdover from the Heath government, would play a no less crucial role in the greatest domestic confrontation of the Thatcher government.

In 1981 there were moments when Mrs Thatcher seemed to be losing her nerve, and events seemed to be running out of control. Unemployment shot upward, to 2.5 million and beyond. It had been a touchstone among the paternalist or One Nation Tories that this was politically impossible: the country would be ungovernable with so many people out of work, the jobless would take to the streets to riot. By a curious paradox that was confuted by the very fact of the welfare state about which Thatcherism was supposedly ambivalent. The postwar Attlee welfare state has been criticized as anachronistic. It addressed the great social evils of the years before the Great War and of the interwar years – abject poverty and mass unemployment respectively – both of which it was assumed in the 1960s and even the 1970s would never return. Unemployment did return, but not with a vengeance, since unemployment pay defused the problem, even if it created an acute financial difficulty for the government. Sceptics within the government were dismayed, and for a time an 'inner-party opposition', notably in the intelligent shape of Sir Ian Gilmour, criticized the prime minister, in the not-too-coded language of the Disraelian tradition and 'One Nation'. What really saved the Thatcher experiment in its early years was the uncovenanted benefit of North Sea oil, which began to flow just as she took office.

The turning point came not in 1979 but in 1981, when she rounded on those dissidents in her own ranks, and in 1982, the year of the Falklands war. First to the tumbrils was Norman St John Stevas, a gifted scholar and writer who changed the life of the Commons, not entirely for the better, by creating departmental select committees, but who was too frivolous and 'leaky' to survive, quite apart from his exhaustingly jocose way of referring to his colleagues as 'John Nitt' or 'Ongoose Maude'. He also spoke of Mrs Thatcher as the Leadereen, and may have been responsible for (along with various other witless sobriquets which were bestowed on her at the time) the very apt 'Attila the Hen'.

His departure in January 1981 was a mere augury of what was to come. Most of that year saw the Thatcher government at a low ebb. The economy showed no sign of improvement, and in the summer the country was swept by riots in one town after another, Bristol, London, Liverpool. This was what the wets had foreseen: monetarism, non-interventionism, high unemployment would lead to disorder and even rebellion. If they wanted the prime minister to say how sorry she was for the poor rioters, they were disappointed. 'Oh those poor shopkeepers', was her instinctive response at the sight of wrecked streets. In fact, the riots were not a general phenomenon but almost entirely confined to 'inner-city' areas, to borrow the American euphemism. If anyone could logically express schadenfreude it was not the wets but Enoch Powell, whose followers did indeed gloat at the fulfilment of his forebodings.

Even before that summer of discontent, at the Tory conference the previous autumn, Mrs Thatcher had said that she had been expected to make a U-turn and that others could turn if they wanted, but 'The Lady's not for turning.'[5] Now at last she turned in on her party and carried out a purge. It might have been called Iain Macleod's revenge. Her first Cabinet had contained a large number of the old guard. There were no survivors from Macmillan's or Home's Cabinets except Hailsham, Lord Chancellor once again, sitting irritably on the Woolsack and muttering 'Bollocks' as his fellow peers spoke. But there were still a number of grandees. Lord Carrington was Foreign Secretary until the Falklands debacle in the spring of 1982, when he was replaced by Francis Pym, one wartime MC (9th Lancers) succeeding another (Grenadiers). One more Grenadier, Sir Ian Gilmour, a rich, clever baronet, was Lord Privy Seal in the first ministry Mrs Thatcher formed, and Lord Soames (a Coldstreamer though not an MC) was Lord President. By the time Thatcher had won her second election and reshaped her government in 1983, Gilmour, Soames, Carrington and Pym had been removed. Four of the four men mentioned in the last sentence went to Eton. The ruthlessness of her class war was startling, and the memory lingered on. The novelist Martin Amis knew Soames through his daughter Emma, and nearly twenty years later wrote: 'But, lor, how much stuff there was about class in those days. Whatever else she did, Margaret Thatcher helped weaken all that. Mrs Thatcher, with her Cecils, with her Normans, with her Keiths.'[6]

With the old guard or without them Mrs Thatcher was in trouble. For several months between the autumn of 1981 and the spring of 1982 her fortunes sank very low. Reacting at last to the takeover of

[5] An example of the excruciating rhetorical style imposed on her by her speechwriters, notably Ronald Millar, an old theatrical party. How many Tories, or anyone, by then remembered the English verse drama revival of the postwar years and Christopher Fry's *The Lady's Not for Burning*?

[6] This last betrayed Amis's solipsism and political innocence. In his own novels, 'Keith' – Little Keith, Keith Talent – is a naff, low-life name; there was only one Keith in Mrs Thatcher's Cabinets, Sir Keith Joseph, a millionaire Old Harrovian baronet and Fellow of All Souls, not the point Amis was trying to make.

the Labour party by the left, a group of leaders of the right of the party, soon dubbed the Gang of Four, announced their departure, and shortly formed themselves into a new party. The Social Democrats enjoyed a startling wave of popularity as the leaders returned to parliament in triumph. In November, Shirley Williams, the gangsters' moll, won the middle-class Lancashire seat of Crosby in a by-election, overturning a Tory majority of 18,000. By the end of the year this Social Democratic party had formed a pragmatic Alliance with the Liberals, and this Alliance was passing 50 per cent in polls, in some of which Mrs Thatcher appeared as the most unpopular prime minister in living memory. As 1982 opened, unemployment reached the unimaginable level of three million, and in March Roy Jenkins won another astonishing by-election victory in Glasgow. By almost universal consent among the political pundits, the Tories could not win the next election, certainly not an outright victory.

Three days before Jenkins's by-election, there was a curious news story which at first was barely noticed. A group of Argentine 'scrap merchants' had landed on South Georgia, an island which was British territory near the Falklands in the south Atlantic. It looked like provocation, and so it turned out at the beginning of April, when the Falklands themselves were invaded. For many years this territorial dispute had been an accident waiting to happen: as one learned historian put it, too important to forget but not important enough to settle. Successive British governments had thought of relinquishing them, most recently Mrs Thatcher's own government, only for Nicholas Ridley as junior foreign office minister to be howled down in the Commons by MPs from both sides insistent that the islands should be kept and that, in an endlessly reiterated phrase, the wishes of the islanders should be paramount. There were barely 2,000 of these islanders and the phrase was obviously absurd: in no other context were the wishes of a handful of people allowed to dictate the policies of a nation of more than fifty million, and one which had long since accepted the contrary principle of the greatest good of the greatest number. Indeed, when it came to building a motorway or power station in the English shires, the wishes of a couple of thousand villagers were almost unfailingly ignored.

Even so, there was a widespread sense that the invasion was a grave challenge. 'It's all over', was Alan Clark's initial reaction to the fall of the Falklands. 'We're a Third World country, no good for anything.' Mrs Thatcher's reaction was not so vehement, and although a task force was assembled and steamed to the south Atlantic, she was nothing like as inflexible as might have been supposed. The reconquest of the Falklands looked a very perilous undertaking in prospect and was a damned close-run thing in the event; there was much pressure on London, not least from Washington, to avoid a full-scale war, and if it had not been for the brutal pigheadedness of the Argentinian dictator General Galtieri Thatcher might have been forced into a humiliating compromise. She was always fortunate in her enemies.

The war divided the country, not as bitterly as the Boer war or Suez, and not along party lines. Enoch Powell was at his worst, bombastically saying – a man who had never heard the proverbial shot fired in anger – that a battle was not worth winning without bloodshed. But on the other hand was Jock Bruce-Gardyne, Wykehamist intellectual, financial journalist, a man with an amiably sinister demeanour, and driest of dries, who as Economic Secretary to the Treasury had out-monetarized any other monetarists. He thought the Falklands war a waste of time, money and blood, and said so in a letter to a friend at the *Financial Times*, which managed to find its way into print.

All misgivings were swept away by events. The forces were irrevocably committed. When South Georgia was recaptured in a blizzard which saw two British helicopters crash, reporters asked the prime minister what would happen next, and she barked at them, 'Rejoice! Just rejoice at that news and congratulate our forces and the Marines.' Then when the Union Jack flew again over Port Stanley, she rejoiced again, for her country and for herself, and she was entitled to.

'But is he lucky?' Napoleon would ask when a general was mentioned. There is an indefinable quality of good fortune which shines on some leaders but not on others: on Salisbury but not Balfour, on Macmillan but not Eden. Margaret Thatcher had it, at least until the end when she wilfully exhausted her luck and used up the political equivalent of a cat's nine lives.

Now in this apotheosis, she seemed unlike any previous Tory leader. She defied categorization. It might even be said that she was not even a conservative: part reactionary, part radical, she was in many ways not a Tory. Her forebears were solid provincial Dissenters, Methodists from Lincolnshire, and a woman with Roundhead roots could not so easily become a Cavalier. Those purges were not simply acts of spite: she clearly had more affinity with other outsiders – plebeian interlopers like Norman Tebbit or Jews like five of her Cabinet ministers – than with traditional 'good society'; whatever else she was, she was never BGBC, as Parisians say, *bon genre bon chic*. She made a romantic cult of Churchill (or Winston as she called him, whether the Churchill family liked it or not), and invoked consciously Churchillian rhetoric when she took the country to war, but the prime minister she really best resembled was Lloyd George, another provincial outsider who had made his way by sheer ability and force of personality, who like her led the nation in a time of crisis, and who, for that matter, was finally deserted by the Tories before he could inflict any more damage on them.

The resemblance included his faults as well as his virtues. A. J. P. Taylor's description of Lloyd George applied word for word to Mrs Thatcher, changing only the gender of the pronouns: 'She had no friends and did not deserve any. She repaid loyalty with disloyalty. She was surrounded by dependants and sycophants, whom she rewarded lavishly and threw aside when they had served their turn. Her rule was dynamic and sordid at the same time.' Unlike Lloyd George she did not give hostages to fortune through an irregular private life, although the business careers of her husband and her ne'er-do-well son were unquestionably helped by her name. Most of all, the words Baldwin had used when advising his fellow Tories to sunder their alliance with Lloyd George applied to Mrs Thatcher. She was 'a great dynamic force', as Baldwin might have said, 'a very terrible thing'.

Even to stress her lack of intellectual depth is by no means an insult. Schiller's famous aesthetic essay *Über naive und sentimentalische Dichtung* distinguished between two kinds of writer, the instinctive and the reflective. His distinction applies to politicians also, and for all her tutoring by Keith Joseph (her exact antithesis in this respect) and others, she was the supreme example of the instinctive politician.

Her attack on the old Tory party leadership was only part of Mrs

Thatcher's social revolution. Ever since Peel's time, the Conservatives had been co-opting one lower social class after another: the radical *Poor Man's Guardian* wrote perceptively at the time that reform itself might have been an attempt not 'to subvert, or even remodel, our aristocratic institutions, but to consolidate them by a reinforcement of sub-aristocracy from the middle classes'. By now the sub-aristocracy had enormously expanded. The special Thatcherite constituency was the C2s, as they were called from the jargon of advertising: the prosperous skilled artisan class between upper working and lower middle. Another not wholly affectionate tag was 'Essex Man', the man who might have grown up in the East End of London but who had moved out further east. His family accumulated impressive quantities of consumer goods, their own house, cars, kitchen and garden gadgets, televisions, videos, hi-fis and, a little later, computers. They holidayed abroad, and even began to buy shares. But they conspicuously did not attempt to acquire the manners and graces of their betters.

Within the higher reaches of the Tory party itself there was a shift of emphasis. By no means all former leaders had conformed to a type, and English society was always more fluid than some observers supposed, a point illustrated by the personal lives of Victorian prime ministers. Peel and Gladstone were both born into the purple of commerce, as Lady Bracknell would have said; Peel married a general's daughter, and Gladstone married Miss Glynne, from a Whig gentry family whose estates passed to the Gladstones. Salisbury and Rosebery were both from the *erste Gesselschaft*, the inner circle of the great territorial nobility; Salisbury married a judge's daughter, and Rosebery married a Rothschild. Nor were tastes and recreations standardized. Salisbury had no interest in hunting or racing, his nephew and successor Balfour preferred golf and lawn tennis to shooting, while Bonar Law played chess and drank milk, as un-Tory as could be.

In the second half of the twentieth century, the thrall of traditional aristocratic culture had far from faded in the party. Tories were either gentlemen by birth or tried to become so by assimilation, with more (Cecil Parkinson) or less (Ted Heath) degrees of success. But that was not true of another of Mrs Thatcher's trusted lieutenants: as Ferdinand Mount once wrote, Norman Tebbit was gloriously common. Tebbit was also, Mount observed, one of the most effective parliamentary debaters the Tories had. He gave no quarter, and enriched the language of politics when he told the rioters and the jobless generally that, when his own father had been unemployed in the 1930s, 'He didn't riot. He got on his bike and looked for work.' Tebbit personified the aspiring new class in the party. He spoke for Essex Man; after all, he was one himself.

Although the Falklands war was not quite an accident of history, it was an extraneous event which was unforeseen and whose consequences were quite unintended. It consolidated Mrs Thatcher's position and her reputation for toughness and for populist determination in the face of what she might have called – would soon call – enemies within as well as abroad. She bestrode the political scene, Iron Britannia in one vivid image. She was reputedly the chief object of sexual fantasy among British soldiers. She was ready for a fresh offensive.

6

Continental Divide

Just before the 1983 election, the *Sunday Times* books section had
the nice idea of reviewing the party manifestos in intellectual and
literary terms like any other new publications, and they were sent to
John Carey, a professor of English at Oxford. No prose masterpiece,
the Labour manifesto was nevertheless of historic importance, marking the subjugation of the party to the hard left. It advocated unilateral
nuclear disarmament, withdrawal from Europe, along with 'an irre-
versible shift of wealth and power to working people and their
families', and was memorably described by the Labour MP Gerald
Kaufman as the longest suicide note in history. This document
presaged the lowest ebb in Labour's fortunes.

Among the party's parliamentary candidates that June who were
obliged to subscribe to the suicide note were two young hopefuls, a
married couple. The previous summer there had been a by-election at
Beaconsfield, the Buckinghamshire seat now in the London commut-
ing belt, from which Disraeli had taken his title (and Burke might
have done), and vacated by the death of the libertarian Ronald Bell.
It was safe Tory territory in any case; with the Union Jack flying once
again over Port Stanley, the result was a formality. Covering that
by-election, I was struck mostly by how very much of a muchness the
main candidates were, all three of them middle-class Oxonian lawyers,
a reflection of the way that politics had become a profession whose
professionals were increasingly indistinguishable. Although the unsuccessful Labour candidate was a personable and persuasive young man,
I cannot claim then to have discerned anything out of the ordinary
in him, still less to have suspected that his career would one day have

huge consequences for his country, and not least for the Tory party.

Next year Anthony Blair found, at the last moment, a safe Labour seat in the north-east, while his wife, Cherie Booth, was standing in a Tory seat in Kent. Having now chummily Tonified himself, like Benn before him, Blair prepared to enter parliament. His heart was being hardened by experience, including an elaborately insulting ritual at the hands of the left in his new seat when Dennis Skinner told a meeting that Blair should never have been chosen. Now he determined to turn the tables, and he began his own Long March through the party, which he would one day capture from the inside, not merely tearing up the suicide note but beating the Tories at their own game.

Since Carey was no Tory, he may have surprised himself by finding how much better written the Conservative manifesto was than the others, but that was not in fact surprising, since it was the work of Ferdinand Mount. He was a journalist and author then serving briefly as head of Mrs Thatcher's policy unit, an experience he later described as 'the longest holiday from irony I ever took'. Neither ironically nor boastfully, he was able to claim that 'Britain is once more a force to be reckoned with. Formidable difficulties remain to be overcome. But after four years of Conservative government, national recovery has begun.' The government had successfully launched its attack on 'uncompetitive, overtaxed, over-regulated and overmanned' industry.

A number of thoughtful younger Tories had outgrown the shibboleths of One Nation, the Middle Way, the Industrial Charter, Butskellism, Keynsianism and central planning, and had rediscovered the virtues of the competitive market economy. Mount was one of them. He was anything but a Disraelian Conservative (even if he did agree with Mr Hatton in *Sybil* that 'There is no title in the world for which I have such contempt as that of baronet'), and the Thatcherite attack on the unions might indeed have been called 'Don't, Mr Disraeli'. At last an attempt was made to reverse the disastrous process he had begun of privileging the unions above the law; and for all the groans and cries of the union leaders, this had struck a chord with their members, as the election would show. Of course, what Mrs Thatcher, Mount or any other Tory could not quite say publicly – though Alan

Clark, needless to say, did so in private – was that their most potent weapon in the battle against uncompetitive and overmanned industry had been the lash of unemployment. Nor did they guess that defeating the unions might prove a brilliant success in the short term which would then turn into its own 'problem of success' by leaving the Tories purposeless after their mission was accomplished.

In the spring of 1983 there was a wonderful moment in the Commons when Denis Healey tried to taunt Mrs Thatcher, and she snapped at him, 'The Right Honourable Gentleman is afraid of an election, is he? Afraid? Frightened? Frit?' Modern politicians are packaged and homogenized, their rough edges smoothed off and their origins toned down, all at a great loss of personal authenticity. Margaret Thatcher had genteelized herself and had been rebranded and polished until she resembled an ordinary suburban housewife, which she was not. When in her anger she lapsed into the Lincolnshire dialect of her girlhood, the real person shone through.

She was not frit. She was ready for an election, and when it came in June she was more triumphantly vindicated than she could have hoped. Mrs Thatcher now became the first prime minister since Attlee more than thirty years before to win re-election after a full term in office, except that she also repeated Attlee's 1945 rather than his 1950 achievement, by winning a landslide: 397 seats to Labour's 209, and a majority of 144 over all other parties. It was devastating victory for her, and for poor Michael Foot a complete rout. The Labour vote collapsed, lower in numbers than at any election for more than forty years and only marginally larger than in 1935, smaller as a percentage of the poll than at any election since 1918.

Another remarkable and portentous feature was the huge vote for the 'third party' which was not quite a party, the electoral Alliance between the old Liberals and the new Social Democrats. For many years the Liberals had been complaining about the unfairness of the electoral system, and never had it seemed so unfair as now. Partly because they were still a pantomime horse, with David Steel's Liberals as the front legs and Roy Jenkins's SDP as the back, partly because the system was as ever so inimical to third parties, and partly because they did not quite break through a crucial barrier, almost impossible exactly to define but nearer 30 than 25 per cent of the vote, the Alliance won only twenty-three seats – or less than one seat in twenty-five – with more than one in four of the popular vote.[1]

In an odd if not mangled metaphor, the Social Democrats had claimed that they were 'breaking the mould' of British politics, but it was actually Mrs Thatcher who had broken the pattern. It was said that she had won thanks to extraneous factors, but then that could be said to some degree of almost any party winning any election. Although she was held particularly to be benefiting from the 'split progressive vote', this was illogical in theory – a third party might just as well be taking votes from the first as from the second party – and simply wrong in the British political context. Sixty years earlier Beatrice Webb had said with unambiguous vehemence that for Social- ists 'the real enemy are the Liberals' rather than the Tories, and for decades past the threatened Liberal revival – which had now at last come to pass – had almost always been seen as a threat to the Con- servatives: when Tory voters were disaffected they voted Liberal, went a conventional assumption based on a good deal of evidence, while when Labour voters were disgruntled they simply stayed at home. The 1983 election itself gave some colour to that dictum. Those voting Tory had actually fallen by nearly 700,000, many of them doubtless moving to the Alliance; and it was just about discernible even then that the subterranean shifts in the political landscape might yet upset the Tories.

Even Mrs Thatcher's rout of Labour meant distant trouble for her party. Under Foot Labour's fortunes had sunk about as low as they could go. It might be that Labour would now disappear, or at least be replaced as the main party of opposition. Or it might be that Labour could survive and, as the song suggests, pick itself up, dust itself down and start all over again. That was the hope of a few stalwarts. And even at that moment of despair Labour had one piece of luck of its own: Benn lost his seat in Mrs Thatcher's landslide. When Foot resigned and an election for leader was held in the autumn, Benn might very well have won and confirmed Labour as a party of the hard left for the foreseeable future had he been eligible, which he

---

[1] Tories: 13 million votes, 42.2 per cent, 397 seats; Labour: 8.5 million, 27.6 per cent, 209 seats; Alliance: 7.9 million, 25.4 per cent, 23 seats; Others: 21 seats.

was not until he could re-enter parliament. For him, 1983 was the moment Goethe speaks of, which, once lost, Eternity will never give back. For Labour, it was a moment offering a distant glimmer of hope. In October Neil Kinnock won the election for leader and began the painfully long and slow process of refashioning the party.

As to the way union leaders had raged and fulminated at Mrs Thatcher, their own members gave a breathtakingly clear answer. The single most extraordinary fact about the 1983 election was that only 40 per cent of trade union members voted Labour. Before it adopted a socialist constitution, before it became a managerialist party of government, before it agonized over nationalization or reformism, Labour had been from the beginning just what its name said, the political voice of the organized working class. And it was that no longer. Here was 'the Thatcher revolution' on display. The political 'cleavage of classes', which Harcourt had said began with household suffrage, had lasted a century, and grown starker when Labour had emerged as a specifically class-based party. Labour had remained the party of the working class from the 1920s until the 1970s, but had demonstrably ceased to be that. Mrs Thatcher had all unconsciously returned to an earlier age when politics ignored class lines.

In truth, there had always been an uneasy relationship between the left and the poor. As Hobsbawm has said, a large anthology could be compiled of socialist writers in the nineteenth and twentieth centuries complaining about the indolence and fecklessness of the working classes, their indiscipline and inability to organize. The left was perennially confused by its mystic cult of the masses, who always felt the right way but always acted the wrong way. There was a fine example of this superior patronage in Oscar Wilde's amusing but frivolous 1892 essay, 'The Soul of Man under Socialism'. Two very different critics saw through it. At the time, Engels was still alive to snort with derision at Wilde and 'a form of socialism which has actually donned evening dress and lounges on sofas'. More than fifty years later, George Orwell quoted Wilde's languidly camp saying, 'I hardly think that any Socialist, nowadays, would seriously propose that an inspector should call every morning at each house to see that each citizen rose up and did manual labour for eight hours', and added grimly that we had learned that this was 'just the kind of thing countless modern Socialists would propose' (not to say that if those citizens were not labouring enough, they could be sent to learn in labour camps).

There was more to it. In a phrase which was still quoted with approval by other salon socialists a hundred years later, Wilde said, 'As for the deserving poor, one can pity them but one cannot admire them.' This line doubtless won sniggers of approval in the Café Royal. But at that very time, it was precisely men from the deserving poor, otherwise 'the self-helping working class' who had come up through the chapels as well as the many plebeian institutions for self-improvement, who were now giving their lives to the labour movement and the cause of socialism.

And ninety years later, it was the deserving poor – the self-helping working class who had helped themselves and deserved to – who had then become a large part of Mrs Thatcher's constituency. One of the crucial social differences in England, often ignored, as important as between patrician and plebeian, bourgeois and proletarian, gentle and common, upper middle and lower middle, was within the working class, between rough and respectable. The respectable working class had been in many ways the backbone of the nation. Disraeli had whimsically described the working class as 'angels in a block of marble'. But when the angel emerged from the stone, he had disappointed Disraeli and his heirs by supporting the Liberals and then Labour. Now the respectable working class had come full circle to become the C2s, and instead of voting for Mr Gladstone or Major Attlee, they were voting for Mrs Thatcher.

With that support she was now free and untrammelled. She had seen off Galtieri, Foot, and the wets in her own party. The last execution was Francis Pym's. He had foolishly said off the cuff during the election campaign that a landslide might be bad for the party, and thus sealed his fate. The prime minister's press officer was Bernard Ingham, a chirpy and chippy Yorkshireman who had once been a minor journalist and an aggressive Labour supporter. With the zeal of the convert he became Mrs Thatcher's most implacable lieutenant, and this took the form, as it had never before under prime ministers of either party, of anonymous delation and non-attributable blackguarding.

Although much maligned, the journalistic 'lobby system' worked perfectly well most of the time and, in any case, it was really as old as human intercourse: 'I'll tell you what's going on if you keep my name out of it.' Background or off-the-record conversation is part of the political culture in most countries, even passing into their languages: 'Bien entendu, c'est off', French politicians say when they don't want to be quoted. In London, correspondents had long been admitted to to Palace of Westminster and to the Commons lobby (hence the name) where they could speak to ministers and MPs in confidence. The system did tend to abuse once the prime minister's press officer began to give daily briefings which could be reported, but only as though the revelations had come straight from the Holy Ghost rather than from human lips. Such abuse became scandalous under Mrs Thatcher, when colleagues who had incurred the displeasure of Number Ten found themselves described as unreliable or 'semi-detached' (the phrase used of John Biffen). Rather as in 1938 a general of the Red Army would read some criticism of himself in *Pravda*, and feel in that moment the muzzle of the executioner's gun at the back of his neck, so a Tory minister now learned from the morning papers that he was out of favour, and knew that he would soon be out of a job.

Not all were banished into outer darkness: some were merely sent upstairs. Whitelaw was of much the same social stamp as the upper-class wets, but he had been a loyal and valuable supporter of Mrs Thatcher from the time when she had defeated him for the leadership. In 1983 he was despatched to the Lords. It was when he finally left the government that Mrs Thatcher said at a gathering of colleagues that 'Every prime minister needs a Willie,' and took some time to understand the sniggers.[2] Needing a Willie was truer than she may have known. Now she reconstructed the government, with Geoffrey Howe moved to the Foreign Office, and succeeded as Chancellor by Nigel Lawson; two names which would one day haunt the prime minister. The phrase 'one of us' which she supposedly used to describe those she relied on may have been apocryphal, but it described her

---

[2] On another occasion she needed to have explained to her slowly what was an admittedly laborious joke about Callaghan, Moses, and 'keep taking the tablets' – both episodes confirming that she had no sense of humour whatsoever.

cast of mind, and most of her government were largely her own people, with the glaring exception of Michael Heseltine.

If the great defining event of Mrs Thatcher's first government was the Falklands war, the great defining event of her second was the miners' strike. Once again she was a lucky general. The coal miners and the National Union of Mineworkers occupied a special place in the emotional life of the labour movement, from the days when mining was the only industry employing more than a million men, and at the cutting edge of the class war. Harold Macmillan was fond of saying sententiously that there were three institutions no wise man took on, the Vatican, the Brigade of Guards and the NUM. In fact the Vatican had often been resisted, the Guards had known defeats as well as victories, and the NUM had been crushed before now, above all in 1926. Whether it would be crushed again depended in large part on the man who had been its president since 1981, Arthur Scargill.

He was no fool. The late John Marriage, a prosperous QC who spent a number of evenings with Scargill when he was acting for him in various legal cases, used to say that he was one of the sharpest and most amusing men he had ever met. Scargill was indeed very clever and very vain, a combination more often found in academic life than in the labour movement. In a just society he would have spent his life irritating his colleagues in a university common room; as it was, in a union leader his vanity was dangerous even before the adulation he had received from the sectarian left. That would have gone to the head of even a naturally humble man. In Scargill's case it was disastrous. He now picked a fight with the Coal Board, and the government, a fight which was in every sense wrong: the wrong battle at the wrong time fought in the wrong way over the wrong question. Scargill made everything much easier for Mrs Thatcher. His insistence that only his union – or he – should decide when pits could be closed, and that every pit should be kept open if it had the smallest quantity of coal left, however uneconomical that made it, was unreasonable to the point of absurdity.

Sixty years earlier the miners had been morally in the right, demanding no more than a living wage and respite from conditions close to serfdom. It was for that that the whole organized working class had taken part with self-sacrificial heroism in the general strike of 1926. They had been defeated comprehensively, not only through bad leadership and hesitancy or because of the government's ruthless lack of scruple, but also because 'the middle class, united, will never be defeated'. The English bourgeoisie had been enlisted to break the strike, helped by an educational system which was designed for physical fitness. Both the strike and its aftermath, when the miners had remained out for months until forced by hunger back to work on worse terms than before, brought out something very nasty in the victors. When A. E. Housman was asked by a Cambridge colleague for a donation to help the indigent miners, he said, 'They tried to starve me, let them starve.' But that in turn left a lingering bad conscience. From the thirties perhaps, certainly from the forties, the Tories had tended toward conciliation of the unions, never more than under Churchill's 1951–5 government, when he who had helped crush the miners in 1926, and had then opposed appeasement in the 1930s, presided over a policy of pure appeasement in one industrial dispute after another. Mrs Thatcher had seen it as her business not only to stop the appeasement but to exorcize the underlying guilty conscience.

Finally Scargill was wrong in the most elementary terms of strategy. For all the supposed rancour between wets and dries within Mrs Thatcher's government, the real ministerial hero of the strike was the arch-wet Peter Walker, Energy Secretary throughout the second Thatcher ministry. As soon as he was appointed, he quietly went about accumulating coal stocks, and arranging alternative means of moving them. The appointment of an American businessman, Ian MacGregor, to run the National Coal Board was not quite a provocation, but his task was clear enough. Large parts of nationalized industries were already being privatized, with more to come, but that was not much of an option for an industry which was looking at an annual loss of £250 million. It was MacGregor's clear intention to invest in profitable modern pits in places like Leicestershire, and to weed out the worst loss-making pits, which happened to be in Yorkshire and Scotland, the respective bailiwicks of Scargill and his henchman Mick McGahey.

And so by early 1984 everything was in place, awaiting only

Scargill's hubristic folly, which came sure enough. He never disguised his aim, which was not only to dictate which pits, if any, could be shut, not only to demand that all miners should have jobs guaranteed for life, but openly to challenge the authority of the government: after the overwhelming election victory, industrial action to bring down Mrs Thatcher 'was the only course open to the working class and the labour movement'. He had not thought through the difficulty of trying to launch a revolution with a wholly unrevolutionary working class and a placid labour movement, including the NUM itself: its constitution now required a 55 per cent majority in a ballot for a strike, and its members had three times voted against strike action. McGahey genially said that 'We shall not be constitutionalized out of a strike', and he and Scargill tried to escalate regional strikes into a national strike by 'a domino effect', until by these means a mining strike did come about.

But to call a strike without a ballot of members was to undermine its moral as well as legal validity from the start. Scargill put Neil Kinnock in a comically impossible position, yearning to support the strike but unable to do so, prevaricating this way and that way, and altogether a sitting duck for Mrs Thatcher's most brutal scorn. The larger union movement was hopelessly divided, with the TUC ignoring Scargill's demand for 'the total mobilization of the trade union and labour movement', with steel workers desperate to keep on working even if that meant burning 'black' coal, with the railwaymen turning a deaf ear to calls for support, and with a half-hearted attempt at such support by the dockers easily thwarted. The traditional ports of Liverpool and Southampton were still controlled by the unions and were closed for a time, but, as part of a new kind of industrial revolution which Mrs Thatcher had encouraged, and now benefited from, most cargo now came through non-unionized ports, and the dockers' sympathetic action quickly collapsed.

Moral validity apart, Scargill's venture was always doomed. To call a national mining strike in the spring, with coal stocks at the highest they had ever been, was a strategic decision to be compared with invading Russia in December. And it was made worse by Scargill's vainglorious assumption that the labour movement as a whole would support him. Even so, his retreat from Moscow lasted more than a year amid increasing violence between strikers and the police, who were marshalled, as never before in British history, to contain the strike, and between strikers and non-striking miners: scabs and black-legs to Scargill, heroes to Mrs Thatcher.

In 1926, there had been complete solidarity, among miners and the whole union movement, with scarcely a man going back to work until the strike was called off. In 1984, even the miners themselves were deeply divided, with Nottinghamshire calling a ballot in which miners voted four to one against a strike and went on working, as many miners in South Wales would have done if they had not been coerced into the strike. Behind Macmillan's and Butler's and Heath's approach to the unions lay that guilty conscience, which Mrs Thatcher simply did not share. She was untroubled by patrician anguish, but then so were many ordinary people. She proved to be articulating the view of 'her people', the C2s and Essex Man, if not of the shell-shocked Tory wets, or of the soft-left intelligentsia. In London during the strike it was very noticeable that if you wanted to see 'Dig Deep for the Miners' buttons, you went to the British Museum Reading Room or an avant-garde theatre or a publishing party. You did not see them worn in working-class pubs.

When the strike finally collapsed, it was clear that there had been, to adapt a phrase from the Labour manifesto, a massive and irrevers-ible shift in the industrial balance of power. Others in the Tory party may have hesitated to gloat, and even Mrs Thatcher on occasions showed some restraint, although she used very telling words to her MPs: 'We had to fight the enemy without in the Falklands and now we have to fight the enemy within, which is much more difficult but just as dangerous.' As if to rub it in, MacGregor published a book on the strike called *The Enemy Within*, which did not quite suggest Churchill's 'In Victory: Magnanimity' or the conciliatory tone some Tories wanted to hear.

To wrap up that victory came another confrontation, smaller in scale but almost more symbolic, between Rupert Murdoch and the Fleet Street printing unions. These had for decades past held the London newspaper industry in a stranglehold which was a parody of what was wrong with British industrial relations, delaying or destroying the printing of a vulnerable product on any whim and in the most blatantly blackmailing fashion. By the 1980s, Murdoch had acquired a large slice of the London newspaper circulation, from *The Times* and *Sunday Times* to the *News of the World* and the flagship *Sun*, and done so with the help of government (see p. 218). Like every other paper, these were being stifled and held back from much greater profitability by the unions' intransigence, by their insistence on using ten men to work a modern press designed to be manned by three, and by plain corruption, those 'old Spanish customs' whose very name was an unjust slur of the land of *siesta* and *mañana*.

After negotiating with the unions, or maybe pretending to, after building a fine new printing plant at Wapping, east of the Tower Bridge, after being told by one union official that he might as well put a match to the new plant, Murdoch acted unilaterally and moved his whole operation to Wapping at dead of night. For months Wapping was not so much picketed as besieged by angry mobs in scenes very reminiscent of Orgreave during the miners' strike, but they were beaten back by a huge police contingent, and then just beaten. Unilaterally did not mean without collusion. Murdoch's pensioner Woodrow Wyatt acted as go-between with Mrs Thatcher, and with the electricians' union who supplied the new workforce, while Andrew Neil, then editor of the *Sunday Times*, later recorded that Murdoch had sought Mrs Thatcher's assurance that enough police would be available to keep Wapping open, 'and she kept her word'.

Once again, opinion was divided. Many journalists, even those who affected to be on the left and to support the labour movement, had come to hate the printers, although some of us had a soft spot for them. When I worked at this time for the *Evening Standard* I enjoyed seeing the chaps 'on the stone' twice a day. They seemed to me the very kind of moneyed leisure class on whom civilization is said to depend. Then again, it was hard to view as any sort of suffering horny-handed toiler a senior printer who worked fewer than twenty hours a week, and was paid more than a family doctor. Few honest people did see the unions as victims. The London correspondent of the *New York Times* was Joseph Lelyveld, no reactionary, and he correctly reported that, although there was a certain amount of sentimental regret for the passing of old Fleet Street, the general feeling was that 'the printers had it coming'. To put it another way, after years of behaving in the most arrogant and brutish way towards weak newspaper owners and managers, the unions had finally found in Murdoch the proprietor they deserved.

On top of the miners' strike, Wapping was a complete victory not merely for the forces of capital but for the principle that industry should be run in the interests of consumers and not producers, the many not the few. That had not always been the basis of Toryism by any means: not in the days of the Corn Laws, not during the renewed protectionism of the 1930s, or in the age of retail price maintenance. Rather it was a notion of whose virtues the Conservatives had periodically persuaded themselves, with the repeal of the Corn Laws and the abolition of RPM. And yet putting into practice that great utilitarian principle was not pure benefit for the Tories. In his book *The Strange Death of Liberal England*, George Dangerfield suggested that by achieving their great victories of 1911–14, by taming the House of Lords, passing Lloyd George's 'people's budget', and enacting Home Rule despite the Unionists, the Liberals had won everything they wanted, had exhausted themselves – and had run out of a *raison d'être*. The Lords' veto had long been the Liberals' great grievance, and their excuse. With that gone, what purpose had they? The unions were Mrs Thatcher's House of Lords. Her victory over them would have most paradoxical results.

At the time of Mrs Thatcher's second election, her possible successors were already being discussed. One was Cecil Parkinson, maybe her greatest favourite, a working-class boy who had gone to Cambridge and prospered, a handsome man of considerable charm. Each of those features is worth glossing. The Tories really were now a party open to the talents, where social origins were by the way. When Reg Bevins had served as postmaster general under Macmillan as the first working-class Tory he was an oddity, and his memoirs later showed how much he had resented the patronage of his colleagues. That would no longer be true twenty years later. As to the university, although the prime minister was an Oxonian, her Cabinets were dominated by a generation who had been at Cambridge in the 1950s and early 1960s. And Mrs Thatcher was undoubtedly susceptible to good-looking men, even if that did not always stop her sacking them.

As party chairman with the nominal office of Paymaster-General for two years before the election, Parkinson took much of the credit for the victory, and he was made Trade and Industry Secretary (a new title after the reorganization of the ministry) in the summer of 1983. He lasted four months in the post, and then his downfall had nothing to do with policy. His mistress of some years became pregnant, expected him to leave his wife for her, and cut up rough when he did not. This overshadowed the 1983 party conference, and the man Mrs Thatcher had seen as her possible successor was obliged to leave the government.

One other minister was a man she very much did not see as her successor, the fascinating and faintly sinister figure of Michael Heseltine. Glamorous and eloquent, he was shrewd without being in any sense intellectual, mildly dyslexic (he had real difficulty writing unaided), flashy, and, in the eyes of what was left of the old guard, not quite sixteen annas to the rupee. Heseltine was a Welsh boy of modest background who had gone to Shrewsbury school. Postponing his National Service until he had finished at Oxford, where he was president of the Union, he had then served in the Welsh Guards rather briefly until he stood at a by-election in 1959 and thus obtained release from the army (precipitating a rush of others doing the same, who thought the £150 deposit a cheap way of getting early demob). Not all of his brother officers were pleased at his subsequent practice of wearing a Brigade tie, or by the cut of his jib in general. One old Scots Guardsman, Willie Whitelaw, had said that Heseltine could never become Defence Secretary: 'His hair's too long'.

Before and then after entering parliament in 1966, Heseltine had made money fast, through rented property in London and glossy magazines. There was a touch of P. G. Wodehouse's Ukridge about him. One of his colleagues recalled how Heseltine, told that owning lodging houses was an easy way of making money, replied angrily that it was on the contrary very hard work. Only that morning he had been up early 'mixing the butter with the marge'. After junior office in the Heath government, Heseltine was a prominent member of Mrs Thatcher's shadow cabinet and then served as Environment Secretary when she formed her first government. He was neither a wet in the full sense nor, for all his red and blue tie, a patrician. Alan Clark delighted in the silly jibe (attributed to Michael Jopling, scarcely a squierarch himself) that Heseltine had 'bought his own furniture', meaning that his *richesse* was *nouvelle*. Two hundred years earlier the Duke of Devonshire had bought his own furniture when he patronized Mr Chippendale, as indeed had the Clark family a couple of generations before Alan when they climbed out of Scottish petty-burgherdom.

As he showed in a notorious incident in the Commons when in opposition, Heseltine had a short temper. At the end of a fractious and noisy debate in 1975, he had picked up the mace which rests below the Speaker and waved it angrily at the Labour benches. Much less an ideologist than a pragmatist, he believed in getting things done, and in his enterprise zones he had regenerated desolate inner cities by the un-Thatcherite means of tax breaks. After the 1983 victory he became Defence Secretary, without even a haircut; and less than three years later his rivalry with Mrs Thatcher led to the great internal Tory crisis of this period, the Westland affair.

Its details were hard to grasp at the time and defy summary now: even the participants could scarcely have given a clear account of its rights and wrongs. Ostensibly the question was whether the British helicopter company Westland, once vigorous, now ailing, should be bought by the American company Sikorsky or a European consortium encouraged by Heseltine. This quickly turned into a conflict of wills. Neither Heseltine nor Mrs Thatcher came out of it well. He looked ambitious and cunning, she ruthless and downright disloyal. At the height of the dispute on Wednesday 8 January, I interviewed Heseltine in his office, surrounded by officials, cautious, calculating, entirely uninformative. In the middle of the next morning, my suitably dull piece was running in the *Evening Standard* when the electrifying news reached Fleet Street that Heseltine had resigned. Not any old resignation: he had stormed histrionically out of the Cabinet; and as one of the distinctly trivial consequences of this episode, I was obliged to rewrite the leader-pager very fast. Although I had had no intimation of his abrupt departure, neither had his colleagues. Some of them ever after believed that it was unpremeditated and a fit of pique (in one version that he had first angrily got up from the Cabinet table to go to the lavatory), and that if someone had called him back when he reached the door, history would have been different.

On the other hand, well before that morning's melodrama the affair had taken on a life of its own, as a showdown between Heseltine and Mrs Thatcher, and her sorry underling Leon Brittan, the Trade and Industry Secretary. Heseltine used press and parliament to conduct an alternative government strategy, explaining his 'European option' in secret evidence to a Commons select committee, briefing journalists, complaining that Cabinet committee meetings were being cancelled, and even that Sir Robert Armstrong, the Cabinet secretary, was writing misleading Cabinet minutes. All this was of course private and 'off'.

Clearly Mrs Thatcher had real grounds for resenting his insubordination, and would have been within her rights disciplining or ditching him, but she and her cabal had been worried about the damage he could do from the backbenches: in Lyndon Johnson's hallowed phrase, she still preferred him on the inside pissing out than on the outside pissing in. Instead, Downing Street resorted to thoroughly base tactics to curb Heseltine. When he wrote a letter to the European consortium, and made it public, the prime minister's office thought they had got him, because of a slight error about the legal position as he stated it. An opinion was sought from the Solicitor-General, Sir Patrick Mayhew, who was instructed to write to Heseltine. So he did, in what he thought was confidence, and in mild terms – the two were old friends – saying that one sentence in the letter 'does in my opinion contain material inaccuracies', which should be corrected if needed.

In any other circumstances it might have rested there, but Mayhew furnished Downing Street with a copy of his letter, which was leaked to the press; the information officer concerned expressed apprehension that she might be breaking the Official Secrets Act, but Ingham said (according to her 'friends' reported in the press at the time), 'You'll fucking well do what you're fucking well told.' When the letter was made public, the *Sun* screamed 'You liar!' at Heseltine, while Mayhew exploded, and his colleague Sir Michael Havers, the Attorney-General, talked of sending the police to Downing Street, until Thatcher and Ingham sheepishly agreed to hold an inquiry (or cover-up), and lighted on Brittan as the fall-guy.

One of Margaret Thatcher's more attractive characteristics was her philosemitism. Her Finchley constituency had a large Jewish population, and those businessmen, accountants and dentists became almost as much her 'own folk' as her Methodist forebears in Lincolnshire. Her Cabinets contained five Jewish ministers in all (Joseph, Lawson, Brittan, Young, Rifkind), not to mention others she patronized inside or outside Parliament, such as Michael Howard, Charles Saatchi and Oliver Letwin. It was this that prompted Harold Macmillan's witticism, which caused so much merriment in Clubland, that Tory Cabinets were once full of Old Etonians but now they were full of old Estonians, as well as the less jocose opinion recorded by Alan Clark at a dinner of Tory MPs that there were 'too many Jew-boys in the Cabinet'. Still, as Sir Lewis Namier used to say (and that great historian had reason to know this negatively), charm has always surmounted most barriers in England, and it transcends ethnicity. Alas for Brittan, few of his colleagues found his charm irresistible, and his unpopularity made it easier for Mrs Thatcher to throw him to the wolves, although she subsequently tried to make it up to him by finding him a job in Brussels.

The other point which later generations might not grasp was that the law officers, Attorney-General (Sir Michael Havers at the time) and Solicitor-General, were by ancient custom appointed by the government but not strictly members of it. Until well into the twentieth century they were not even paid a salary, but had instead the very lucrative compensation of being able to 'mark their own briefs' or choose which cases they wanted, apart from those such as treason and poisoning where they traditionally prosecuted in any case. The Attorney-General was head of the Bar, the standard-bearer of his profession; and the law officers were the government's legal advisers, providing it, as any other barrister would a client, with advice which was meant to be detached, honest – and confidential. This was not mere sentimental pretence; it wasn't until the Blair government and the Iraq war that the law officers came inside the 'Big Tent' as part of the Downing Street team.

But then Westland was a frightening display of the worst thing about 'Thatcherism', not only its unscrupulous ruthlessness but its destructive contempt for traditional institutions and conventions. At one level Westland was simply a trial of strength between two tough, ambitious politicians, and a piece of dirty work at the crossroads, which took on a life of its own beyond the original rights and wrongs. And yet there was a very important question lurking in the background, as it had been for generations. If it was a choice between him and the open sea, Churchill had told de Gaulle, he would always choose the open sea, which meant the empire and the United States as much as the oceans themselves. In 1986, shortly after the Westland episode, Mrs Thatcher went further than Churchill when she gave Washington permission to bomb Libya from British air bases. This decision put her at odds with the rest of Europe, it was opposed in Cabinet by several ministers, including Tebbit, it was criticized by several Tory papers, the whole of the rest of the government tried to dissociate themselves from it, and it was conspicuously not reciprocated by the Americans. It was an ominous precedent.

But could England turn her back on Europe? There was an ambiguous answer under successive Tory governments. Macmillan had sent Heath to try and effect British entry into the Common Market and Heath had failed, but ten years later, now prime minister himself, he succeeded. In the 1970s the Labour party was more divided than the Tories over Europe, and certainly no less Europhobic on balance: in 1976 Roy Jenkins had left British politics in despair (and for a comfortable billet in Brussels) because of this. But the Tories were more and more divided, as Common Market was transmuted into European Community[3] and then into European Union.

Some Europhile (in extreme cases Euromanic) Tories, Heseltine notable among them, always recognized that the destiny of this whole European project was economic, monetary and finally political union. When Tony Blair years later told the Labour conference that no one had ever wanted a United States of Europe he was ignorant or disingenuous or both. That was precisely what many men had dreamed of and advocated, from the nineteenth-century Italian radical Carlo Cattaneo onward, and what Churchill himself had foreseen after 1945 (what role he saw for his own country in it is another and cloudy matter). That was what Tory Europhiles, if they were honest, looked forward to.

On the other side the party's Eurosceptics, as they came to be called, often more accurately Europhobes, increasingly resented the whole

---

[3] Strictly speaking Communities: in 1973 the United Kingdom joined three of them, the European Economic Community, the European Coal and Steel Community, and the European Atomic Energy Community.

enterprise, and if they in turn were honest, they regretted ever having entered and now wanted to get out. That was just what Enoch Powell did advocate, though now from outside his old party. But if the empire had gone and (as Powell insisted) the Commonwealth was a sentimental delusion, and if England were not to be part of this United States of Europe, what role did she have other than to serve as an American client state? This whole question, this continental divide, was to loom over Mrs Thatcher's last years in office, to precipitate her departure, and to poison her party for at least the rest of the century.

7

Celtic Fringes

For all the economic problems the new prime minister had inherited in 1979, the gravest challenge the government of the United Kingdom faced at this time was the conflict in Northern Ireland, and republican terrorism spreading from there to England. It impinged very closely on Margaret Thatcher. At either end, her premiership was marked by the killing of two of her nearest political friends by Irish terrorists, and her eleven years in office were punctuated by many more murders, some of them also close to her. Her campaign manager for the leadership in 1975 was Airey Neave, who was killed just before she entered Downing Street, her first PPS as premier was Ian Gow, who was killed shortly before she left. In between, the Irish Republican Army tried to kill Mrs Thatcher and her whole Cabinet and did kill several more of her colleagues.

Those were only a few of the characteristic deeds of the IRA. There had been another incident a year before Mrs Thatcher became prime minister, when the IRA fire-bombed La Mon House hotel near Belfast and burned to death twelve party-goers, all of them Protestants, to make as clear as possible the IRA's project of communal murder. One more came in November 1987, when the IRA bombed a religious service in Enniskillen on 'Poppy Day', killing eleven people, again all of them Protestants. They had been commemorating the dead of two wars, in the latter of which the United Kingdom of Great Britain and Northern Ireland had played a crucial part in defeating a Third Reich which Irish republicans had done everything they could to help and whose enthusiasm for which they proclaimed. Nobody could complain that the battle lines, political and moral, in this conflict had not been clearly drawn.

Nor was Ulster the only problem for the Tories on the fringes of the British Isles. Whatever other difficulties they had faced in Macmillan's day, the Union seemed solid, and the Tories looked like a national party. The dozen or fewer Ulster Unionists at Westminster voted as a block with the Conservatives, in 1955 the Tories still held six seats in Wales, and in that year they actually won a majority of seats in Scotland. Within thirty years, even in Mrs Thatcher's prime, they were further on their way to becoming a southern regional party. The Union was fracturing, with a renewed and ultimately successful demand for devolved parliaments in Scotland, Wales and Northern Ireland. And this was the supreme example of where the Tories, having won so many political battles, lost the argument and let others take control of the narrative.

For several decades around the turn of the twentieth century the Tories became known as the Unionists. This advertised their opposition to Irish Home Rule, and, more particularly, the nomenclatural shift made possible their alliance with and then absorption of the Liberal Unionists who had broken with Gladstone over Home Rule in 1886. Long before that the Tories had already been a Unionist party in the sense that they had profited politically from the creation of the United Kingdom of Great Britain and Ireland through the two Unions of 1707 and 1801. Both the Acts of Union were passed through coercion and corruption, and both had pragmatic rather than principled origins (as had the sixteenth-century absorption of Wales). The Union of 1707 between England and Scotland was a defensive measure for economic, religious and dynastic purposes, above all to protect both countries, Scotland if anything more than England, against a restoration of the Catholic house of Stuart – no idle threat, as the adventures of 1715 and 1745 showed.

It worked, and brilliantly. A backward and corrupt country on the verge of national bankruptcy, Scotland was now dragged kicking and screaming into the eighteenth century, to its immense advantage, economically, culturally and intellectually. The story of Georgian Scotland is instructive, not least in terms of later nationalist romance. In that long century from the accession of the first George in 1714 to the death of the last in 1830, political life in Scotland was extinguished. The country was ruled despotically, by the Duke of Argyll and then by the Lord Advocate; forty-five Scottish MPs, mostly primitive Tories, were returned to the House of Commons at Westminster by an electorate which in 1790 numbered throughout Scotland in total about 3,000.

And this was the greatest age in Scotland's history, the age of the Edinburgh enlightenment, of Hume, Adam Smith, Raeburn, Cockburn, the age when Edinburgh was truly the Athens of the North. Such collective explosions of genius cannot be explained in political or social terms, except that they evidently confute any coarse idea that 'national freedom' means cultural creativity. If anything, the opposite is the case, as many examples suggest, including Ireland and Israel in the twentieth century. For that matter, contemporary with that Scottish enlightenment, from 1750 to 1830, political life in most of Germany was also extinguished, under the decaying Holy Roman Empire and the principalities of the *ancien régime* and then their makeshift replacements; and this was the age of Goethe, Schiller and Grillparzer, of Mozart, Haydn and Beethoven.

That Union worked for other reasons. Linda Colley's admirable and influential book *Britons* described the way a British nation had been forged – deliberately ambiguous word – under the Hanoverians, by the experience of war, by the expansion of empire, and by Protestantism. For some reason this book and its thesis were disapproved of by the fogey right, although what she said, with much illustration, seemed unarguable. By the nineteenth century there really was a British nation. And as the British empire continued growing towards its apogee, Scotland was a junior partner in the great enterprise, but very much a partner none the less.

In 1801[1] this united Great Britain was united in turn with Ireland, a second Union which was not a success, for equally obvious reasons. The 'United Kingdom' of Great Britain had been quite an odd affair: whatever sacrifices Scotland had made, she kept her own Scots law (in many ways superior to English) and her own Presbyterian established Kirk. No Hanoverian monarch even visited Scotland for more

---

[1] The Union came into being at the beginning of that year though it is sometimes dated 1800, the year the Act of Union was passed.

than a hundred years until George IV's hilarious visit of 1822 (when he sought to humour the natives by donning a kilt, or, as Macaulay put it, by 'disguising himself in what, before the Union, was considered by nine Scotchmen out of ten as the dress of a thief'), still less attended services of the Church of Scotland. A few decades later Queen Victoria found her favourite home at Balmoral and began attending the local kirk, with the bizarre consequence that she was an Episcopalian in one country but became a Presbyterian when she crossed the Tweed northward.

Such quaint anomalies were nothing compared with the second Union, which was based on the implicit – and absurd – assumption that Ireland too was a Protestant nation. The Protestant Episcopalian Church of Ireland, the established church in that country, was united with its sister-church, the Church of England, and four of its prelates were sent each session to sit in the House of Lords, along with representatives of the Irish temporal peerage. Irish MPs, all Protestants at first, were sent to the Commons in what seemed merely equitable numbers at the time, though they ceased to be that, one way and then the other, as the century advanced. By the early 1840s, the population of Ireland was eight million or more, which was half as much as the population of Great Britain, and it could have been argued that Ireland deserved a third of all MPs. The catastrophe of the Famine, followed by decades of emigration, meant that Ireland, uniquely in Europe, had a smaller population in 1900 – or in 1940, or even in 2000 – than in 1840; and by the end of the century, Ireland was grossly over-represented in the Commons with 105 Members, or nearly a sixth of MPs. Since these Members were by now four-fifths nationalists, there might have been some unconscious relief in seeing the back of them, even on the part of Englishmen who called themselves Unionists.

If Catholic emancipation had helped wreck the old Tory party, the Home Rule crisis of 1886 was vital in the development of the modern Conservative party. It was a peculiarly bitter period, and it encouraged further the political 'cleavage of classes'. Even after the split in the Liberal party, its ranks still included a very few of the higher aristocracy, such as Lords Spencer and Ripon, as well as the fascinating figure of Lord Beauchamp, who helped turn out the lights of Europe when, as Lord President of the Council, he formally declared war on the king-emperor's behalf in 1914.[2] But most of the upper classes had left the Liberals for good and those who did not were brave to weather the consequences. London Society, encouraged by Queen Victoria, did its best to ostracize Home Rulers; Brooks's Club, once the heartland of Whiggery, was almost torn apart by political blackballing, each side doing down the other. And those old Whigs who remained faithful were less important politically than the ones like Hartington who defected, who were in any case less important in turn than the defectors from the other end of the Liberal party, Chamberlain and the Radicals. Within not many years the defectors of 1886 had become hard to distinguish from Salisbury's party. The Liberals put off another Home Rule Bill until the parliamentary balance after 1910 dictated its return. The Tories, or Unionists, not only fought that tooth and nail but also fought Welsh disestablishment, not distinguishing very successfully in either case between 'ought' and 'is'. 'Ought' Ireland was Protestant, when in fact its inhabitants were overwhelmingly Roman Catholic; 'ought' Wales was Episcopalian, when in fact for generations it had been swept by Dissent, when the chapels were, along with the language, the central strand in Welsh identity, and when in many villages the only members of the Established Church were the squire and the parson. For a High Tory such as Lord Hugh Cecil, Welsh disestablishment was nevertheless another national apostasy, while for a young Unionist on the make such as F. E. Smith it was an opportunity for vulgar rhetoric.

The defeat of the first Home Rule Bill of 1886 had greatly benefited the Tories in terms of domestic British politics, as Salisbury cynically exploited the question for all it was worth with short-sighted glee. The second Home Rule Bill of 1893 had passed in the Commons after Gladstone's heroic last attempt to bring justice to Ireland, but had been defeated in the Lords, giving notice that as long as the upper house held its veto there would be no further such measure. Salisbury

[2] He later closed a different chapter for the old order when he left the country to avoid prosecution for homosexual offences, subsequently inspiring – *mutatis* very much *mutandis* in terms of sexual orientation – the exiled voluptuary Lord Marchmain in *Brideshead Revisited*.

made it plain that he opposed Home Rule not in the name of democracy (in which he never pretended to believe) but of Property: his cause was 'All who have land to lose . . .' A hundred years or more later it is indeed comical to look back and see the way that he and landowning Irish Unionists like Lord Lansdowne were obsessed by the idea that an autonomous Ireland would represent a grave threat to the existing social and economic order, which just goes to show how wrong you can be. At the same time, something quite unforeseen and unintended had happened. Successive London governments, principally Tory governments, had tried to kill Home Rule by kindness, legislating to relieve misery and then, on a startlingly drastic scale, to bring about land reform by breaking up and distributing the huge estates. This did not in the event kill the demand for self-government, but it turned the Irish from a people of starvelings and outlaws into a nation of sturdy farmers and traders; and it meant that when Home Rule was at last granted in the name of a Free State Ireland would become, as the intelligent Tory Lord Crawford predicted at the time, 'the most reactionary corner of the Empire'.

But in the course of the Ulster crisis of 1912–14, something happened which was also unforeseen and even odder. To their amazement, or without quite recognizing the fact, the Tories found themselves in the right. In their own favourite terms, they were entirely in the wrong, as they tried to thwart the imposition of Home Rule on Ulster by non-parliamentary and even violent means: the party of Crown and constitution came near, uniquely in the past century, to fomenting insurrection and civil war. With the words, 'I can imagine no length of resistance to which Ulster will go, which I shall not be ready to support, and in which they will not be supported by the overwhelming majority of the British people', the Unionist leader Bonar Law defied the law of the land.

With their proposal to paralyse the government by voting down the Army Annual Act, die-hard Tory peers, led by the fox-hunting Lord Willoughby de Broke, would have disarmed their country as Europe trembled on the brink of war. With the Curragh incident of March 1914, many army officers, Tory Unionists to a man, effectively turned mutineer. With his secret intrigues on behalf of the Ulster rebels and the Curragh mutineers, General Sir Henry Wilson, the director of military operations, betrayed the trust of the state he served. Ten years later Wilson was assassinated by IRA gunmen; he might with more justice have been executed for treason.

And yet, funnily enough, the Tories were turning out to be in the right in terms of democracy and self-determination. No myth became more powerful, but was more absurd, than that the British government wilfully partitioned Ireland from malice aforethought and as a ruse, when it should and could have created a self-governing united Ireland against the fiercely held wishes of the Unionists of Ulster. In his books *The Strange Death of Liberal England* and *The Damnable Question*, George Dangerfield was one of those who made this case. It was wholly false. Earlier the Tory Lord Randolph Churchill had cynically 'played the Orange card', but this was a very apt metaphor: at the bridge table, one card is played to take the other three and win the trick, and Lord Randolph's object was to use Orange resistance not to break Ulster away from the rest of Ireland but to keep the whole of Ireland within the Union.

That remained Balfour's policy also, and then Bonar Law's, or ostensibly so, insisting that the Tory principle was opposition to Home Rule at all, with or without special treatment for Ulster. In complete contradiction of any idea of wilful partition, the Cabinet in the summer of 1916, after the Easter Rising, reviewed the options, and its minutes recorded that 'the permanent partition of Ireland has no friends'; even after the war, the London government still hoped for a self-ruling united Ireland under the Crown, and Lloyd George's 1920 Government of Ireland Act was based on that objective: while partitioning Ireland for the time being into twenty-six counties and six, it provided for their reunification, though again of course under the sovereignty of London, which republicans flatly rejected.

In the event, partition arrived edgewise, by degrees, unloved on all sides whether Nationalist or Unionist, Tory or Liberal. But once the principle of partition was grudgingly accepted, the Tories found themselves for the first time with an immensely strong moral argument. This was something Bonar Law grasped. A son of the manse, his father a dour Presbyterian minister from Coleraine in County Londonderry, he was the only British prime minister ever to have had a close personal attachment to the Ulster cause (and the only one ever to be born outside the British Isles, in New Brunswick, where his father had gone to serve).

Because of that background, or perhaps despite it, he understood the Ulster question better than almost anyone. When the Ulster crisis of 1912 was at its height, a Roman Catholic Tory, the sonorously named Lady Ninian Crichton-Stuart, wrote to Bonar Law with the hope that nothing he and his party did would stir up sectarian animosity against her co-religionists. He replied that he hated religious bigotry, which was true: despite his childhood (or perhaps because of it) he had grown up an agnostic, and was anything but a zealous Protestant or Orange fanatic.

But try 'reversing the picture', he said to Lady Ninian. Suppose that by the accidents of history the settlement in Ireland had turned out the other way after the great conflicts of the sixteenth and seventeenth centuries; that the mass of the Irish people in the southern three provinces had become and remained staunch Protestants (he might have added that less likely things had happened elsewhere in Europe); that they had acquired a strong national consciousness and were now demanding an autonomous parliament in Dublin; but that the same historical vagaries had left a compact and organized community of a million Roman Catholics in eastern Ulster, 'who looked with horror upon the idea of being governed by Orangemen and claimed the right to continue under the control of the British Parliament. In that case, whatever the reason, I should think their claim was just; and in the same way, whether the reasons which actuate the people of Ulster are sound or not, I think that their claim is one which this country cannot without dishonour disregard.' In parliament he asked similarly whether 'any prime minister could give orders to shoot down men whose only crime is that they refuse to be driven out of our community and deprived of the privilege of British citizenship'.

After the Great War, he also made what remains, in the context of Ulster and of very many other national conflicts besides, another unanswerable point. The Ulster people were being condemned – as they would be again seventy or eighty years later – for making no concessions, when 'what is being asked of them is not concession but the surrender of everything they have been fighting for', and this over 'one simple issue – that they will not be put under a Dublin Parliament without their consent. In my opinion *the fact that they do not consent is enough. It is not for us to judge whether they are wise or foolish in refusing.*' The words here italicized demolish the whole 'republican' case then and since, and many other irredentist cases as well.

That really was the nub of the matter, and it became more acute as the extreme version of Irish nationalism called republicanism developed its venomous and sterile character. It claimed to be reviving the Gaelic language and culture, it was most certainly bent on narrow clericalism which would turn the independent Irish state for generations into one of the narrowest theocracies in Europe, and all the while it continued to make an irredentist demand on Northern Ireland. That is what Stephen Gwynne, the old Home Rule MP for Galway, meant in 1918 when he saw his own party being swept away by Ourselves Alone[3] and he said, 'If Ireland as a nation means what de Valera says it means, it does not include Ulster.'

Although the Tories found themselves inadvertently in the right, they accepted the Free State with ill grace and managed to forget their decades of bitter opposition even to a modest degree of autonomy, and there must have been many sensible Tories who later thought in their hearts what George V – a sensible conservative himself – said to Ramsay MacDonald in 1930: 'What fools we were not to have accepted Gladstone's Home Rule Bill. The Empire would not have had the Irish Free State giving us so much trouble and pulling us to pieces.' For half a century after the Treaty, the English turned their back on Ireland, both parts of it. A lamentable moment came almost unnoticed at Westminster shortly after the creation of the Stormont statelet, when the Speaker ruled that the Commons could no longer discuss the internal affairs of Northern Ireland, which meant that much authentic injustice (if not as much as republicans claimed) was permitted under the authority of, but not with proper invigilation by, the national parliament, and that the Ulster Catholics were treated as second-class citizens (although not treated in the same way as black South Africans under apartheid, or German Jews under Hitler, two of the specific comparisons republicans have made). In David Trimble's

---

[3] A good fascist name, though widely known by the version 'Sinn Fein' in the official 'first language' of the Irish state which no one actually spoke.

brave words when he received the Nobel Peace Prize in 1998, Northern Ireland under Stormont was a cold house for Catholics.

During that half-century, from the creation of the statelet under the 1920 Government of Ireland Act until its suspension by the Heath government in 1972, Ireland was almost forgotten by the English. The southern Unionists were abandoned to their fate, A. J. P. Taylor wrote, 'although they became a cosseted minority, a contrast indeed to the Catholics of Northern Ireland'. The first part of that was simply wrong, as so often with Taylor's sweeping phrases. Leave aside all other evidence and look merely at population statistics. At the time of partition, the Roman Catholics in six-county Northern Ireland were about 34 per cent; by the end of the century they were at least 44 per cent and maybe increasing. At the time of partition, the Protestant minority in twenty-six-county southern Ireland, later the Republic, was more than 12 per cent, by the end of the century it was less than 2 per cent. If those figures applied to respective minorities in any other two adjacent European territories, no one would have adduced it as evidence that the latter minority had been cosseted.

Then events horribly caught up with the English when violence erupted in Ulster at the end of the 1960s. No honourable Tory – or any Englishman – should properly have objected to the slogan of the original Ulster civil rights movement: 'British rights for British citizens.' Men and women who were, whether they liked it or not, British subjects, residents and taxpayers, were entitled to the protection of the Crown, which many of them did not receive. But before those wrongs could be righted the problem had taken on hideous new dimensions. Even during the Stormont period there had been still more anomalies within this none-too-United Kingdom, beginning with the bizarre fact that two of its four component parts, the kingdoms of England and Scotland, both had established churches, though quite different ones, while the other two, the principality of Wales and the province of Northern Ireland, did not. When conscription had been brought in during the Great War it did not at first apply to Ireland. Numbers of Irishmen joined up voluntarily, and fought and died, though fewer proportionately than from England and Scotland. Then the generals and their fellow-Unionists insisted that it should be applied to Ireland also, one of the greatest displays of Tory pigheadedness there ever was, which united Catholic Ireland in opposition, was condemned by the bishops, and led to a general strike closing the whole country outside Belfast, including the bars. It was a dismal idea even from the perspective of those who proposed it: calmer army officers pointed out that any attempt to enforce conscription would require more military manpower than it could possibly raise.

Following that episode, and then the creation of the Free State, the truth had dimly dawned that abandoning Ireland to its fate had freed the Tories from an incubus. They no longer had to defend the indefensible by retaining the three Catholic nationalist provinces forcibly against their will. Any specifically Tory tradition in Ireland had died by the twentieth century. Large numbers of Ulstermen called themselves Unionists, but they were that purely in a 'single-issue' sense and would many of them naturally have been Liberal or later Labour voters. Indeed the settlement, such as it was, left the internal politics of both parts of Ireland in a condition of infantile paralysis as late as the beginning of the twenty-first century. In the north politics were divided over a partition which had taken place more than eighty years before, and in the south by a civil war fought in 1922–3, the rights and wrongs of which few Irish people under fifty could even explain.

Although Mrs Thatcher said that 'Any Conservative should in his bones be a Unionist too', she did not always give the impression that she felt this in her own bones, and the Tories did not have an impressive record in this period, either in principle as Unionists or as honest rulers of Ulster: Labour were much better, in 1968–70 and again in 1974–9. When the province flared up in 1969 the Home Secretary – while Stormont existed, the London minister ultimately responsible for Northern Ireland – was James Callaghan, who made a much better fist of it than his immediate Tory successor. Maudling never had a grip of the troubles, treating the situation with the insouciance which was his trademark, agreeing fatally to an ill-thought-out plan for internment, and summing up his own feelings as his flight left Belfast once: 'For God's sake bring me a large Scotch. What a bloody awful country!'

In 1972 the recrudescence of violence reached an appalling level, with scores killed by the IRA, and a number of demonstrators shot by the army in Londonderry, which inflamed Irish and American opinion much more than anything the Provos did. All this was contemplated by the Tories with a sense of hopelessness. Almost more alarming than Maudling's thirsty weariness was the fact that, in his last period as Foreign Secretary, Lord Home[4] suggested in a confidential memorandum that Great Britain might have to extricate herself from Northern Ireland: 'The real British interest would be served best by pushing them towards a United Ireland rather than tying them closer to the United Kingdom.'

Even at the time the Heath government was making such a mess of Ulster, the Tories could still claim to be a British national party, before that phrase was appropriated. Although the Liberals, and then Labour from as early as 1923, took most seats in Scotland, the Unionists won a slight majority of Scottish seats in 1900; in 1945 the Tories were still hanging on well, with twenty-nine Scottish seats to Labour's thirty-seven, and as late as 1955 – one of those political facts so unlikely as later to excite disbelief – the Conservatives won most seats in Scotland, thirty-six to Labour's thirty-four.[5] Thereafter the story was one of decline and fall, until the collapse of 1997. In Wales the most seats the Tories ever won was fourteen out of thirty-eight at Mrs Thatcher's 1983 landslide. Throughout these Celtic extremities, the whole period was one of melancholy, long, withdrawing roar for the Tories, and they became the party everyone loved to hate, the losers in the game of narrative in Scotland as well as Ireland, before their final rout in England also. Indeed in Ulster, despite their long and somewhat corrupt connection with the Unionists, the Tories quite never grasped the point: it was not that Ulster Unionism had a particularly good case, it was that Irish republicanism had an absurdly bad case.

To muddy the waters still more came the saturnine Enoch. At the first 1974 election, when Powell gave up his seat in the Midlands and implied that his followers should vote Labour, he looked towards Ulster; he was chosen as a Unionist and returned as MP for South Down at the second 1974 election. It was to be one more display of Macleod's saying, 'Poor Enoch, driven mad by the remorselessness of

[4] Like Hailsham, he renounced his peerage but then returned to the Lords with a similar title.
[5] There was also a solitary Liberal, Jo Grimond in his northern fastness of Orkney and Shetland.

his own logic.' The academic rigour he liked to flaunt simply did not apply in Ulster, and the truth was that Powell, though exceedingly clever, was unusually lacking in judgement.[6] Above all, his politics were increasingly ideological and doctrinaire, turning round that obsessive word sovereignty. His acolytes followed him, and in the case of Northern Ireland as in the case of European integration, obsessively screeched about sovereignty when they should really have been talking about democracy.

And yet Powell did not manage to influence Mrs Thatcher much on the subject of Ulster when she became prime minister. Shortly before, she had lost a friend. Neave was a belligerent, not universally popular MP who had had an adventurous war, including a spell as a prisoner in Colditz. Mrs Thatcher had rewarded him for running her leadership campaign in 1975 by making him shadow spokesman for Northern Ireland, and he was playing an active part in the 1979 general election campaign when he was killed by a car bomb as he left the Palace of Westminster. The bombers were ostensibly a breakaway or splinter group from the Provisional IRA, although such terms always needed to be qualified: little happened in Catholic republican Ulster without the knowledge and at least tacit approval of the 'Provos'.

Shortly after the election the IRA carried out a series of ferocious attacks. One bomb killed eighteen British soldiers at Warrenpoint in County Down, and another blew up the holiday boat carrying Lord Mountbatten off the coast of County Sligo. Along with Mountbatten, the elderly Dowager Lady Brabourne was killed, as well as her and Mountbatten's fourteen-year-old grandson. This was a doubly eloquent statement. The IRA had always excelled at killing women and children, and Mountbatten had been one of the famous military leaders of a war in which the Irish Free State was neutral throughout and in which the militant Irish republican movement was not neutral at all. In 1940, Sean Russell, 'chief of staff' of the IRA, went on a clandestine mission to Berlin and met Ribbentrop, Hitler's foreign minister later hanged at Nuremberg, concluding cordially that 'Our

[6] That was true even in his literary or scholarly life. He wrote a cranky work of history, about the mediaeval House of Lords, a crankier study of the origins of the Gospels, and passed the crankiest test of all by becoming obsessed by the idea that Shakespeare's plays were written by someone other than Shakespeare.

ideas have much in common.' And as a Dubliner might have added, a truer word he never spoke. It was more than fifty years later that the admirable Dr Joseph Hendron, a Belfast MP for the moderate Catholic Social Democratic and Labour party, called Sinn Fein 'a sectarian and fascist organization', while John Banville, the most eminent Irish novelist of his generation, said despairingly: 'Those of us who have always thought of the IRA, and indeed Sinn Fein, as neo-fascist, are deeply worried by the kind of respectability they have won now in Dublin, London and Washington.' If the democratic government of a great power could not win a popularity contest against a small gang of pro-Nazi child murderers, what battle for hearts and minds could it win?

Following those murders, the problem was acutely illustrated by Mrs Thatcher's first test, when a group of IRA prisoners went on hunger strike. After Stormont was prorogued and direct rule introduced in 1972, Whitelaw had been appointed as Northern Ireland Secretary, and the first of a line of upper-class buffers who were for some reason considered appropriate for the province. In a disastrous decision, Whitelaw had allowed IRA prisoners to enjoy special status, conceding their own claim that they were political offenders. That was reversed by Roy Mason, who was Northern Ireland Secretary in Callaghan's 1976–9 Labour government, and easily the best holder of the office there ever was. Mrs Thatcher rightly refused to make any concessions to IRA blackmail, but when one of the terrorists, Bobby Sands, killed himself by starvation, nationalist Ulster, southern Ireland, and Irish America were swept by a wave of indignation, much greater than the crocodile tears which Irish and Irish-American politicians shed when the IRA murdered women and children. Even in England, a large part of *bien-pensant* opinion sympathized with Irish nationalism and viscerally disliked the Ulster Protestants, and while Powell, with his tendency to conspiracy theory, was probably wrong in thinking that Mountbatten had been killed with the help of the CIA, he was not wrong in thinking that many people in the Whitehall establishment – or even people in his former party, as Home showed – quietly hoped to be shot of the troublesome province.

At the Tory conference in Brighton in October 1984 Mrs Thatcher looked in on one small evening party at the Grand Hotel, where as it happened I was talking to Norman Tebbit and one or two others, before making my way elsewhere. A few hours later, a huge IRA bomb ripped two floors of the hotel apart. Dozens of people emerged from the hotel in various states of undress and more or less badly hurt, Keith Joseph elegant and quizzical in silk dressing-gown, some in shredded clothes. Lord Gowrie organized somewhere for the dazed evacuees to sit, and Peter Morrison, who later played a minor but crucial part in the Tory story as Mrs Thatcher's last PPS, said dreamily that it was 'Probably some Young Conservatives playing silly buggers with the fire extinguishers.' It soon transpired that several people had been killed, among them the amiable MP Anthony Berry, and the wife of John Wakeham, the chief whip. Norman Tebbit's wife Margaret was so badly injured that she became permanently confined to a wheelchair. By pure accident the prime minister was a room away from one where she might have been, and where she would have been killed; or in Alan Clark's unhappy comparison: 'Mrs T had been saved by good fortune (von Stauffenberg's briefcase!).' And he added, 'But what a coup for the Paddys. The whole thing had a smell of the Tet offensive. If they had just had the wit to press their advantage, a couple of chaps with guns in the crowd, they could have had the whole government as they blearily emerged.' It was not the Tet offensive, and Mrs Thatcher was at her bravest and best when she addressed the conference later in the day.

But her officials, under American pressure and with the connivance of the Dublin government, were still engaged in the desperate search for a 'political solution'. This next took the form of an Anglo-Irish agreement suggesting a new role for the Irish Republic in Northern Ireland. The details of that mattered much less than the fact that the agreement was negotiated between London and Dublin, and with politicians of the nationalist Social Democratic and Labour party kept privately but fully informed, while Unionist leaders were just as deliberately kept entirely in the dark. It then seemed to come as a surprise when the Unionists reacted violently. Powell told Mrs Thatcher in the Commons that 'the punishment for treachery is to fall into public contempt', and the Unionist MPs precipitated by-elections by all resigning their seats, marking the final estrangement between Ulster and the Conservative party.

In all of this there were messages for the Tories, if they could have read them, one very ominous. They, more than any, should have understood the vanity of human wishes and the limits of human action. For years past plenty of people involved in the conflict, including senior British generals, had said that there was no military solution in Ulster but this missed the conceptual point. There was no victory available in the terms of Alamein or Normandy, no start line, no objective, no plan of campaign, and even to think in such terms was straightaway to go awry. The alternative to a (supposedly impossible) military solution was a (supposedly possible) political solution, and it became clearer and clearer what that meant. From the late 1960s Conor Cruise O'Brien had seen through the republican case, the tradition in which he had been brought up, and resolutely opposed the IRA ever after. He would be asked, he once wrote, what answer he proposed to the Ulster problem, and he would answer: 'None.' The language of problem and answer was not apt to the case. In Ulster there was not a problem but a conflict, which would persist as long as the province contained a large, conscious Protestant community and a militant republican movement. Any search for a political solution was likely to be transitory, and likely also to exacerbate rather than heal the division between the communities, which is precisely what has happened twenty years after the Brighton bomb, when Protestant and Catholic are more segregated than ever before.

Ten years after Brighton, I wrote an essay on Ulster in the *Spectator*, in a mood of bleak pessimism and echoing Cruise O'Brien, to which the late Martyn Harris responded in the same magazine. What would happen, he confidently averred, was that the British would withdraw, leaving behind a power-sharing government and that the Unionists would be 'bribed or bullied into accepting it'. That was an accurate description of the subsequent 'peace process' and Belfast Agreement, but he also derided Cruise O'Brien's and my view that there was no political solution available in Northern Ireland, and wrote that this was 'really a Unionist position in disguise'. It was not a bad point to make – except that those who made it should have recognized that, if saying that no political solution was available was really a Unionist position in disguise, then logically and by the same token what was called the search for a political solution was really a nationalist position in disguise. That was what it looked like to the Ulster majority.

The graver problem was of public opinion, and it applied to this whole story of the death of Tory England, which may be said to have begun in those Celtic fringes. Mrs Thatcher had been brought to power by the collapse of the Callaghan government's cynical devolution plans. As the 1980s went by, that subject did not go away. Scottish recalcitrance irritated Mrs Thatcher, as did the determination of the politicians and people of Scotland to acquire internal home rule while they continued to be heavily subsidized by the English taxpayer, which is what 'devolution' meant. She tried to persuade them of the errors of their ways: in her 'Sermon on the Mound' to the General Assembly of the Church of Scotland in 1988, she preached the Presbyterian virtues of self-help and individual autonomy, in which the Kirk had once believed but did no more. It was no good. The Tory decline in North Britain continued. At the 1987 election, which Mrs Thatcher won easily throughout the United Kingdom, the number of seats the Tories won in Scotland had already been halved, from twenty-one out of seventy-two four years earlier, to ten. In Wales, where the Tories had won fourteen out of thirty-eight seats in 1983 – their best tally during the twentieth century – they dropped back to eight. It was a harbinger of impending catastrophe.

There was another kind of disaster only months before Mrs Thatcher fell, when Gow was killed by another car bomb, at his home in Sussex. He was a genial, pompous man, something of a parodic fogey, who claimed to be unaware how to catch a London bus, but who was more human in his way than many Tory MPs, and had at least some interests outside politics (he and the late Duke of Devonshire once discussed mournfully, with occasional interpolations from myself, the sad disappearance of Eastbourne – Gow's parliamentary seat, and a fief of the duke – as a Sussex county cricket ground). More to the point, he had served as Mrs Thatcher's very close friend and counsellor. He was her parliamentary private secretary during her first government, and the best she ever had, although his very devotion may have irritated her. 'Like many men who find their love unrequited,' his friend Alan Clark said, 'he was becoming more and more subservient and attentive. The stooping, obsequious family retainer, speaking very often in a special high-pitched tone that was almost tearful.' It was she who was tearful at his funeral, maybe half-consciously realizing the victory Irish republicanism had won by persuading even a Tory prime minister to propitiate it, while it murdered those close to her. In truth, unionism in the broadest sense had won many battles, political, economic, cultural. That was true even of the supposedly autonomous Irish Republic, which never acquired true economic let alone military independence, while its attempt at cultural or linguistic independence, through the Gaelic revival, was a total and abject failure. In Ulster itself there was, on the one side, Irish 'republicanism' and 'Ourselves Alone', a supposed political party which was in reality the front organization for, and controlled by, a gang of terrorists engaged in communal killing, child murder and ethnic cleansing, not to say a fascist movement with a long history of antisemitism and ardent support for Hitler. On the other side was the country which had invented parliamentary government and which, in the summer of 1940, had flown the standard of freedom against the Third Reich. And yet the IRA remained heroes throughout much of the world, admired by millions of Americans, seen as misguided but understandable even by many English people, revered in Europe. In 2004, the supposedly left-wing Paris daily paper *Libération* devoted an entire page to a gushing tribute to Bobby Sands, who had streets named after him in several French towns. Much of the world had accepted the narrative proposed by the enemies of the British state, of the Conservative party, and of liberal democracy. If the Tories could not win that argument, which could they win?

8

'Not exactly vulgar . . .'

Even without much help from the Celtic fringes, Mrs Thatcher had no difficulty in winning the 1987 election: an extraordinary and historic achievement. Salisbury had won three elections but not consecutively, the Tories had won three successive elections in the 1950s but under three successive leaders. Never since Lord Liverpool or the great Reform Bill – which is to say since a time when conditions were so different as to make comparisons almost meaningless – had one leader won a hat trick of three elections in a row. And although the number of seats the Tories won fell from 397 to 376, their share of the poll was the same and the numbers voting for them increased.[1] Labour staged a modest recovery, though Kinnock was still dismayed to be beaten so easily, and the Alliance, not always behaving in a very allied way, held its own in terms of seats on a reduced poll. Reading those runes suggested that there might yet be problems for the Tories. Labour had nearly fallen through the floor in 1983 but was now recovering. Even if there were still substantially fewer people voting Labour than at any election from 1945 to 1979, the party was on a gentle upward curve. Much harder to spot at the time was that the secret of success for the third party might not need to be proportional representation, which neither of the two larger parties was ever willingly going to grant, but could be tactical voting.

For the time being Mrs Thatcher's problems were inside her own party, with the continuing – though much evaded – questions of her succession, and of Europe. She had another and deeper problem. Her

[1] Tories: 13.8 million votes, 42.3 per cent, 376 seats; Labour 10 million, 30.8 per cent, 229 seats; Alliance 7.3 million, 22.5 per cent, 22 seats; Others: 23 seats.

first governments had carried out a formidable programme of loosely coherent reforms, libertarian in inspiration and underlain by the idea of individual freedom and responsibility. Labour and her other enemies were baffled politically. Ending exchange controls, privatizing industries, curbing the unions, selling council houses, had all been opposed by the left and sometimes greeted with a lack of enthusiasm within the Tory party. But they had all been popular with the electorate, and they had all demonstrably worked. Not only was Labour quietly moving away from the ultra-left position of the early 1980s and the longest suicide note, it was increasingly clear that any future Labour government would leave most of those reforms in place.

Any further reforms were another matter. 'Thatcherism' had not run out of steam, but it began to look as if it was flailing around blindly, and as if the government, driven on by Mrs Thatcher's sheer bad temper, was conducting a broad attack not only on vested interest but on many of the very institutions – local government the supreme example – which Conservatives should have been encouraging. Disraeli may not have been a profound thinker, but some of his cynical aphorisms were still apt. 'Conservatism discards Prescription, shrinks from Principle, disavows Progress; having rejected all respect for antiquity, it offers no redress for the present, and makes no preparation for the future,' was by no means a bad description of Mrs Thatcher's brand of Conservatism 140 years after *Coningsby* was published. And to say, however facetiously, in the same novel that the Tory party 'treats institutions as we do our pheasants, they preserve only to destroy them' might have been a motto for the later years of the Thatcher regime. Her disdain for universities, for the temples of high culture, for the learned professions of medicine and law (even her own Bar), was temporarily invigorating, but then debilitating. But the most shocking work of destruction was her onslaught on local government.

It was a fantasy cherished by some wets that vigorous representative local government was an English tradition reaching back to the Domesday Book and beyond. In fact, until the nineteenth century, the boroughs had been ruled by corrupt municipal corporations and the shires by lord lieutenants and justices, magnates and country gentlemen appointed by the government. Still, they were a supremely self-confident class, and they maintained a tradition of local autonomy which passed smoothly to modern representative local government as created by Tory governments, with the 1888 Act introduced by C. T. Ritchie in Salisbury's government and the 1928 Act introduced by Chamberlain in Baldwin's. The 1980s saw a complete reversal. The Thatcher government centralized administration in every field, destroyed the Greater London Council, the (admittedly unsatisfactory) successor to the LCC which the Tories had once created, and then set about wrecking the system of local government finance. There was even a terrifying moment when one Cabinet meeting under Mrs Thatcher actually discussed the possibility of abolishing local government altogether. Looking back, even her admirers would have to admit that she had a lot to answer for.

Although having been one of the earlier candidates considered *papabile* to succeed Mrs Thatcher, and now rehabilitated and brought back into the Cabinet after the election as Energy Secretary, Parkinson's realistic chances had gone. So had Tebbit's: after steering the Tories to the third victory as party chairman, he had decided to leave frontbench politics. Heseltine had very much not been rehabilitated. He said that he had absolutely no regrets about resigning, since he knew what his fate would have otherwise been: frozen out, undermined, briefed against, and finally despatched to Wales or Northern Ireland, the Tory equivalent of the power station in Omsk. He now had a clear mission, and he was on his own:

> Down to Gehenna or up to the throne,
> He travels the fastest who travels alone.

Despite all the appearance of infighting and backbiting, and those earlier purges, the Thatcher government was by this time quite stable at its higher levels. Hailsham had been Lord Chancellor for all eight years of her first two administrations, which was far too long. He had been kept on as an act of kindness on the prime minister's part, had become a minor embarrassment, and was now replaced by Michael Havers as another 'kindness. In the 1980s, White's and Pratt's had been succeeded by the Garrick as the club where you could most easily convene a Cabinet committee at the bar. It might have consisted of Nigel Lawson, Geoffrey Howe, Cecil Parkinson and, very far from least, Havers. He would later be recalled with affection and even awe by other Garrick members as a most amiable man who, when Attorney-General for Mrs Thatcher's first eight years, and then briefly Lord Chancellor, was able to arrange his workload so skilfully that he could spend two or sometimes the best part of three hours lunching at the club several days of the week. His final appointment was not a success, however, and he lasted less than six months before he made way for the unlikely figure of Lord Mackay, a dour Scotsman and extreme Presbyterian who would not speak to Sunday newspapers since they broke the Sabbath. He was once nearly expelled from his fissiparous little kirk for attending the memorial service of a colleague in a Roman Catholic church, but he was also a distinctly better lawyer than many who have sat on the Woolsack.

He most certainly did not tipple at the Garrick or anywhere else, although most of his Cabinet colleagues were more relaxed, as were London politics at this time. Having already edited the *New Republic* in Washington, Michael Kinsley spent a year in the late 1980s working for the *Economist*. Many interesting and remarkable sights met his eyes in London, but the most extraordinary was when the magazine held its weekly lunch and entertained as chief guest a Cabinet minister. This man drank a couple of gin and tonics as aperitif, several glasses of wine with his meal, and then a glass of brandy. In Washington (and whatever might have been the glorious older traditions of the three-martini lunch, or of senators' 'striking a blow for liberty' over a bottle of bourbon with Vice-President 'Cactus Jack' Garner), any serious politician would by then as soon be seen snorting cocaine in front of journalists as polishing off that much drink. The Tories had not quite forgotten what they had owed to the licensed trade, or 'better England free than England sober'.

As for the great offices of state, as they are sonorously known, Mrs Thatcher had four Home Secretaries in all, Whitelaw for four years, Brittan for a little more than two, and then Douglas Hurd for another four, until the government began to fracture in late 1989 when he was replaced by David Waddington. Until that point she had only two Chancellors, Howe for four years and then Lawson for more than six. Howe had moved to the Foreign Office in 1983, where he served for six years, longer than any Foreign Secretary since Sir Edward

Grey's epic and tragic tenure from 1905 to 1916. Both Lawson and Howe were to be impaled on the question of Europe, although not before they had done important work in their departments. Lawson brought the Thatcher revolution another stage closer to completion when he reduced income tax to a level unknown since the 1930s.

In some ways Lawson was more Thatcherite than Thatcher, whose own commitment to privatization and the free market was qualified by her prejudices and her electoral instincts as Member for a constituency of affluent property-owning democrats. To the end her government failed to make one crucial 'Thatcherite' change of transferring the control of interest rates to an independent Bank of England. That had to await the arrival of the wise monetarist Gordon Brown at the Treasury in 1997. She had originally been unenthusiastic about selling council houses because it was unfair on those who already owned their homes, and she resisted another vital move of ending the income tax relief on mortgage interest. Along with her suburban voters, she actually liked rapidly rising house prices, and it was a measure of her intellectual limitations that she never grasped the fact that, far from being somehow separate from general inflation, this was its single most dangerous motor.

Nor did she see that the problem with booms is that they too often turn to busts. That was just what happened shortly after her third election victory. In the autumn of 1987, Wall Street crashed, not on the scale of October 1929 but badly enough to take the London Stock Exchange a long way down with it. This coincided with the most dramatic and destructive storms England had known since the eighteenth century, which destroyed vast woodlands, almost as though Providence were warning the prime minister. There were to be sure dangers ahead, not least another boom-and-bust. House prices had been shooting up far ahead of incomes and prices generally, but they stopped, and began to fall, leaving many voters first stuck with houses hard to sell and then trapped in negative equity, when they could only sell their houses for less than they had paid for them with huge mortgages. Not everything was happy in Middle England.

When Palmerston had once compared the deft management of the force of opinion with the skill that enabled a man at the helm of a ship to control the mighty winds of heaven and the waves of the ocean, he had said something profoundly true and important. The rest of the nineteenth century and then the twentieth would prove his claim that those who 'avail themselves of the passions, and the interests, and the opinion of mankind' could effect a sway over human affairs far greater than that which merely belonged to the power of the state. His younger contemporary Marx may have been the more brilliant mind, but Palmerston, the flippant and amorous Irish aristocrat, was in this the more far-seeing. Men did not merely follow brute force, nor yet their objective interests; and as Karl Kraus had prophesied all too accurately, ideological factors would trump economic interests throughout the twentieth century.

One slow but inexorable shift in the current was under way, the ebbing of socialism from its mid-century high water mark. Around 1950, socialism in the sense not so much of the welfare state but of state direction of the economy was very widely seen as the inevitable pattern of the future. Nye Bevan had not been alone in thinking that Soviet Russia was bound to overtake the West economically, nor Tony Crosland in thinking that the problem of economic growth was solved. That was an easy assumption to make in western Europe during the *trente glorieuses* of the *Wirtschaftswunder*, the glorious thirty years of economic miracle in France, Germany, several other European countries, and indeed in England. It needed the shocks of the sixties and seventies to show up such complacency. The failures of both Labour and Conservative governments between 1959 and 1979 gave a new impetus to older doctrines of the free market.

By the time she reached Downing Street, Margaret Thatcher had gathered around her skirts her own group of court intellectuals, some of them from that tradition, some not, some more impressive than others. Not a few of those who became her ardent supporters had begun life on the left, from the historian Hugh Thomas, to Paul Johnson, a former editor of the *New Statesman* who had once called for the abolition of all traditional institutions from the Brigade of Guards to the House of Lords and who had been enraptured by the student revolt in Paris in 1968, to the extreme case of Sir Alfred Sherman, who for a time ran the Centre for Policy Studies, the innocuously named right-wing think-tank, and later became an advisor to

Radovan Karadzic. Thomas had written a history of the Spanish Civil War, Sherman had actually served with the International Brigades as a devout Communist. There was nothing unusual about this rightward tendency, which had been a phenomenon throughout the century and throughout the west. The revealing truth about many of these was that they had become right-wingers, but not Tories. It was no doubt because of their idiosyncrasy that they had an affinity with Mrs Thatcher, although in their bellicose intransigence transferred from left to right they also illustrated Newman's saying that convictions change but habits of mind endure. They encouraged her own cantankerous opposition to many of her colleagues, as well as her disdain for much custom and tradition.

One or two imaginative writers also had an affinity with Mrs Thatcher, though not many. Kingsley Amis was another defector from the left (in fact another former Communist) who became a devotee, although his own balletic leap from left to right was so huge that he found her something of a liberal trimmer. But if Thatcherism had a bard, as Kipling was the bard of imperialism and Yeats of Irish nationalism, it was Amis's great friend Philip Larkin. She was the first politician he had responded to since the austere socialist Sir Stafford Cripps, Larkin said. On one occasion when they met, she quoted, or rather misquoted, a line of his as 'Her mind was full of knives' (*recte*: 'Your mind lay open like a drawer of knives'), in a way which suggested that she had once read the poem. It was an interesting Freudian slip, and her own version of the line said something about her personality; 'Not that I don't kiss the ground she treads', Larkin added.

He had already shown himself a proto-Thatcherite, or had at least captured one side of her spirit. With all the big talk of individual freedom and economic discipline, Mrs Thatcher's creed sometimes boiled down to the policy of the *Daily Beast* as outlined by Lord Copper: 'Self-sufficiency at home, self-assertion abroad'; both parts of that struck a chord with Larkin. He mourned the passing of a lost (and possibly imaginary) world, and he stared in the face the hedonism of the 1960s with its 'Bonds and gestures pushed to one side', whose flavour he caught still more brilliantly in the lines:

> And every life became
> A brilliant breaking of the bank,
> A quite unlosable game.

He despised the Wilson government's imperial retrenchment which would 'bring the soldiers home' instead of guarding distant places and keeping them orderly, because

> We want the money for ourselves at home
> Instead of working. And this is all right.

He hated the way England had become, years before Mrs Thatcher reached Number Ten,

> First slum of Europe: a role
> It won't be so hard to win,
> With a cast of crooks and tarts

until the day comes when

> all that remains
> For us will be concrete and tyres.

When his admiring friend John Betjeman died, Larkin was offered but declined the Poet Laureateship; Mrs Thatcher should have made him her own court poet.

All the same, Amis and Larkin very much did not represent the broader literary classes. So far from learning to love Thatcherism, with every year that passed the dominant academic or cultural intelligentsia hated this prime minister as they had never hated any before. Macmillan had been cruelly mocked, by Peter Cook in *Beyond the Fringe*, in the infant *Private Eye*, and then Wilson and Heath in turn had been guyed in the same magazine in the form of 'Mrs Wilson's Diary' and 'Heathco'. In turn came the 'Dear Bill' letters in the *Eye*, ostensibly written by Denis Thatcher. These captured him with uncanny accuracy, to the point that phrases like 'little cookie-pusher' and 'right marker in the shits' brigade' became more real than the man himself (although in private he could be even more of a saloon-bar bigot than the spoof suggested).

That squib was almost good-natured; there was nothing whatever amiable about the response to Margaret Thatcher of academia and what were neatly dubbed 'the chattering classes'. She grated on this lumpen-intelligentsia with unique dissonance. It was not difficult to mock in turn the *bien-pensant* consensus, in its smug assumption of virtue and its 'liberal' intolerance. In his book *Our Age*, Noel Annan analysed that consensus with the insight of one who had very much belonged to it. Although he did not write with much warmth about the Cambridge critic F. R. Leavis, Annan knew what Leavis had meant when he spoke of a 'confident new orthodoxy'. It was this consensus which had largely governed England for decades, and had assumed it would go on doing so, and it was that confident orthodoxy which was appalled when, in the 1980s, it was challenged for the first time.

During the first Thatcher years the new clerisy chafed and gnashed its teeth but bided its time, as the prime minister laid about her at Labour, Galtieri and Scargill. Then, in early 1985, she came up against a more intractable foe in the form of her old university. In so many ways she should obviously have been seen as a credit to Oxford, its first woman graduate, and its first science graduate, to reach Number Ten. Previous Oxonian prime ministers had been made honorary Doctors of Civil Law (the gong appropriate to statesmen) as a matter of course, the latest of them Wilson and Heath; one Balliol man, Macmillan, had been elected Chancellor of the University in 1957 by Convocation, the alumni of the university, and he was to be succeeded in 1987 by another, Roy Jenkins.

But Mrs Thatcher was in some ways a very atypical product of that costive and complacent academy. She fitted in neither with its traditional culture of lightly worn learning and port-seeped languor nor with its more recent progressive tinge. Even in her own time Oxford had still retained a Tory flavour, but by the 1980s the SDP had been greeted in few places more eagerly than in the home of lost causes, still whispering the last enchantments of the Attlee age. An opportunity to block an honorary degree was available to Congregation, the dons or faculty, and in 1985 they duly took it. Their pretended cause was the government's 'cuts', notably in higher education, but that really concealed a much deeper visceral dislike. A few *Thatcherisant* dons were disgusted. The eminent classicist Sir Hugh Lloyd-Jones made the point that he had detested and despised Wilson, but that Wilson was an Oxonian prime minister and it would never have occurred to Lloyd-Jones that he should not have a degree.

That episode was only a foretaste of what was to come. In 1987 the chattering grew louder and more anguished. Even at that election, the opinion of the cultural elite was startlingly at odds with what proved to be the wishes of the people. One or another *vox* not very *pop* suggested that, if the franchise had been restricted to writers and artists, Mrs Thatcher would have been swept away. Sundry members of the cultural elite were asked how they would vote. Some were engagingly frank about their self-interest. 'As an artist,' the composer Sir Michael Tippett said, 'I'm impelled to vote Labour, since it's the only party committed to double the arts budget', which was echoed by the actor Antony Sher: 'As a member of the arts [*sic*] I am heartened by [Labour's] pledge to double the arts budget.' Another key word was used by the philosopher and lover of both indoor and outdoor games, A. J. Ayer, who was going to vote for the Alliance without much hope it would win, 'but at least it is not philistine'.

Those responses were comparatively restrained. More and more, the mark of Thatcherphobia among 'members of the arts' was its sheer verbal violence. Michael Frayn merely thought that it was necessary to vote whichever way offered 'the best hope of getting the present barbarians out', while Julian Barnes saw the chief function of the election as 'to turn out Mrs Thatcher and her spayed cabinet, whose main achievement in the last eight years has been the legitimization of self-interest as a public and private virtue'. Most forthright of all was the television playwright Dennis Potter, who thought that the most appropriate response to the election 'would be to hawk up a gobbet of contemptuous spittle onto the ballot paper'. He manfully overcame this impulse, to continue his analysis: 'Mrs Thatcher is the most obviously repellent manifestation of the most obviously arrogant, dishonest, divisive, and dangerous British government since the war. All that really counts is getting these yobs and louts away from the swill bucket.'

Alas, the louts stayed at the bucket, the barbarians weren't turned out, the hopes of Labour and the Alliance were dashed, while Mrs Thatcher and her spayed government kept almost exactly the same percentage of the poll as four years earlier and, on a higher turnout, won more popular votes than any party before. How could the British people have paid so little attention to the views of university common rooms, members of the arts, and literary north London? Why did they not even share the intense personal revulsion so many *belles âmes* felt for Thatcher herself? It was not that anyone could seriously think the English, let alone the Scots or Welsh, loved the Lady. At that election a point was made very shrewdly by James Reston, the veteran commentator of the *New York Times*, revisiting his native island.[2] By then, he said, the American people had ceased to think that President Ronald Reagan was doing the country much good, although they were still fond of him personally. The British by contrast had never much liked Mrs Thatcher herself, but they still thought she was the woman to run the country.

That was a view, amazingly enough, which was shared even by some eminent artists and writers. The novelist Anthony Powell admired her while admitting that she had no conversation apart from politics, while the painter Francis Bacon said sensibly enough, 'It simply isn't the point of politicians to be pro-art. I don't know if she admired painting all that much, but it doesn't matter.' He was seconded by the novelist and critic Peter Ackroyd, who said that he preferred a leader who honestly didn't pretend to be interested in the arts to a cultural phoney.

More tellingly, Annan perceived why Thatcher was so hated by the chatterers, in a way which illuminated the weakness of their position. The Webbs had believed that all the world's ills could be righted through the efficient compilation and application of statistics by a superior caste such as themselves. Although the Fabians (or at least the Webbs) were quite as philistine as Thatcher was ever accused of being, another thread was woven in, personified by Keynes, a great and immensely influential political economist who became the first head of the Arts Council. When Oliver St John Gogarty was made first film censor of the Irish Free State he had said that his mission was 'to prevent the Californication of Ireland', and Keynes, from an aesthetic rather than moral perspective, had been no less publicly determined to fight the values of Hollywood on behalf of European

[2] 'Scottie' Reston was so nicknamed because he had been born in Scotland and brought to America as a small boy.

High Art. In both economic and cultural terms, Annan saw, the new elite had assumed that, under whatever government, the country would be run not only by, but for them. The Tories had had a few of their own 'members of the arts', cultivated politicians like Sir Edward Boyle and David Eccles, who gave the party some veneer of cultural sophistication, but they were now gone.

That complacent assumption had been broken by Thatcher as decisively as she broke the miners' strike. She appealed over the heads of the clerisy to the common people. She instinctively recognized, what never occurred to the confident new orthodoxy, that all state subsidy of the arts' represented a net transfer of wealth from poor to rich, and was in that sense deeply undemocratic. She rode on the backs of the yuppies, another much derided group in the 1980s, with the most extreme species being the 'barrow boys' of the City. In 1986 came 'Big Bang', the comprehensive deregulation of the City by the removal of its own former restrictive practices. In its wake these young market traders of modest birth and education had shoved aside the indolent Etonians and made fortunes which they conspicuously did not spend on the fine arts of civilization.

It was that unapologetic *enrichissez-vous* spirit of the Thatcherite era that Peregrine Worsthorne, a Tory journalist who lived spiritually in the 1930s, or perhaps the 1830s, memorably denounced as 'bourgeois triumphalism', a phrase which delighted the chattering left. Even more fascinating was another phrase used by his near contemporary, the Marxist historian E. J. Hobsbawm, who had joined the Communist party in 1936 (the year of the Moscow Trials) and was, by the time Bolshevism was thrown onto the dust-heap of history fifty-five years later, the only intellectual adornment that British Communism could still claim. Although Hobsbawm had intelligently dissected the left's failures, he was still repelled by Thatcherism, with its 'anarchism of the lower middle classes'. As another historian, Tony Judt, pointed out, this neatly combined two bugbears of the old left: a loathing of anarchism, or the idea that people could live together in society through co-operation and mutual aid, without a vanguard party (not to say secret police and labour camps) to keep them in order; and a contempt for the petty bourgeoisie, a class which had a tendency to think for itself and try to control its own life.

The trouble was that the lower middle class, let alone the working class, outnumbered the educated and fastidious literary class. Mrs Thatcher herself was in some ways truer to her origins in her lack of serious artistic interests. She made a political point when she favoured the opera festival at Glyndebourne, which managed very successfully with no state subsidy at all. Her only concession to subsidized culture was to attend the Royal Opera, where Sir Robert Armstrong, her Cabinet secretary, was secretary to the board, and which she recognized as a great national institution. When that company came near to extinction during the closure of Covent Garden in 1998, it gave an extraordinary concert performance of the *Ring* at the Albert Hall. The cycle was attended by, among others, Paul Channon, who had been arts minister in 1981–3, and his wife Ingrid. Talking to them in the interval about the crisis, I said that it would never have happened under Mrs Thatcher. 'It would not,' Channon agreed. 'Whatever Margaret knew about art, she recognized excellence.'

On the other hand she disliked the subsidized National Theatre, and never went there again after her theatrical speechwriter took her to see *Amadeus*, whose foul-mouthed portrait of Mozart shocked her sense of propriety.[3] She would have been still more shocked if she had seen Howard Brenton's *The Romans in Britain*, which was grossly indecent (and utter tripe), or *Pravda*, David Hare's witlessly feeble satire on the mass media and Rupert Murdoch. Apart from anything else, these pieces comically displayed the sheer arrogance of the cultural elite. Writers and artists had always hoped for the patronage of the mighty, and in turn from Horace and Virgil onwards they were expected to sing for their suppers by fawning on their patrons. Now for the first time writers assumed that they would be generously paid by the government to insult the government.

After her third electoral triumph, the hatred of Thatcher among the cultural elite and the chatterers began to acquire a pathological and paranoid tinge. Another survey of chattering opinion in 1988 found the admirable poet Peter Porter shuddering at the 'bullying, stupid and brutal' Mrs Thatcher, while Jonathan Miller, the opera director

---

[3] She might have been on better ground if she had echoed James Fenton's sharp verdict that Peter Shaffer was 'the worst serious English playwright since John Drinkwater'.

and all-purpose pundit, went further than any others. He hated the prime minister's 'odious suburban gentility' and the way she appealed to 'the worst elements in commuter idiocy'. She was 'loathsome, repulsive in almost every way', and the question of why the bulk of the cultural establishment was so hostile to her was silly: 'It's the same as why the bulk of the human race is hostile to typhoid.'

One left-liberal group was named Charter '88 after the year of its creation, and an anti-Thatcherite magazine was launched called *Samizdat*. But both names deliberately echoed the resistance in eastern Europe: there had been a Charter '77 in Czechoslovakia, and *samizdat* was the Russian name for dissident underground publication. Most of these Chartists were comfortable professional men and women; the magazine was edited by Ben Pimlott, a charming man, an excellent political historian,[4] and a salaried professor at London University. His keen intelligence was not seen to best advantage when he compared himself and his colleagues with persecuted Russian writers, or Czech professors who had been reduced to working as janitors and cleaners.

On top of that came the news of what called itself the 20 June Group. This was the ultimate gathering of Bollinger Bolsheviks (originally Churchill's tag for Nye Bevan), the supreme expression of radical chic, the very image of Engels's 'form of socialism which has actually donned evening dress and lounges on sofas'. Its prime movers were the playwright Harold Pinter and his wife Lady Antonia Fraser, whose first husband Hugh Fraser we have met as an engaging romantic Tory MP and forlorn-hope runner for the leadership in 1975. At their house in Holland Park they assembled a cadre of *résistants* which included John Mortimer and Melvyn Bragg,[5] as well as Margaret Drabble, Fay Weldon and Salman Rushdie (before a threat from another regime than Thatcher's forced him into hiding). What the name 20 June commemorated is now lost in the mists of the late 1980s; given *Samizdat* and Charter '88, it's perhaps a relief that these martyrs did not call themselves the 20 July Group after the men who had tried to kill Hitler in 1944. That might have appealed to two

[4] Whose biographies of Hugh Dalton, Harold Wilson and the queen all cast useful oblique light on our story.
[5] Subsequently to become Sir John and Lord Bragg at the hands of the Blair government, by way of *médailles de la résistance*.

playwrights. In 2004, the genial and amusing Peter Nichols looked back on the heady days of that resistance group: 'It's not easy to remember, now, how difficult it was at the height of Thatcher's regime to speak out against her.' And Pinter scented persecution everywhere. When asked about his group he said, 'We have a precise agenda and we are going to meet again and again until they break down the windows and drag us out.' All of these people instinctively spoke and wrote as if England at this time were an occupied country ruled by a military dictator, rather than governed democratically by the most electorally successful prime minister in political history.

Any overtones of snobbery which might have been detected in Worsthorne's and Hobsbawm's words now swelled into a great crescendo. One fastidious enemy of Mrs Thatcher after another complained about the butchers and taxi-drivers who supported her, and about the *garagistes* in her own Cabinet. Lady (Mary) Warnock, the philosopher who was head of Girton College, Cambridge, was repelled by Mrs Thatcher's lower-middle-class manner; her clothes and hair were intolerable, 'packaged together in a way that's not exactly vulgar, just *low*'. The lack of caution these critics displayed was quite remarkable. There had always been a strong vein of snobbery on the intellectual left, but it might have been supposed that, by the eighties, *soi-disant* radicals could have found a better reason to dislike a Tory prime minister than the fact that she was so common. And there was also an unmistakable sense of bitterness and rejection, when the masses had so disgracefully continued to support Mrs Thatcher. In their hearts, many of these critics felt like Algernon in *The Importance of Being Earnest*: 'Really, if the lower classes don't set us a good example, what on earth is the use of them?'

At the same time, there was more than a hint that these haughty anti-Thatcherites were not truly 'men of the left'. Of course the true left did not love Thatcher, but it often felt a wary respect for her, and it was a frequent complaint on the left of the Labour party at the time that Neil Kinnock was not fighting the corner for socialism as she was for capitalism. Even those further to the left could admire her. Raphael Samuel was a beguiling social historian and sometime Communist. Only months after her fall, he saluted Margaret Thatcher and her innate, if untutored, sense of history.

On Russia and eastern Europe, if not on southern Africa, on enterprise culture if not on education, and even in her brutal treatment of uneconomic pits and the coalfields, she showed an intuitive capacity to seize on what was new and developing – perhaps the first condition of the historical imagination – and she clearly cares passionately about the past, or at least her version of it.

He instanced her 'excited intervention' in the debate over how history was taught in schools; her superbly tactless lecture in 1989 at the time of the *bicentenaire* of the French Revolution, telling the French that it was the English who had invented liberty (a good Whig sentiment rather than Tory); and her invocation of 'Victorian values'.[6] In all of this he found that: 'One of the unnerving things about Mrs Thatcher for anyone on the left was that she spoke our language, or at any rate addressed our traditions, far more convincingly than she did those of her own party.' Her strength and weakness within that party had been her outsider status, which was just what Samuel admired her for. She

had no feelings for the traditions of the British ruling class or – despite her invocations of Churchill – for the imperial dimensions of British history, whence her impatience with the Commonwealth and her indifference to royalty. A lifetime of active politics seems to have insulated her from, rather than drawn her into, the mystique of Westminster and Whitehall.

She reached out instead to the provincial England of her childhood, constructing an alternative national epic in which there was a merchant-adventurer in every counting house, a village Hampden in every store . . . She spoke in accents not of church but of chapel, and in her radical contempt for paternalism it is not difficult to find echoes of her Northamptonshire shoe-maker forebears. Her version of Victorian values was of a piece with this, invoking the plebeian virtues of self-reliance and self-help rather than the more patrician ones of chivalry and noblesse oblige.

This tribute from a serious and thoughtful radical was not only touching but significant, not least because Samuel was himself very much outside the liberal *bien-pensant* consensus. He was thus conspicuously free of the sheer sneering superiority of Thatcher's critics

[6] The phrase was first proposed by Brian Walden in a television interview, Mrs Thatcher concurring.

from within that consensus, whether One Nation Tories or north London liberals or those whose distaste was connected with a deeper resentment. Just as the labour movement had never been quite sure whether the capitalist system was on its last legs and needed only a final push to be toppled, or was healthy enough to be milked over and again, so the cultural-intellectual left had never quite decided whether it liked increasing prosperity or not. Orwell used to say in his glum way that true socialism would mean that most people would be worse off, and not just the rich, but 'Vote Labour and get poorer' was never likely to be an election-winning slogan. Labour's underlying claim had long been that it could act as an agent to take money off the undeserving rich and redistribute it.

But then what? The astonishing prosperity of the postwar years had brought more material prosperity and sheer wealth to greater numbers of people than any Victorian exponent of the market economy, let alone Marx, had ever dreamed of, but the left was not sure what to make of it. Throughout the 1950s and 1960s there was a continuing bleat against the get-rich-quick society, a sheer revulsion from the explosive production and consumption of goods, including labour-saving goods. An anthology could be compiled from this time of left-wing complaints about the proliferation of cars, televisions and even washing machines (which last could have seemed a luxury only to men who had never tried to wash a week's laundry for a large household by hand).

Now, more than thirty years after Macmillan's complacent but correct words, there was a fresh howl of disappointment. The novelist John Fowles complained about 'the self-centred notions of the new conservatism'. He was shocked by 'this rightward and selfward tendency in most of the electorate since the 1950s', a cult of personal advantage made worse now by 'the ethos of the grocer's daughter'. Still more frenziedly, the poetaster Adrian Mitchell shrieked that 'Thatcher's vision is a little plastic credit card.' The most horrible manifestations of Thatcherism for Mitchell were 'unisex aerobic centres, sado-video centres and plonk bars. And it was under Thatcher that you were first offered Filofaxes, mangetout peas, jacuzzis and compact bloody discs.'

However risible or simply contemptible all this may have seemed, it had a corrosive effect on Mrs Thatcher and the Tories. 'How many divisions has the Pope?' Stalin asked when the political position of the Vatican was mentioned. It was a foolish question. Rigorous reactionaries such as Joseph de Maistre had once extolled the glorious alliance of altar, throne and scaffold. During the nineteenth century that alliance tottered, as the Church was beset by liberalism, nationalism, rationalism and, the most dangerous ism of all, industrialism. The two classes which had supported it, aristocracy and peasantry, both dwindled, and Catholicism found that it had to appeal to argument, and enter the arena of democracy, which it did with considerable success. Even at the apogee of Stalin's own career, the weight of the Catholic Church helped turn the crucial 1948 election when the Communists might even have taken Italy by electoral means. By the end of the century the Church was embattled and declining and in some countries even imploding, but it was still there.

In a comparable way, even when socialism was dead as practical politics, it survived as a sentimental myth, even in England where the mass party of the left had not even been Marxist. There was a pervasive if indefinable sense that the left was somehow nicer than the right, a perception which the Tories at their bloodiest and most brutal had done nothing to discourage. Even when the Thatcher government was seen to be doing harsh but necessary work, it had always appeared dislikeable, even to many of those who voted for it. As *1066 and All That* had seen the Cavaliers and Roundheads, Labour at its worst could still seem Wrong but Wromantic, and Mrs Thatcher's Tories at their best as Right but Repulsive.

By the time Mrs Thatcher departed, literary-intellectual sentiment had become almost totalitarian in its unanimity. This was nicely caught in Martin Amis's novel *The Information*. Two writers, one more successful than the other, are talking about politics.

'That would be Labour, of course.'
'Obviously.'
'Of course.'
'Of course.'
Of course, thought Richard, yeah: of course Gwyn was Labour. Obvious not from the ripply cornices twenty feet above their heads, not from the brass

lamps or the military plumpness of the leather-topped desk. Obvious because Gwyn was a writer, in England at the end of the twentieth century. There was nothing else for such a person to be. Richard was Labour, obviously. It often seemed to him, moving in the circles he moved in and reading what he read, that everyone in England was Labour except the government ... All writers, all book people were Labour, which was why they got on so well ...

It was easy to laugh at that complacency which Amis nailed so well, writing several years after the fall of Mrs Thatcher. She was contemptuous of her sneering critics, and would have been entitled to point out how grossly their resentment at not being taken seriously had been translated into odious condescension, and for that matter to ask what was wrong with Filofaxes and compact bloody discs. All the same, those patronizing chatterers were not simply impotent bystanders. Throughout the 1980s there was an undercurrent of hostility toward the prime minister, even on the part of those who voted for her; even on the part, as events would show, of her own MPs and Cabinet ministers. The shade of Palmerston warned about the danger of neglecting the narrative argument; so had Beatrice Webb when she said, 'There is no such thing as spontaneous public opinion. It all has to be manufactured from a centre of conviction and energy.' For all her successes, Margaret Thatcher had not done that, and it was an omission for which she would pay, as would her party.

9

November Criminals

Throughout 1989 and 1990 trouble deepened for Mrs Thatcher, her government, and for much of what she represented. At home, that is; abroad was a quite different story. As we have seen, at the *bicentenaire* in July 1989, Mrs Thatcher offered her own interpretation of a French revolution which had changed history, and had been hailed by later revolutionists as their great precursor. The Bolsheviks regularly invoked the memory of Robespierre and Marat, and in the 1930s the French intellectual left used the example of the original Parisian terror to justify Stalin's purges. With its claim to be the heir to all revolutions, Communism had seemed to be reaching an apogee in the middle years of the twentieth century.

That was when the twenty-five-year-old Margaret Roberts first stood for Parliament. In 1950, she had proclaimed the need to 'rise up and fight totalitarianism' in her first election address, and had said quite correctly that the nature of Communism could be seen in China, where more than a million people had been put to death in the year following the Communist seizure of power (she did not know then that there would be another seventy or more million to come before Mao had finished). The following decades saw what often seemed the irresistible advance of Communism, with Khruschev's boast that 'we will bury you', Castro's takeover in Cuba, and then another tide of victory in Indochina. Pol Pot took the socialist principle of equality to its logical conclusion by setting out to make the population of Cambodia all perfectly equal once they were all equally dead, and in 1975, months after Mrs Thatcher became Tory leader, South Vietnam fell to Communism as the Americans scuttled from Saigon.

At that moment, it was barely possible to discern that within fifteen years the whole structure of Soviet Communism would have dissolved like cloud-capped towers and palaces, an insubstantial pageant leaving not a rack behind. Even when they came, the events of 1989–90 seemed dreamlike in their improbability. Rumbles of discontent throughout eastern Europe turned into vast explosions of public protest, Communist governments – or 'Communist', since regimes which called themselves that had everywhere been long predeceased by Marxism-Leninism as a doctrine in which anyone in those countries actually believed – swayed and crumbled. And then on 9 November 1989, a more momentous and more heroic date than 14 July 1789, the Berlin Wall came down.

Many people could claim a share of the credit for that, above all the heroic resisters of east Europe, the men and women whose Charter '77 and whose *samizdat* had been grotesquely echoed in England. Credit also went to Ronald Reagan, who had been much mocked when he accurately called Soviet Russia an evil empire. But few in the west could claim more credit than the woman who had told the electors of Dartford nearly forty years before, 'We believe in the democratic way of life. *If we serve the ideal faithfully, with tenacity of purpose, we have nothing to fear from Russian Communism.*' It was Margaret Thatcher who had, as opposition leader, acquired the nickname of the Iron Lady after she addressed the continuing moral challenge of Communism, notably in an exceptionally thoughtful and well-informed speech written by Robert Conquest, the great historian of the crimes of Communism. It was she who had gazed at the Berlin Wall in 1982 and said the Soviet leaders knew very well that 'their pitiless ideology only survives because it is maintained by force. But the day comes when the anger and frustration of the people is so great that force cannot contain it. Then the edifice cracks: the mortar crumbles.' At a time when plenty of western politicians, on the right as well as the left, had been content with 'peaceful coexistence' for the indefinite future, she had said that 'one day liberty will dawn on the other side of the wall'. Eight years later, few men or women of her age were so vindicated.

Alas, tenacity of purpose was what her Tory colleagues had come to dread, not least the tenacity with which she hung on to office. Many prime ministers had done quite short stints at Downing Street.

To take only postwar names, Eden and Home were not entirely forgotten even though they had neither of them served as much as two years. Lloyd George and Attlee had served historically crucial premierships lasting six years, which had set a kind of par for the course, only beaten until then in the twentieth century by Asquith with more than eight years. In 1985 Mrs Thatcher surpassed Lloyd George, and Asquith in 1987.

For years the unspoken assumption had been that she would find a good and dignified moment to stop, but as each year passed it became ever clearer that there would never be such a moment. What was more, by the time she overtook Asquith she had accomplished her predestined will, in Yeats's phrase. The unions had been tamed. Inflation had been brought down. Economic growth had revived. Large swathes of nationalized industries had been privatized. Hundreds of thousands of council houses had been bought by their owners. The Falklands had been retaken. The tendency toward centralization within the European Community had at any rate been checked. Lawson had reduced direct taxation to a lower standard rate than for decades and to a top marginal rate which would have seemed impossible ten years earlier.

She might have left it there, but leaving it there was not in her nature, and, having taken the credit for those successes, she now had to take the blame for the accumulating failures of her last years in office. Two epigraphs might have stood for those years. 'In der Begrenzung steigt sich erst der Meister', said Goethe: the hand of the master is shown in recognizing limits, or genius is knowing when to stop. And Acton said that 'Power tends to corrupt and absolute power corrupts absolutely.' Mrs Thatcher did not know when to stop. Even when 'the Thatcher revolution' had been carried out, she could not imagine standing aside, to the point where that project came to look almost like crazed Maoist permanent revolution, a project which of course could not be entrusted to other hands, which might betray it.

It was not merely a matter of personal foible or failing. Mrs Thatcher had insisted in 1975 that 'We must have an ideology. The other side have got an ideology. We must have one too.' There was something to be said for that at the time, although the way the ideological, anti-European, unilateralist and sometimes Trotskyist left was trying to take over the Labour party, and the consequences thereof, might have been seen more as warning than example. But she forgot that Toryism is fundamentally unideological, and must be; that any ideas it picks up are makeshift and never immutable. Peel converted the Tory party, or a section of it, to Free Trade, while the Tariff Reformers tried to convert them back again; some Tories were appeasers, while Churchill was a resister; many Tories had accepted the managed economy and the welfare state, some had clung hard to the faith of the free market and competition; from the 1960s, some Tories passionately supported European integration, while some passionately opposed it. Forgetting that policy must be adaptable, and exalted by her self-belief, Mrs Thatcher had cut a legislative swathe through one institution after another, in the end alienating very many quite different sections of society on whom a Conservative government might be thought to depend: doctors, lawyers, academics and in fact just about every group except the police.

This culminated in the debacle of the poll tax. Having identified a real problem – the excesses of supposedly (but in reality none too) representative local government, and the inequities of the way the existing rates or property taxes were operated – the Tories managed to come up with a doctrinaire and abstract answer which created quite as many problems as it solved, a new levy on rich and poor alike which predictably led to even deeper resentment than had the rates. Later, the poll tax would illustrate the old saying that success has many parents but failure is an orphan, and pinning down responsibility would not be easy. The tax was a levy on individual residents rather than on the value of real property and was first dreamt up inside the Department of the Environment (that Orwellian name), but it was promoted with enthusiasm by men in the party machine and the Tory press, and it did not at first distinguish left and right. Chris Patten was, if not a dripping wet, clearly on the liberal wing of the party, and he failed to kill off the misbegotten tax when he moved from Overseas Development to take over at Environment in the summer of 1989.

Then there were two clever men who had been at Eton and Cambridge together, Oliver Letwin and Charles Moore. Letwin was the son of remarkable parents, Bill and Shirley Robin Letwin, Jewish-

American academic neo-conservatives *avant la phrase* who had settled in London and become popular and hospitable members of a rightist coterie graced by distinguished names – Michael Oakeshott, Elie Kedourie – even if its tone was sometimes lowered by dissipated bohemian journalists. After Trinity, Princeton, Cambridge again, and a learned treatise on *Ethics, Emotion and the Unity of the Self*, and before a spell at Rothschilds and then a parliamentary seat in 1997, Letwin had served in the prime minister's Policy Unit during the second Thatcher government. There he was one of the razor-sharp minds who latched on to the poll tax (as it became universally and understandably known; one mark of the most desperate government loyalists, in parliament and press, in 1989–91, was their insistence on calling it by its Newspeak name, 'the community charge'). His friend Moore became in some ways the central figure in Tory journalism, successively editor of the weekly *Spectator*, the *Sunday Telegraph* and the *Daily Telegraph*, and, though not one of its begetters, defended the poll tax until the very bitter end.

That bitterness had been foreseen by some Tories, of both stolid or subtle intellect. Willie Whitelaw was asked late at night in 1987 what he thought about the tax, and replied, with heaving of the shoulders and reddening of the face, '*Trouble.*' After his sojourn running the prime minister's policy unit in 1982–3, Ferdinand Mount had returned to columnizing. He recognized before most people the problems of the poll tax and diagnosed its likely problems, but his warnings went unheeded at the time they mattered. Even the prime minister saw the trouble, but only too late in the day. The Thatchers had bought a house to move to, if or when they ever left Downing Street, just the kind of 'des. res.' on which the rates had been so high; when she looked at the figures, Mrs Thatcher said almost with surprise, 'It's not fair that Denis and I should be gaining so much on our house in Dulwich when others on £180 or £190 a week are having to find so much to pay.' That was what hundreds of thousands of street protesters – and even some people she knew and trusted – had been trying to tell her all along.

For Mrs Thatcher the deeper problem was the sense of invulnerability and even of infallibility which events had bred in her. As her third ministry went by and economic indicators began to go wrong, it became ever clearer that Lawson's attempt to loosen the economy had unleashed inflation again. The government's unpopularity was attested by terrible opinion polls. But had they not been terrible during her first term, before the Falklands? And in her second, after the Westland debacle? 'Absolute power' may not be the word for any British prime minister, but after her three victories she felt unassailable, and the effect was certainly corrupting.

One sign was her use or abuse of patronage, which was very flagrant. All parties had immemorially used honours for political purposes, and for raising funds (although Labour did not do so in a blatant way until Tony Blair). This had become an open scandal under Lloyd George. Some of his recommendations were grossly unsuitable – one of them, Sir J. B. Robinson, so outrageous that the House of Lords actually blackballed him for his peerage after it had been gazetted. Lloyd George privately defended the sale of honours by saying that when a rich man paid money and received a peerage it was the end of the matter, whereas in America a millionaire who paid money to a party was expecting to buy political influence and commercial advantage. That might have seemed a disingenuous argument, until the arrival of New Labour showed that it was possible to combine the worst of the British and American systems.

However that might be, under Thatcher there was more quo for every quid than at any time since Lloyd George. The building magnate Sir Robert McAlpine, the property developer and newspaper owner Victor Matthews, the hotelier Sir Charles Forte and the industrialist Sir James Hanson were only some of the large donors to party funds whom she ennobled. An honours committee which was supposed to weed out names rarely drew the line, although it reportedly did so with Rupert Murdoch. Again, the parallel with Lloyd George applied. Like him, Mrs Thatcher was a provincial Dissenter by origin, like him she had an innate disdain for the traditional establishment, and as with him that disdain could turn into contempt, and even an indifference for normal standards of decency.

Apart from her thoroughly cynical use of the honours list, she made appointments across whole areas of public life with a partisanship not seen since the eighteenth century. Under Walpole and the long Whig hegemony, no clergyman however scholarly or saintly could join the bench of bishops if he were a Tory; under Thatcher, few people were preferred who were seen as unsound. The Arts Council was meant to be above politics, promoting culture in the disinterested and high-minded spirit of Keynes. Shortly after Mrs Thatcher became prime minister, her financial wizard Alistair McAlpine (son of Robert), who did so much to keep Tory coffers filled, was appointed to the Council, and Richard Hoggart was removed from its vice-chairmanship, because 'Number Ten doesn't like him.' The secretary-general of the Council, Roy Shaw, said that McAlpine's appointment was like making an atheist a bishop (some people might have thought that had already happened), which was unfair since McAlpine was not only yet another genial cove at the Garrick lunch table but a collector of considerable taste. Still, it was without doubt a political appointment in a field where at least a pretence of non-partisanship had long been kept up.

One name stood out in the Thatcherite list of dishonour. Woodrow Wyatt was a young MP in the 1945 parliament, on the socialist left wing of the Labour party, insisting that 'at present the country is far to the left of Labour Ministers', and not without talent, as a journalist and later as a businessman. Quite soon he began to move rightwards. In the 1950s he became a television journalist and did good work exposing the Communist attempts to take over the electricians' union. He lost his seat, found another, then saw his political career fortuitously but definitively ended by the death of his friend and patron Gaitskell. He was given a column in the *Sunday Mirror*, where he wrote in bluff, undistinguished fashion, and then moved in 1983 to the *News of the World*, owned by his friend Rupert Murdoch. Mrs Thatcher had him knighted that year, and made him a peer in 1987.

Both in his column and in the Lords he was an obsequious supporter of the prime minister, and he also acted as her intermediary with Murdoch. That was bad enough. Wyatt was a racing enthusiast, and his original appointment as chairman of the Horserace Totalizator Board in 1976 by Roy Jenkins, a Labour Home Secretary, seemed unexceptionable at the time. But Mrs Thatcher renewed it, and then again, by when it had become clear that Wyatt was a fat windbag with no remaining qualifications whatever for a sinecure which was very well paid, was entirely undemanding, and allowed ample scope for entertaining his friends. It might seem ungrateful for anyone who enjoyed that hospitality to say so, but Wyatt's patronage by Mrs Thatcher was such a shocking piece of jobbery as to represent a real debasement of public life. And although such things, like Ingham's brutal blackguarding of ministers who had fallen out of favour, seemed to serve a short-term purpose, they corroded such moral foundations as the regime had.

More than that, they contributed to the terrible fall that was coming. What transpired gradually, and at the last with horrific clarity, was that, for all her achievements, Mrs Thatcher had lost the support of her colleagues, notably those once closest to her. Howe and Lawson had both been with her from the start. Howe had the longest tenure of any of her Cabinet ministers, just over ten years from the morrow of victory in 1979; Lawson had served with him in the first and most able Treasury team, and then succeeded as Chancellor for six years from the 1983 election. Both were gifted men, although the lugubrious Welsh Howe and the abrasive Jewish Lawson were antithetical personalities; Geoffrey was a nice chap, it could be said, but you wished you knew what didn't make him tick, whereas it was all too clear what made Lawson tick.

Slowly but surely, the two had each had enough of Mrs Thatcher. Their final fallings out with her were ostensibly – and in some ways actually – over policy, and in particular relations with Europe, but the importance of personality in political history should never be underestimated. Lawson had been almost the only man who stood up to her hectoring in Cabinet, even on one truly historic occasion telling her to 'Shut up prime minister, and let someone get a word in edge-ways,' words Howe could never have used. Mrs Thatcher was famous for her kindness towards her staff, secretaries, cleaners and the like. She was tolerant about the foibles of her intimates, some of whose sexual and alcoholic defalcations required a good deal of tolerance. And she treated her principal colleagues abominably, to the point of regularly insulting and humiliating them. Maybe there was some psychological urge behind this, which went beyond her very tense position as a woman commanding men; and there may have been in some measure a psycho-sexual reason why those men put up with it.

In July 1989 there was a reshuffle. Mrs Thatcher's hostility to Europe by now led her to see Howe as an unreliable ally at the Foreign

Office. She offered him the Home Office, and, as Robert Harris wrote, 'Howe failed to spot the scaffold which was being erected for him.' He asked instead to be made leader of the House and Lord President, and to be called deputy prime minister, which she reluctantly granted: Howe had a considerable following in the party, and it would have been perilous to sack him. The next morning, and veritably as day follows night, Howe read stories defaming him in one newspaper after another, the most brutal of which stories, in the *Daily Mail*, said that his new role 'had already been downgraded by Downing Street. It was suggested [by 'Whitehall sources', sc. Ingham] that the titles he has acquired are constitutional fiction – and in any case the prime minister does not think they matter.' This humiliation was a briefing too far; David Howell, who had served in Mrs Thatcher's first Cabinet, found the episode 'nauseating and intolerable', and was so far from alone that when Howe next entered the Commons he was cheered for more than a minute by the Tory benches. Mrs Thatcher and Ingham had not only found a way to breathe new life into a dead sheep, they were infuriating the parliamentary party.

Then in October Lawson finally resigned, after increasing disagreements with the prime minister over economic policy but on the immediate sticking-point that she had insisted on retaining the academic monetarist Sir Alan Walters as her private economic adviser. His resignation speech was comparatively restrained, but damagingly suggested that she had lost control of economic events. When Lawson told her of his intention to resign, she did not even mention it to Howe but discussed it instead with Ingham and Charles Powell, a former Foreign Office man who had been seconded to Downing Street and had become part of her inner circle, or bunker. Resentment of this cabal was growing steadily. None other than Lord Hailsham, Mrs Thatcher's Lord Chancellor for her first eight years, said that what Ingham had done was 'dishonourable conduct'. In addition, a former junior minister, Sir Barney Hayhoe, spoke for many on the Tory benches when he said that the best way to restore confidence would be to have Ingham and Powell 'moved to quieter pastures before the end of this year'.

They stayed grazing noisily where they were, but they could not stop Sir Anthony Meyer. This rather vague and diffident septuagenarian baronet, Etonian, Scots Guardsman (wounded in action), diplomatist before entering parliament where he never rose beyond the humble rung of PPS, availed himself of the procedure which allowed him to stand against Mrs Thatcher as leader, so that in December the party held its first ballot for nearly fifteen years. Meyer won thirty-three votes to her 314, but it was a portent, less stalking-horse than ranging shot. He had showed that it could be done.

In the spring of 1990 the poll tax was at last introduced, and the consequences were all that might have been expected by the gloomiest pessimists. By March, the Tories had lost a by-election in mid-Staffordshire to the biggest swing since 1933, Labour led in a Gallup poll by 24.5 per cent, and Mrs Thatcher achieved another distinction in becoming the most unpopular prime minister since polling began. The party could smell defeat in the air; there was a mood of palpable panic even before Howe resigned in November. Two years later, Chris Patten's election campaign came up with the slightly strained colloquialism 'double whammy' to describe Labour's tax plans; the two resignations truly were a double whammy for the prime minister, a hook and an uppercut which pummelled her sideways. In his resignation speech, the dead sheep at last bit back. He had been continually undermined by Thatcher as he negotiated with other countries, he claimed; in a simile aimed at sporting England, Howe said that serving Mrs Thatcher in Europe was like being sent out to the wicket to find that the captain had broken his bat. He ended his devastating speech with an unmistakable call for others – by which he could mean only one man – to stand up and be counted. The next day Heseltine announced that he would challenge the prime minister for the leadership.

For all the brutality of her regime, it could now be discerned that Mrs Thatcher had lost her grip, or even her will to power. Two men illustrated this in quite different ways, Tim Renton and Peter Morrison. During her first two governments, she had had two chief whips, Michael Jopling and then John Wakeham, who was succeeded in 1987 by David Waddington until Lawson's resignation precipitated a largely unwanted reconstruction of the ministry. John Major moved from Foreign Office to Treasury, Douglas Hurd took his place as Foreign Secretary and was replaced as Home Secretary by Waddington. His successor in turn was Renton, an affable Etonian with an

Oxford First in history. A good deal more to the point than his educational background, the new chief whip was – and was known to be – a henchman of Howe, whose PPS he had once been.

'It is important to consider to what and to whom the loyalty of a chief whip should be directed,' Macleod had written in 1964:

Not, I think, to any individual ... He must, if he is a faithful servant of the party, think first and last of the party. He, too, in the classic phrase, must be 'a good butcher'. It follows that if a Chief Whip becomes convinced that the prime minister is a major liability to the party he would be failing in his duty not to consider alternatives and, if need be, to press for change.

Maybe Renton knew that eerily prophetic passage. Mrs Thatcher now had a chief whip who was indeed convinced that she was a liability and was ready for change. Renton later admitted that he should arguably not have accepted the job, 'as there was too great a philosophical divide between us', but accept it he did, and thanks to that startling miscalculation Mrs Thatcher found at the critical moment that this vital personage was not even neutral, but foe rather than friend.

Despite her earlier class war against the patrician wets, and her subsequently saying that she did not want Hurd to take over since he was one of the 'Old Etonian Tories of the old school' who would go back to the former complacent, consensus ways, she was far from having any rooted prejudice against that particular school. After Ian Gow had served so well as her PPS in her first government, all his successors were Etonians and men of means, partly because she thought it was unfair to expect someone who needed an earned income to do the job. The last of these PPSs was Peter Morrison, vaguely amiable or amiably vague, sexually unhappy,[1] bibulously indolent. In this last November when the election was forced by Heseltine, he became her campaign manager, with disastrous consequences. No serious attempt was made to see which way the party was moving, to canvass, or even to assess the votes. Events showed that Morrison had not properly understood how to conduct the leadership campaign, or the electoral system.

[1] The PPS is often described as a bag-carrier, but when, on the occasion of Morrison's appointment, the Tory MP Jeremy Hanley said 'At last Margaret's got herself an aide who knows how to carry a handbag', it was a gibe his audience understood.

Others had understood it, all right. The most shocking revelation Renton would make years later was not about his own (arguably improper) role but about that of (Sir) Andrew Turnbull and one or two other officials. Turnbull had been the prime minister's principal private secretary since 1988. This was not a political appointment: he had come from the Treasury and would later be Cabinet Secretary. But he intervened during the leadership election to try and alter the party rules, so that the 15 per cent surcharge in the ballot would again apply, as it originally had, to votes cast rather than to eligible voters. As it happened, the brilliant Treasury mind got something right on this occasion: that seemingly recondite change would have altered history. And yet it was absolutely none of Turnbull's business as a salaried civil servant so much as to express an opinion on how the party conducted its internal affairs. Mrs Thatcher's kitchen cabinet had truly become an unconstitutional force in the land.

As to poor Morrison, his performance was summed up by Alan Clark: 'Now he's sozzled, there isn't a single person working for her who cuts any ice at all.' On 20 November the prime minister set off for Paris, for the international summit to reorder Europe after the collapse of Communism, leaving matters in Morrison's unsteady hands. On the afternoon before the vote, Clark found him in his office, fast asleep but, when woken, confident about events. Clark was not, and warned him that MPs could not be trusted to state their true intentions. When Morrison blithely said of the Wintertons (a married couple of MPs), 'Funnily enough, I've got them down as "Don't Knows",' Clark shouted at him, 'What the fuck do you mean, "*Don't know*"? This isn't a fucking street canvass. It's a two-horse race, and each vote affects the relative score by two.' That conversation was a little vignette of Mrs Thatcher's fall: while she bestrode the stage in Europe, her team in London had no idea what was going on.

For all that, the story of her fall had a tragic quality. She was in Paris when the news came through that she had beaten Heseltine, but by 204 to 152 votes, which was, thanks to the system, four votes too few. Another ballot was required. She said defiantly that she would fight again, but on her return the baroque drama unfolded. Cabals and conclaves of ministers were held that night in different places in and about Westminister to discuss what was to be done; a consensus soon emerged that she was fatally wounded and could not survive. She saw her Cabinet ministers, not all together, when she might still have overawed them, but one by one, and one by one they told her the truth. If she stood in a second ballot she would lose to Heseltine, an outcome most of the Cabinet wanted to avoid. Malcolm Rifkind had been Scottish Secretary for nearly five years, a gifted and astute Edinburgh Jewish advocate to whom she had never really warmed. Now he braced himself to tell her that he would not vote for her in a second ballot; whether every member of her Cabinet had done so on the first ballot is something history would never reveal, although when Alan Clark was told beforehand that they were bound to, he said, 'Like hell.'

In the morning, fighting back tears, she told her Cabinet that she was standing down: 'It's a funny old world.' She still had a further ordeal, or so it seemed, her final speech as a rejected prime minister; a potential last humiliation even some of her enemies were dreading. Instead, her swansong was a wholly magnificent performance, the best Commons speech she had given in thirty years, taking cues from the left-winger Dennis Skinner opposite, smiling ironically when a voice on her own side said she was better than the rest of them put together, laying about her with her old zest: 'I'm enjoying this.' For the Tory MPs it was an awful occasion, reminding them what she was made of, what they had done, and what sort of people they were.

Toward the end of his career and his life Gladstone made his last heroic attempt to find a just settlement for Ireland, and the octogenarian prime minister steered the second Home Rule Bill of 1893 through the Commons almost single-handed with one grand speech after another, in a way which humbled his most bitter enemies, few of whom were more bitter than Lord Randolph Churchill. Outside the chamber one evening during that epic display, he stopped a Liberal Unionist, one of those who had broken with Gladstone in 1886. 'And that is the man you deserted,' Lord Randolph said. 'How could you do it?' Many a Tory MP must have asked himself inwardly during Mrs Thatcher's last speech: 'That is the woman we deserted. How could we have done it?'

In one light, the defenestration of Mrs Thatcher could be seen as a supreme display of Tory toughness, but that was not the whole story. An MP talking to Paul Johnson shortly afterwards said, 'I'm afraid it means we've become a party of cowards.' 'And shits.' 'Oh, we've always been that.' This was true enough. The Tories had sacrificed Mrs Thatcher to save their own skins, and it seemed for a time that they had succeeded. But what had happened, and the way it had happened, had an effect on the party which was in the full sense demoralizing. The consequence showed that the party had not lost its capacity for surprise. Apart from those grim interviews, what had shown Mrs Thatcher that the game was up was the curious evasiveness of her senior colleagues about endorsing her formally for the second ballot. John Major, her improbable heir, absented himself with a very convenient attack of toothache, and then with an adroitness which belied his cheeky innocent grin was soon organizing his own campaign. Something else had gone wrong. In 1975, Tory MPs had deposed Heath, and then followed through the logic of their action by choosing her who had challenged him. In 1990, they deposed Thatcher, but lacked the courage to do the same thing.

Once she had tearfully accepted that her time was up, the man who could apparently thwart Heseltine was Douglas Hurd, the Foreign Secretary. But he proved to be yet another of those who 'should' have been Tory leader as orthodox opinion saw it, but who were rejected by the inner consciousness of the party. In the MPs' ballot Hurd was comfortably beaten by Heseltine, who was beaten in turn by John Major (Major 185, Heseltine 131, Hurd 56). Since the technical requirements for a 'majority plus' had still not been met, there should strictly speaking have been one more ballot, but Cranley Onslow, the chairman of the 1922 Committee, high-handedly decided that it was no time for strict speaking, and declared Major the winner.

Even in the aftermath, no one quite knew what had happened. John Biffen put it memorably when he was asked about the destruction of his friend turned foe: 'You know those maps in the Paris Metro that light up when you press a button to go from A to B? Well, it was like that. Someone pressed a button, and all the connections lit up.' Putting it another way some months later, Enoch Powell said to me that it was really quite simple: 'A prime minister who has lost the support of her Cabinet cannot continue,' which was of course true, but the *petitio principii* (as Powell might have said) was why she had lost it. Looking back later, Mrs Thatcher still spoke on television with barely suppressed rage of her colleagues and their '*Treachery!*' Her feelings were subjectively understandable, and it was true that the behaviour of the Cabinet was by definition disloyal, but then, from Heseltine to Lawson to Howe and at the last to the whole party, she had never asked herself what she had done to earn their loyalty. Quite apart from her sheer bullying, she had repeatedly betrayed those she now accused of betrayal.

There were darker portents. It was a reflection on her leadership that there had been no obvious – or even wholly satisfactory – candidate to take her place, and it was a reflection on the Tories that they had got rid of her in the way they had. If the methods used by the Tories to choose a leader had once been, in Humphry Berkeley's phrase, more appropriate to the enstoolment of a chieftain, then the Great Matricide of 1990 was reminiscent of the ritual sacrifice of an ageing chieftainess in an attempt to placate the gods. So far from doing so, its long-term consequences were catastrophic for the party.

Following her deposition, Hurd said in a radio interview that it should not happen again, and she said the same thing herself later. That might have made them sound like bad losers, but they had a valid point. Hurd meant that a party in opposition could do what it liked with and to its leader, but that when a party was in office and its leader was therefore head of government different considerations applied: the British prime minister should be removed only by the people at a general election or by parliament in the clean open air of the Commons. That was well said, but Hurd was too close to politics himself to see the background. Those pusillanimous MPs had acted as they did not for the good of the nation but out of pure self-interest.

In 1983 Mrs Thatcher had got 397 Tories returned to parliament, and then four years later 376, which was still substantially more than at any election before her since the war. And these were now professional politicians from a new class who were in politics as a trade, and for the money. By his later years, Julian Amery seemed a survivor from a remote era. He used to say that, 'When I was young, a man would go into parliament because he was somebody. Now a man goes into parliament to become somebody.' That might have sounded like a High Tory's high dudgeon, but several objective measures testified to this change. There was the disappearing by-election,[2] which showed that, once elected, MPs now hung on to their seats as long as possible. And there was the inability or unwillingness of parliament to throw ministries out or to change prime ministers. Every British government between 1837 and 1874 fell following a vote in the House of Commons, a golden age when parliament really was master of the executive. During the twentieth century that happened just twice: in 1924 when the first, minority Labour government of MacDonald inevitably lost a confidence vote, and in 1979 when Callaghan's troubled Labour government was finally despatched in the same way.[3]

By the late twentieth century, politics had become a trade, and a well-rewarded one; being an MP was a nice little earner. It was not so much the salary as the expenses (with some MPs claiming well over £100,000 a year), along with the perks, handshakes or severance pay for MPs who lost their seats, and pensions, which would once have been considered a grotesque idea but which were now an accepted mark of that professionalization. If MPs acted as they had so often done in the past, and voted openly to bring down a government, it would be likely to precipitate a general election, when many of them might lose their seats and no longer be able to pocket those expenses. The destruction of Mrs Thatcher was one oblique reflection on this lamentable development.

In other ways the Great Matricide did not appease Providence so much as provoke more turmoil. Plenty of MPs – as well as many journalists – never accepted the verdict of that November. At the *Daily* and *Sunday Telegraph* in particular, there was a knot of Maggobites, as they might have been called, Maggie's Jacobites who still drank to the Queen Across the Water, pined for her return, actively undermined her successor, and practised something like Leninist 'revolutionary defeatism'. The atmosphere was poisoned, and myth-making flourished, and all because the deed had been done in the dark.

In the autumn of 1918, the German army was in retreat on the

[2] See pp. 45–6.
[3] The change of prime minister in May 1940 might be included as the consequence of a Commons vote, which was technically on the adjournment, in practice a vote of confidence, but Chamberlain won that vote comfortably; he was only persuaded by the large defection from his usual supporters that he should resign.

Western Front after its commanders' last throw of the dice, and yet German soldiers were almost everywhere still on foreign soil. The German generals recognized they could not last much longer, and they let the Entente powers know they could have an armistice, which was to say technically a ceasefire and not a surrender. The commanders, who had seen nearly one-and-a-half million French and a million British soldiers killed, and who knew that their armies had long since reached the very limits of endurance, were ready to accept that ceasefire, which duly came about at the eleventh hour of the eleventh day of the eleventh month. But the upshot was disastrous. Soldiers returning to Germany were told that they had not lost the war at all, and they were told this not only by the nationalist right but by the Social Democratic leader Carl Ebert, who said to troops parading in Berlin that 'No army has overcome you.' This belief was nourished until the Versailles Treaty was announced in July 1919. All Germans were outraged by it, and many wanted to reject its terms, until the generals had to tell the politicians that it was quite impossible to resume fighting. In consequence of all this, a myth was able to take root that the army had not been defeated on the battlefield (as of course it had been), but had been stabbed in the back by the 'November criminals', treacherous Jews and corrupt civilians in Berlin.

For Mrs Thatcher's admirers, for the irreconcilable right of the party, and for the increasingly overwrought Maggobites of the Tory press, a comparable *Dolchstosslegende* was now in the making, their own stab-in-the-back myth. After all, she too was *im Felde unbesiegt*, undefeated on the battlefield of three elections. She too had been stabbed in the back by the Conservative party's own 'November criminals'.

With all the fevered rivalries and hatreds of the Conservatives, it was quite true that Margaret Thatcher had won one last great triumph, against totalitarianism. It was poignant but fitting that the disastrous news of the election reached Paris where she was attending a conference to recognize the new shape of the world after that triumph. In her role as a world leader, she fell like Wolfe or Nelson, at the moment of her greatest victory. Her own party was another matter. The Tories believed that they were free from an embarrassing encumbrance; in truth they were now doomed to intestine strife of a bitterness they had never known before.

10

'An addict of almost every
sexual vice . . .'

Before now the Tories had done improbable things and chosen unlikely leaders, but none quite as unlikely as this. Heath in 1965 and Thatcher in 1975 had been surprising; Major was astonishing. He emerged from the rubble of November 1990 almost unobserved. One instant biography was even called a little apologetically *The Quiet Rise of John Major*; the biographer might rather have borrowed Kitty Muggeridge's phrase, 'risen without trace', or for that matter Robert Musil's 'man without qualities'. A few months later I was talking about our new prime minister to Enoch Powell, who said, 'I simply find myself asking, Does he really exist?' It was a question the British people asked with a shrug of the shoulders, but which was to drive Europhobes, Tory press and fogey right to ever greater frenzies of exasperation and rage as the party entered its most self-destructive phase.

In one light it was very creditable that someone of such modest background could rise so high, but there was without doubt something odd and implausible about Major. Before the second ballot in November, he had said that he disliked the artificial distinction between blue-collar and white-collar workers,[1] and that 'In the next ten years we will have to continue to make changes which will make the whole of this country a genuinely classless society.' It might have seemed a curious aspiration for a Tory leader, well beyond Eden's property-owning democracy, Macleod's aspiration to equality of opportunity, and Macmillan's claim that the class war was over.

[1] An American socio-sartorial distinction by origin: in England the middle class had been known as 'black-coat'.

But then Major himself was classless in the sense that he barely corresponded to any known social category. Disraeli was the son of an amiable Jewish antiquarian living near Gray's Inn, Bonar Law the son of a dour Presbyterian minister from Ulster by way of New Brunswick, Heath the son of an industrious carpenter in Broadstairs and Thatcher the daughter of a Grantham grocer, but Major's origins were obscure to a different degree. He was not even called 'Major',[2] but was the son of Thomas Ball, who changed his name first to Major-Ball, a music-hall entertainer who had turned to making garden gnomes. John grew up in straitened circumstances in south London, left school with scarcely any O levels, let alone A levels, to his name, and tried without success to get a job on the buses. A good deal of odious snobbery would be directed at him, but there is no denying that this was an improbable *Bildung* for the heir to Pitt and Salisbury.

He had finally found work in a bank and spent some time in West Africa, which led the journalist Simon Hoggart to speculate ingeniously that Major was really a Nigerian. He appeared to be white, but then there were black Britons, so why should there not be white Nigerians? Most tellingly of all, Major spoke like a man who had learned English from a crumbling British Council phrasebook, using expressions like 'Fine words butter no parsnips', which had long since been unknown on anyone else's lips. It was reminiscent of the (maybe apocryphal) stories of luckless German agents who were dropped into wartime England and immediately identified because they had acquired their knowledge of the country's speech and dress from P. G. Wodehouse. John Major might have been parachuted in. Not merely his accent ('wunt' for 'want') but his whole manner seemed to have been constructed by someone who didn't know where he came from, or didn't know modern England very well.

His political career was likewise elusive. Major had begun in local government, as a councillor in Lambeth, had stood unsuccessfully for parliament on the other side of London in the two 1974 elections,

[2] It was to become almost a habit with the Tories to choose leaders who did not quite know their real names. Iain Duncan Smith added the second 'i' to Ian, Michael Howard was born Hecht.

and had found a solid seat in Huntingdonshire in 1979.[3] He stepped on to the ministerial ladder immediately he entered the Commons
and ascended in the traditional way: PPS, junior whip, Lord Commissioner of Her Majesty's Treasury (the grandiose official title of a
government whip). In the second Thatcher government Major held
junior ministries and was parliamentary under-secretary and minister
of state at the Department of Health and Social Security.

Then in her third ministry he finally entered the Cabinet, as Chief
Secretary to the Treasury. During the musical chairs of 1989, with
the departure of Lawson and the humiliation of Howe, Major became
in quick succession Foreign Secretary for all of three months, and then
Chancellor. Even so few people guessed that when the music finally
stopped he would be sitting at Number Ten. It was an instructive
story. 'Risen without trace' was maybe a little unkind of someone
who had served assiduously, and who was admired by civil servants
for his application and his ability to master documents, but his career
did have a flavour of 'I polished up that handle so carefullee / That
now I am the Ruler of the Queen's Navee!' Mrs Thatcher had promoted him and favoured him as her successor, even if *faute de mieux*,
but even then she complained that he had only known parliamentary
life in office, and had never endured the character-forming experience
of opposition.

To take a name from another age, his career was the antithesis of
Asquith's. After sailing brilliantly through Balliol to a prominent
career at the Bar and in journalism, Asquith had entered parliament,
and then in 1892, at thirty-nine, after six years as an opposition MP
with no ministerial experience at all, was appointed Home Secretary
by Gladstone. From 1895 to 1905 the Liberals were out of office, and
it is another fascinating reflection on the changing political culture
that, when offered the party leadership in the Commons, which meant
the prime ministership one day, Asquith declined it. As his son told a
friend, he was 'a poor man and dependent on his practice at the Bar'.
Sir Henry Campbell-Bannerman was chosen instead, duly became
prime minister in 1905, and only resigned in favour of Asquith

[3]Known since 1983 as Huntingdon. One of the minor vexations for anyone writing
about politics in this period is the fidgety way the Boundary Commissioners kept
changing the names of constituencies for little reason or none at all.

in 1908 because of mortal illness. It is unimaginable that Major would have done as Asquith did, quite apart from the fact that, from 1936, the leader of the opposition was an officially recognized and salaried post.

So much else had also changed between the 1890s and the 1990s. In the nineteenth century MPs were paid nothing, but Cabinet ministers were paid a great deal. The Home Secretary's £5,000 salary was worth the equivalent of at least £250,000 a hundred years later – really even more because of the comparative shift of advantage between rich and poor since the days when Asquith could afford to live in a rented house in Cavendish Square with more than twenty servants. But then again there were far fewer ministers. This was one of the least remarked but most important changes of the past hundred years. In Salisbury's government of 1900 there were nineteen Cabinet ministers and in Major's government of 1990 there were twenty-two; but ministers outside the Cabinet had doubled in numbers, from forty-one to eighty-one. Whereas only Cabinet ministers had once had parliamentary private secretaries, now most junior ministers did, whether they needed them or not. When Alan Clark was pressed to take a PPS, he suggested Terry Dicks (a wonderfully vulgar right-winger, who thought all state subsidy of the arts meant giving taxpayers' money to poufs) and no more was heard of it.

As Clark knew very well, the reason for the absurd increase in Commons PPSs, from nine to forty-seven between 1900 and 1990, was that the whips saw this as a way of enlarging the solid 'pay-roll vote', without even paying: although unsalaried, every PPS was still expected to vote loyally for the government at all times. In that time the number of ministers in the Lords had declined while those in the Commons had increased altogether from thirty-three to eighty-two; if PPSs are included, the tame government vote had increased from forty-two to 129. That meant that in 1900 forty-two out of 670 MPs – or forty-two out of 402 Tory MPs – were 'on the staff' of the government, but in 1990 it was 129 out of 659 MPs, or 129 out of 376 Tory MPs.

These figures may seem abstruse, but they are acutely significant. In proportionate terms, the number of those ministerial MPs had gone from little more than a tenth to more than a third of the parliamentary party, a very grave weakening or even corruption of parliament, especially when accompanied by the ever-increasing payment of all MPs, and then the racket of parliamentary expenses. And this had affected the Tories quite as much as any other party. It was they who should have held out against this professionalization, just as it was they who should have done everything to strengthen rather than erode local government, but instead they joined in with zest. Now the party had produced a leader who was a pure man of the political machine.

It was not that Asquith had been a privileged aristocrat. He was from a family of Yorkshire Congregationalists (admittedly the most upmarket brand of Dissent in the north); he had gone to the City of London School rather than an ancient public school and had prospered without any advantage of birth or wealth but entirely on his merits and the *carrière ouverte aux talents*. The comparison exactly illustrates Amery's saying: Asquith had gone into politics because he was somebody, Major went into politics in order to become somebody. His detractors might have said that he had scarcely done so when he woke up to find that he was prime minister, and that so far had barriers been broken down that British politics was now a career open to those with no obvious talents at all.

Maybe Major, in Churchill's phrase about Attlee, was a modest little man with a good deal to be modest about. But then that was just why the Tories had chosen him. After a decade of the sheer noise and anger of Mrs Thatcher, they wanted a quiet life, and they were happy enough with a leader who did not continually keep them on parade and on their toes. Even before the November ballot Clark had caught the mood of many of his colleagues: Major was 'infinitely preferable' just because he was calm and sensible. A few months later Alan Watkins compared the parliamentary party with a chap whose wife has left home and who could now spend the day loafing around in a dressing-gown, drinking from a mug instead of a cup, and neglecting to shave.

If there was an element of inadvertence about the choice of Major, the Tories had been making other and more conscious statements when they rejected his rivals, foreshadowing their coming difficulties. It was not only that the party in 1990 failed to follow its own logic in the way it had done in 1975, and back the challenger who had had the courage to take on the incumbent, and it was not even that challenger's colourful personality. The Tories swerved away from Heseltine because of his warm support for what was just about to become the European Union. Sixty years earlier, it was high praise to say of a Tory like Austen Chamberlain that he was 'a good European'; twenty years earlier the party had been more Europhile than Labour; by the 1990s 'European' was a grave insult, the Europhobic right was threatening the party from the inside, as the fellow-travelling left had once threatened Labour, and the question of Europe was becoming deeply corrosive for the Conservatives.

As to Hurd, the failure of his candidacy said something almost more revealing about what the party had become. Once Mrs Thatcher had tearfully announced her departure so that Hurd could with decency put his name forward, he had been supported by some of the more solid elements in the government, Kenneth Clarke, William Waldegrave and Malcolm Rifkind; and he was supported also by the grand old men Home and Whitelaw. Even if some other illustrious blasts from the past such as Carrington and Gilmour backed Heseltine (to the displeasure of Waldegrave, who was said, with a touch of exaggeration, to regard them as class traitors), Hurd was all in all the establishment candidate.

And yet that gave him no pride or pleasure. He went to some lengths to disavow both his upbringing as the son of Lord Hurd, previously Sir Antony, a farmer and agricultural journalist, and his education at Eton and Trinity, Cambridge. It was true that Douglas had been a scholar of both, but he resorted to absurd poor-mouthing, as the Irish say, when he insisted that there was nothing in the least unusual about his background, and that his father had only tenant-farmed 500 'not particularly good' acres on the Marlborough Downs. The subject so disturbed him that he became almost distraught: 'I was brought up on a farm. I don't know how we get into all this. This is inverted snobbery. I thought I was running for leader of the Conservative party, not some demented Marxist sect.'

Not Marxist, but increasingly a sect, sometimes a little unhinged – and ever more uneasy about class. Nicholas Budgen was a right-wing monetarist and opponent of immigration, as well as a gossipy fox-hunting man and sometime amateur jockey. He voted for Hurd, but conceded that Major's campaign was cleverly run by men such as David Mellor: by presenting Major as 'the boy from Brixton' they had 'forced Hurd to apologize for Eton and Cambridge'. In 1964, Macleod had angrily rounded on the Etonian cabal in the party, while Macmillan had praised Home as a man who represented the old governing class at its best. There could not be a more dramatic example of the way that Macleod had posthumously won this particular duel than that being an Etonian was now thought an active disadvantage, and that Hurd felt the need to dissociate himself from the old governing class. Anyone with an impartial view of English history would know just how good that class can be, Macmillan had said; good or bad, it had now fallen into unmistakable discredit.

In all this the Tories were the victims of a larger change. Eight years before Macleod's *Spectator* diatribe, Evelyn Waugh had written an essay in the now mercifully forgotten 'U and non-U' debate about upper-class language and usage, at a time when Waugh was himself a close observer of the magic circle of patrician Tories, at White's and in the drawing rooms of Pam Berry and Dot Head. Some of what he wrote was painfully snobbish, although some was also very acute, as when he said that habits of speech 'are not a matter of class but of society and on the whole English people do not congregate exclusively or by preference with their social equals', while class differences had little practical effect 'in the matter of talking together, eating together, sleeping together' (the last certainly true of many Tories, classless to a fault in that respect). But at the same time he did not think it absurd to mention 'my attempt to behave like a gentleman'.

Twenty years later, at the time of Mrs Thatcher's ascent, Waugh's son Auberon reviewed some footling book on 'How to Be a Gentleman'. He said still more acutely than his father that books of this kind were now pointless, since they gave the rules to a game which no longer had any prizes: 'apart from pansies, foreigners and shady businessmen', no one wanted to be considered a gentleman any more. But even he did not then foresee that a man vying for the leadership of the Tory party would one day be desperate to avoid the taint of gentility, and that other Tories would share his apprehensions. The party's preference for Major over Hurd betrayed an unmistakable loss of nerve on the part of those who had for so long ruled England.

To begin with, the boy from Brixton enjoyed a happy honeymoon with the party and even with the nation. He had embarked on his incumbency at Number Ten by saying that 'I want us to build a country that is at ease with itself', a sentiment that did not seem so foolish to begin with. The Tories looked a party more at ease with themselves, not least because, in terms of base self-interest, the coup against Mrs Thatcher appeared to have done the trick. In September 1990 the Tories' Gallup poll rating was 34.3 per cent, by December it was 44.6 per cent. The government remained surprisingly buoyant through much of 1991, and for a time Tories could congratulate themselves that they had done the right thing in terms of winning the next election, which Major might have called sooner but in the end postponed until parliament was nearing its full term the following spring.

Any appearance of ease was illusory. Just as ten years before, in the first days of the Thatcher government, the economic outlook was bleak. Unemployment was rising again on a steep curve, and businesses began to fail across the country. Norman Lamont, who had succeeded the new prime minister as Chancellor, insisted that recession and unemployment would control the inflation he had inherited and that this was, as he told the Commons in May 1991, 'a price worth paying'. The jobless and bankrupt might have retorted that he was not the one paying it, although even there they only had to bide their time. In October he assured the Tory conference that 'the green shoots of economic recovery are appearing once again', which sounded as if it were tempting fate.

Shortly before Mrs Thatcher was ejected, Saddam Hussein had invaded Kuwait, and she had stiffened President George Bush the Elder's resolve to drive the Iraqis out. This was duly accomplished after Major had taken over, although Saddam remained in power in Baghdad and the war raised as many questions as it answered. Other international problems accumulated. At the end of the year, Major attended the Maastricht conference which prescribed further European integration and steps on the road to political as well as economic union. With some skill he negotiated British exemptions from the single currency and the 'social chapter'. The treaty thus amended had to be ratified by every member-state, either by parliamentary vote or referendum; trouble was in store from a vehement faction of the Tory party which was now in no mood for even amended treaties, and which more and more openly followed Enoch Powell in wanting British withdrawal from Europe.

A number of European heads of government liked the new British prime minister personally, if only by contrast with his predecessor. After Major met Helmut Kohl, the German chancellor's office let it be known that the premier had been granted a signal mark of favour: he was told that they could *sich duzen*, use the intimate '*Du*' or 'thou', though quite what difference that made to the monoglot Major was not clear. Perhaps Kohl was speaking German when he persuaded or bullied Major and the other heads of government at Maastricht to take a fateful step (the Bonn government itself having been egged on by right-wing polemicists in papers such as the *Frankfurter Allgemeine Zeitung*) of recognizing the independence of Croatia and Slovenia, followed by Bosnia, even though the nationalities problems in those territories had plainly not been resolved.

When Major did call the election in April 1992 it was more in hope than expectation of victory. It seemed sure that this was the election the Tories were fated to lose at last. They had been in power for thirteen years, just they had in 1964 – until then the longest period any party had held office uninterruptedly during the twentieth century – and although Labour did not repeat the slogan 'Thirteen wasted years', there was a very widespread sense that the Tories' time was up. The Thatcherite economic miracle was apparently turning sour, and the prime minister, for all his affability, was no Baldwin or Macmillan in terms of political skill, not to say that he was faintly absurd and already a target for mockery. Going into the last weeks, most opinion polls either put Tories and Labour neck and neck, or Labour fractionally ahead.

And yet it was all right on the night for Major, which was very much not all right for the pollsters. Shortly before the election, Gallup had the Tories on 37.4 per cent and Labour on 37.8 per cent; in the one count that mattered, on Thursday 8 April, the figures were 41.9 per cent and 34.4 per cent. On a turnout of 77.7 per cent, the highest since February 1974, Major became the first ever – and unquestionably the last ever – party leader in British history to win more than 14 million popular votes. As usual this produced more parliamentary seats than were proportionately deserved. The Tories had sixty-five seats more than Labour; less comfortably, they had twenty-five over all parties. Unhappiest of all were the Liberal Democrats, as the Alliance had now become, whose vote unexpectedly fell.[4] For the polling organizations this was a calamity which led to much soul-searching. Politics was for these organizations both sideline and loss-leader. They made comparatively little money from the newspapers, broadcasters and parties which commissioned such polls, but the more accurate a pollster was at an election the higher stood his credit in the business that made his real money, consumer market research. To have got it as badly wrong did not impress supermarket chains who wanted to know which brand of dog-food would sell best.

What had happened? According to that old saw, opposition parties don't win elections, governments lose them. Another maxim dreamt up that very year by Bill Clinton's campaign team said, 'It's the economy, stupid.' This slogan was itself stupid. Kraus had seen through that kind of reductive vulgar-Marxism as the century was beginning; towards its end, the French writer Raymond Aron echoed Kraus by saying that it was a denial of the whole experience of the century to suppose that men would sacrifice their passions for their interests. If it had been just the economy, then the Tories should have lost in 1992 (and won in 1997). As to the first notion, that was stood on its head in 1992. Remarkable as the result was, and although Major was entitled to take credit if only on the principle that he would have taken the blame for a defeat, the truth was that the opposition lost the election. Neil Kinnock's ludicrous performance at his last rally in Sheffield, grinning, gesticulating, hubristically claiming victory and muttering incomprehensibly like a pop singer, passed into political legend as an example of self-destructive folly, though it merely confirmed the voters' suspicions as they shied away from Labour.

But the pollsters' cock-up had a darker implication for the Tories. The exculpatory phrase 'margin of error' had taken on fresh meaning when Gallup underestimated the Conservative vote by 4.3 per cent,

[4]Tories: 14 million votes, 41.9 per cent, 336 seats; Labour: 11.9 million, 34.4 per cent, 271 seats; Liberal Democrats: 6 million, 17.8 per cent, 20 seats; Others: 24 seats.

and NOP overestimated Labour by all of 6.8 per cent. And yet this was not mere incompetence on the part of those organizations. The fact was that the people polled were not telling the truth. Throughout the 1980s Mrs Thatcher was admired rather than loved, supported because the British thought she was doing the right thing, even by people who found her dislikeable or almost intolerable, and for many voters there was something faintly shameful about voting Tory, even as they did so. The anti-Thatcherite chatterers had done their work. To be a committed Tory now seemed disreputable.

At the 1948 Italian election, a crucial battle in the larger Cold War, when it looked as though the Communists might take power democratically, the Christian Democrats had used the clever slogan, 'In the polling booth God can see you but Stalin cannot.' Thatcherism had told people that in the polling booths their bank managers could see them but the *Guardian* could not. Voters could follow their interests rather than parading their consciences. And yet many people still felt uneasy about the Tories. Just how uneasy was demonstrated three years after Major's victory. Polls asked how people would vote next time, which showed correctly that Labour would win a landslide in 1997; they were also asked how they had voted last time, which showed even more interestingly that Labour had won easily in 1992. It was as though the electorate was trying to forget what it had done, and awaiting the opportunity to shed its guilty burden.

There were other ominous signs for the Tories. Christopher Patten was one of a gifted generation of Oxford Conservatives. He had been in Parliament since 1979, and in 1990 had been made party chairman by Major, in which role he had managed the successful campaign, but as luck had it he lost his own seat at Bath to a Liberal Democrat. The news of Mark Bonham Carter's defeat in 1959 had been cheered at Tory parties; now the news of Patten's defeat was cheered by some of those attending the lavish party thrown by the *Daily Telegraph*, where his crime was to be a 'European'. Patten went on to be the last governor of Hong Kong, a European Commissioner, and Chancellor of his old university, and might have thought himself well out of politics. The jeers that evening at the Savoy hotel gave a foretaste of the hatreds which were to eat up his party.

Other governments before now had lost direction and run out of steam well before their time was up, from Gladstone's ministry formed in 1880 to Attlee's formed in 1945, but in those cases the decline took a matter of years. With the government Major formed after the 1992 election, it took a matter of months. Before the year was out the Tories were in a pitiful condition, and it began to look as if the election might have been what, in a brutal but vivid phrase, the City calls dead-cat bounce, when a plummeting stock stages a brief but misleading recovery. The hard knot of anti-Europeans on the Tory benches had bided their time until after the election, and then began their attack against ratification of the Maastricht treaty, a guerrilla campaign which became the most prolonged and damaging rebellion by Tory MPs in generations. They were greatly cheered by the referendum in Denmark which rejected Maastricht (before the Danes were told, in the best spirit of modern European democracy, to go back and vote again until they got it right), they were egged on by Lady Thatcher, as she had now become after leaving the Commons, and they were encouraged also by a section of the right-wing press. One of the leading rebels was the newly elected MP Iain Duncan Smith, something which would not be forgotten ten years later.

Even before the fall of Thatcher, the Tories had often looked shabby or shady, but they had at least retained some credit for economic competence and also, if not for honourable conduct, for being more or less serious. They were about lose both for good. Although Mrs Thatcher had insisted that she would never get into bed with a single European currency, her Chancellor Nigel Lawson had seen to it that the pound flirted with the Deutschmark by shadowing it (she claimed without her knowledge), and then came premarital liaison when sterling joined the European exchange rate mechanism. It was later claimed, needless to say, that we had joined at the wrong rate, though in truth there is never a 'right rate'; what was certainly true was that sterling was in a weak and vulnerable position by 1992.

In September that weakness was seized on by George Soros and other international speculators, who began a run on the pound quite in the 1931 spirit. Wednesday 16 September turned into a day of high drama, awesome and hilarious by turns, as interest rates were raised again and again throughout the day, eventually reaching 15 per cent, and a huge part of British reserves was wasted in a doomed attempt to shore up sterling inside the exchange rate mechanism. All ended in humiliating failure when British membership of the mechanism was suspended. Although the Major government lasted another four and a half years, it was never a glad confident morning again.

That day was immediately dubbed 'Black Wednesday', although some Europhobes who had always hated the ERM tried to call it White Wednesday, and twelve years later Sir Alan Budd, by then Provost of Queen's College, Oxford, but in 1992 chief economic adviser to the Treasury, suggested that it had been grey at worst. Whatever its political repercussions, the ERM episode had been providential, he said; sterling had really entered at the right time and left at the right time, altogether 'an economic triumph' which marked a turning point in the control of inflation and made all subsequent successes possible. However that might be in hindsight, Budd had forgotten Maitland's rule, that events now far in the past were once in the future, and that what matters is how they were seen at the time. For the Tories September 1992 was what the July measures in 1966 had been for Labour, a crippling blow to prestige.

No subtle distinctions were made, nor silver linings sought, by the press, which turned against the government savagely and never turned back. Several papers demanded Lamont's resignation or dismissal, and Max Hastings, editor of the *Daily Telegraph*, threatened him with 'implacable liability' if he did not go. But Major had already shown his determination to hang on to colleagues like grim death in the case (where grim was definitely the word) of David Mellor. Mellor had been rewarded for his part in securing Major's succession with a seat in the Cabinet as Chief Secretary to the Treasury and then after the election he had moved to the risible post of National Heritage Secretary, or 'Minister of Fun' as the tabloids called him, all too aptly.

A veteran Conservative used to give one piece of advice to young men newly arrived at Westminster: 'If you're going to roger a woman, make sure it's a woman who's got more to lose than you do if you're found out.' Mellor was a particularly gross example of a Tory who quite forgot this wise rule. In the summer of 1992, thanks to a talkative and ambitious mistress who revealed their sordid connection, he became a national laughing stock, although whether he indeed wore the Chelsea football kit for his bedroom antics, as the lady claimed, history does not relate. He received little sympathy from his colleagues. Clark had recorded more than three years earlier that 'everyone loathes' Mellor and, apart from MPs, public regard for him was not increased when he forced his unfortunate family, from whom he was soon to separate, to stand smiling over a country gate in an unsuccessful attempt to spirit away his disgrace. After weeks of derision, and after the Black Wednesday debacle had completely unnerved Major, Mellor was finally forced to relinquish his vice-like grip on office and salary, not because of those antics which so delighted the nation and for which alone he would be remembered by posterity, but because he proved to have accepted hospitality from another lady, connected with the Palestinian cause, contrary to official regulations.

Trivial in itself, this episode rang the tone for the next four years. Mellor's final and involuntary departure from the Cabinet less than a fortnight after Black Wednesday left a nasty taste, and set a pattern. Some would have said he personified the word 'sleazy', and Major made himself look both foolish and feeble in hanging on to a discredited colleague before finally abandoning him. This and Black Wednesday were made worse by the continuing Maastricht rebellion, with up to twenty-two Tory MPs repeatedly voting against the government. And as if that were not all bad enough, Alan Clark returned to embarrass his colleagues further. Returned, because from a mixture of caprice and depression he had chosen not to stand again in his Plymouth seat at the election. He may also have simply miscalculated and guessed that Major would lose, and by December he was raging in his diary, 'I SHOULD NEVER HAVE LEFT THE HOUSE OF COMMONS.' But he was still in the wings, ready to make trouble.

For many years past all British governments had been compromised by the manufacture and export of arms, and Clark was not the most dramatic victim of this dubious traffic. Jonathan Aitken had enjoyed a gaudy career in journalism, politics and business, and from the time he founded the James Bond Society at Oxford (its president and only member met in a white dinner jacket to drink shaken not stirred martinis, which pretty girls were invited to share) he had seemed one of the 'Young Meteors' of the title of a book he published in his twenties. He had been an MP since 1974 but had never been preferred by Mrs Thatcher, for personal reasons: in the course of an energetic amorous career he had seduced and then dumped her daughter. 'He made Carol cry', the prime minister said by way of explaining why he remained on the backbenches. But he had finally been promoted by Major as 'defence procurement' minister, an area in which he certainly had expertise, having long worked as an intermediary in the arms trade. It was a connection which would have unhappy consequences for him and his party.

But not unhappier than the consequences of Clark's period as trade minister in 1986–9. A machine-tool company called Matrix Churchill had wanted to export to Iraq products with an undoubted military capacity, an activity naturally illegal given Saddam's record even before Kuwait. They prudently sounded out Clark, who allowed them to think that the government would wink at this. But left and right hand did not know what the other was doing, and the directors of the firm were prosecuted for illicitly selling weaponry to Iraq. The trial began on 10 October, but collapsed dramatically on 10 November when Clark gave evidence. Asked by Geoffrey Robertson, the defence counsel, whether his earlier statement that 'the Iraqis will be using the current order for general engineering purposes' had been true, Clark said, 'Well it's our old friend being economical, isn't it?' 'With the truth?' 'With the actualité.' His words effectively cleared the defendants, and led to an official inquiry at which Clark gave still more indiscreet evidence; they were all too typical of him.

He made a career out of outraging the conventions; or, as Geoffrey Howe said, he 'couldn't see an apple-cart without wanting to overturn it'. Clark has already played more than a walk-on part in this story, and from time to time he entertained fantasies of a much larger part, even of the party leadership. He was not quite what is usually meant by larger than life, but he was, in another phrase, all too human, a very rich, handsome, clever, arrogant roué, with some reputation as a writer of history books, although none of those had anything like the astonishing success of his *Diaries* when the first volume was published in 1993. Most journalists liked him,[5] for reasons not far to

---

[5] Auberon Waugh was an exception, regarding Clark as a posturing show-off.

seek. He was good company, good value, good copy, and if you are good to the press you will get a good press, something Clark's near-namesake and mortal enemy Kenneth Clarke also demonstrated.

For all Clark's snobbery, his own origins were in no sense at all aristocratic. As was said of the Mountbattens, the origins of the Clark family are lost in the mists of the nineteenth century. They were Scottish spinners who had made a fortune in cotton thread, enabling Clark's grandfather to lead the life of the Edwardian idle rich, with a yacht, as well as houses in Suffolk, Scotland, London and the Riviera, and maybe not surprisingly he drank himself to death out of sheer boredom. His son Kenneth became a famous art critic and curator and bought a castle in Kent where Alan lived, along with an estate in the Highlands, a flat in Albany and a house in Zermatt.

With his real gifts, Alan Clark's most salient characteristic was his recklessness. At a party late one evening during the Tory conference in the early 1980s, a flamboyant member of Mrs Thatcher's Cabinet was dancing over-energetically with a girl from the BBC, observing which performance an awestruck journalist said, 'The man's a sexual kamikaze pilot.' The words could have been applied to Clark also, whose adulteries became something of a national spectator sport. And yet his great strength was that he didn't give a damn. When he was a minister, the left-wing *New Statesman* heard a piece of gossip which it thought would destroy him: he had said that an African seeking extradition might have to 'go back to Bongo-Bongo land'. The magazine challenged Clark, expecting a glib denial at worst or a resignation at best. Instead he killed the story with the words, 'I don't remember saying it, but it sounds like me.'

One evening in late 1989, when he was Minister of State at the Ministry of Defence, we bumped into one another in Clubland and our conversation turned to the appeasement period. I mentioned the notorious memorandum which the Admiralty, desperate to avoid war, had prepared in 1935 saying that the Mediterranean fleet could not possibly take on the Italian navy. Just what sorry nonsense this was became clear several years later when the Royal Navy was obliged to fight the Italians in hugely less favourable circumstances, and won one famous victory after another. It had been a wretchedly pusillanimous document, I suggested. 'You think the admirals were bad then?' the defence minister replied crisply. 'You should see them now. I have to deal with them the whole time. What a bunch of cunts.'

This candour made him a fascinating witness to the age; the mistake would be to take him at his own evaluation, as a politician, an historian, or even an *homme sérieux*. He liked to hint at religious yearnings: after lunching with Lord Longford and the fashionable Catholic priest Father Michael Seed, Clark wrote, 'I don't wholly dismiss all that, and will read Newman over Good Friday,' before returning to thoughts of his latest mistress. In truth, Clark had more in common with the dissolute squire who left his village church at the end of a rare visit one Sunday with the words, 'Well, anyhow, I haven't made a graven image.'

Even without Clark, the Tories were upsetting plenty of other apple-carts, and by now there seemed to be a pattern to the government's self-destructiveness. During the American presidential election that autumn, Downing Street did not just openly favour the re-election of George Bush the Elder against his Democratic challenger Bill Clinton, but actually helped the White House by passing on discreditable information about Clinton's youthful sojourn in England. It did not occur to them that Clinton might win and that there would then be an icy *froideur* between Washington and London. Clinton later said that he did not want any permanent damage to Anglo-American relations, 'but I wanted the Tories to worry about it for a while'. So they did, and it was yet further evidence of lack of judgement from a regime which was losing its grip.

Some of the indignation now directed against the government was synthetic. When William Waldegrave, a clever man who had held a succession of Cabinet offices, told a Commons committee that ministers sometimes had to lie – as before a devaluation, when it was necessary to deny that it was about to take place, in order to prevent a speculative squeeze – even this statement of the obvious was held against him. But some derision was well deserved, and the pattern of stubbornness and ineptitude was now followed with Lamont. A pawky, genial if slightly louche Orcadian, he had had one or two private tribulations of his own: he had let his London flat to a young woman who proved to give new meaning to 'the smack of firm government', and he had once turned up in the Commons with a black eye, administered, rumour had it, after a poignant altercation. Even when both eyes were blackened politically that Wednesday in September he declined to go quietly, or at all.

Writing about Gladstone, Roy Jenkins observed with wry puzzlement that nineteenth-century prime ministers had the greatest difficulty hanging on to their Cabinet ministers, who were forever resigning impetuously for small reason or none, whereas twentieth-century prime ministers had as much difficulty getting rid of theirs. It did not occur to him that this was yet another reflection of the professionalization of politics, and that even though Victorian ministers were well salaried, they had other sources of income, and other lives. Now, even when everyone knew that a minister should resign, and even when he himself knew that in his heart, he could not face life without office and without emoluments and privileges.

It was Gladstone who had told the young Asquith that if he ever became prime minister, 'you must steel your nerves and act the butcher'. This was something Major proved unusually bad at, partly from good nature and partly from weakness, as he showed by keeping Lamont through the bleak winter which followed the debacle. During the Newbury by-election campaign in the Tory heartland of Berkshire the following May, Lamont said 'Je ne regrette rien', which echo of Edith Piaf might have seemed pleasingly cheeky until the Liberal Democrats took the seat. Major regretted that very much, and finally dropped his Chancellor. As if to show how little love was now lost inside the party whose secret weapon had once supposedly been loyalty, Lamont turned on Major in the Commons with the unoriginal but deadly phrase 'in office but not in power'.

Although he was no spell-binding orator, Major had a few phrases up his own sleeve. In 1993 he made two speeches which gained considerable attention, along with even more eloquent off-the-record *obiter dicta*. In April, he invoked an England of 'long shadows on county grounds, warm beer, invincible green suburbs, dog lovers and pool fillers and – as George Orwell said – "old maids bicycling to Holy Communion through the morning mist"'. If his speechwriters had looked more closely at Orwell's great essay 'The Lion and the Unicorn', they would have seen that what he said was:

The clatter of clogs in the Lancashire mill towns, the to-and-fro of the lorries on the Great North Road, the queues outside the Labour exchanges, the rattle of pin-tables in the Soho pubs, the old maids biking to Holy Communion through the mists of the autumn morning – all these are not only fragments, but *characteristic* fragments, of the English scene.

That was itself acute, and far from mere romanticism. In one of his more clever than profound observations, Balfour had said that 'Conservative prejudices are rooted in a great past, and Liberal ones in an imaginary future.' It would be nearer the truth to say that reactionaries had oftener conjured up a vision of the past as unreal as any progressive vision of the future. Rather than Orwell, Major sounded more like a pale imitation of Baldwin seventy years before:

The sounds of England, the tinkle of the hammer on the anvil in the country smithy, the corncrake on a dewy morning, the sound of the scythe against the whetstone, and the sight of a plough team coming over the brow of a hill, the sight that has been seen in England since England was a land, and may be seen in England long after the Empire has perished and every works in England has ceased to function. For centuries the one eternal sight of England.

But to say all that was humbug in 1924, when English agriculture was both in crisis and already being mechanized; scythes, anvils and plough teams would soon be only of antiquarian interest. By the time Major spoke, plough teams had vanished along with Orwell's clogs; the old maids were fewer than ever, with the Church of England declining numerically to a tiny sect; warm beer had been replaced by cold lager; and the shadows fell on empty county cricket grounds. The England which Major had tried to evoke was not quite a fantasy, but it was a shell: this vision of 'Tory England' looked more and more like a theme park or what the French call *la mode rétro*, self-conscious and artificial.

Then at the party conference in the autumn Major spoke of 'the old values – neighbourliness, decency, courtesy'. They were still alive, he said, and it was 'time to return to those core values, to get back to basics, to self-discipline and respect for the law, to consideration for others, to accepting responsibility for yourself and your family and not shuffling it off on other people and the state'. Leaving aside the limp rhetoric, this was a most ill-judged statement, and the phrase 'back to basics' would haunt him. For all the exaggeration of Mrs Thatcher's chattering foes, by now it was not only sectarian leftists who believed that neighbourliness and decency had been eroded at least as much by the individualistic materialism of the 1980s as by any progressive doctrines or 'permissiveness'.

To make it worse, Major asked his ministers for their own prescriptions as to how the country could be taken back to those basics, and this turned out to mean raw authoritarian social and penal policies. Michael Howard was Home Secretary from May 1993 until the end of the Major government. He set the tone at that party conference by proposing in Soviet fashion a twenty-seven-point programme for crime prevention, which largely consisted of locking up as many people as possible. Howard never asked himself why the British were such an innately evil people that proportionately so many more of them than of any other European country needed to be imprisoned at any particular time. The mood was heightened by Peter Lilley as Social Security Secretary, who related (after Gilbert and Sullivan) the 'little list' of scroungers and social degenerates he wanted to deal with. The two seemed to suggest that if the unruly populace were to be taught self-discipline and respect for the law, it would have to be by brute force, an ironical upshot of the Thatcherite revolution and its supposed roots in personal freedom and responsibility.

Later Major tried to insist that 'back to basics' had no specific resonance towards private conduct or morality, but that was exactly the spin – an ever more important word and concept, borrowed from American politics – put on it by his press officers at the time – another case where off-the-record briefing went awry. It was duly so interpreted by the newspapers, and it duly went as wrong as could be. Sex scandals continued to erupt on the Tory visage like a plague of boils, and along with the other, financial kind of 'sleaze' they did the party huge damage on its downhill slide.

To suppose that corruption and carnal licence had been unknown before then would be grossly unfair to our island story. Lust has been part of human nature since the Garden of Eden, and the sexual and political lives of rulers have often been closely intertwined. The Church of England itself owed its origin to the erotic appetites and marital complications of Henry VIII, and those subsequent kings of England who did not have irregular sex lives were very much in the minority; kings would often enough promote their mistresses and their mistresses' offspring to high rank, unless like James I and William III they promoted the ephebes who were the objects of their unnatural affections. Many prime ministers also did their bit. Gladstone's peculiarity took the form of encounters with prostitutes, unconsummated, though clearly carrying a strong sexual charge. After such meetings he would whip himself; in his own words he 'courted evil'.

And yet, although tormented, self-righteous and sometimes priggish, Gladstone was not a hypocrite. He said – and this without any implication that they were unfit for office – that he had known eleven prime ministers and that seven at least of them had been adulterers. One of those was Palmerston, whose career had been much assisted by living in open concubinage with Lady Cowper, the sister of Melbourne, another prime minister. Gladstone saw the political career of his younger colleague Sir Charles Dilke destroyed by a lurid divorce case, and then his antagonist (for a time his ally) Charles Stewart Parnell brought down by another. Even then, for all his bitter differences with Parnell, Gladstone was not outraged when it transpired that the Irish leader had been for many years the lover of another man's wife: 'What, because a man is called leader of a party, does that constitute him a censor and a judge of faith and morals? I will not accept it. It would make life intolerable.' Although political opponents were always tempted to use such lapses from faith and morals, they learned the hard way that vice knows no party line.

Nor did it obviously impair political ability. In the twentieth century, Lloyd George lived almost openly with his mistress during the Great War, and he did after all win his war, as Churchill won his a quarter-century later when he consumed what many doctors would now consider the daily intake of a functional alcoholic. The Tories were periodically embarrassed during the second half of the century by minor or major scandals, here a junior minister forced to resign when found with a Guardsman in Hyde Park, there another minister obliged untruthfully to deny adultery. Eden was the first prime minister to have been divorced, despite the severe warnings expressed in the *Church Times* in 1952, in advance of his succession to Number Ten, that this would weaken the fibre of the nation.

When the Macmillan government was shaken by the Profumo affair, there had been two sensible contemporary verdicts. The Tory MP Lord Lambton said that Profumo's connection with Miss Keeler might have been a security risk if it had been platonic. And Evelyn Waugh told one of his most pious friends that newspaper talk of 'the greatest scandal of the century' was absurd. 'To my knowledge in my lifetime three prime ministers have been adulterers and almost every cabinet has had an addict of almost every sexual vice.' He was doubtless thinking of, among others, a rich and elegant Tory Cabinet minister of his acquaintance who was known (by those who knew these things) to have been energetically homosexual not only before his marriage but after.

Almost exactly ten years after Profumo's resignation some of us were taking a pre-prandial drink in the 'French Pub' in Soho to make the wine and food at the subsequent *Private Eye* lunch more bearable, when Auberon Waugh arrived looking more than usually pleased with himself. 'Tony Lambton's been caught at it!' 'At what, Bron?' 'Dipping his wick.' It was true enough, and that earlier verdict of Lambton's rang loudly with historical irony now that he in turn had been caught out. It seemed the party was fated to endure such episodes at decennial intervals: Lambton's downfall was followed in 1983 by Parkinson's, and then in the early 1990s by a series of preposterous escapades, damaging not so much in themselves as for what they said about the incompetence, shabbiness and cronyism of the party. It may not have been strictly the case that Tories were more libidinous than others, but even their seemingly staidest elements were often more exotic than the public knew. One Speaker, a former Tory minister who had been briefly and unhappily married, would attempt to console himself in his later years with young reporters asked back to the Speaker's House. I was not one of them, but thirty years ago I was given lunch by an unusually fat and florid MP who broke the ice by asking, 'I don't suppose you're into fladge?'

So no one should perhaps have been surprised by what happened in the 1990s, except that the scandals came so thick and fast that it was hard to keep up with them. One minister resigned when he had to confess having fathered a child out of wedlock (at least keeping to the party line, as the mother was a Tory councillor), and then an MP admitted he had shared a bed with another man. Farce turned to tragedy when a minister's wife shot herself after a quarrel, and when a young MP was found dead, although that episode had its ludicrous as well as melancholy aspect. He was wearing women's underclothes, there was a tangerine in his mouth, and it appeared that he had inadvertently asphyxiated himself while engaged in some form of auto-erotic gratification. Before then the Tory party had been keen enough on diversions such as adultery, sodomy, or indeed fladge, which were maybe reprehensible but at least comprehensible; it now contained addicts of sexual vices no one had ever heard of.

Even Major himself was haunted by a secret. In the late 1980s he and a colleague spent some time together in the evenings and had at last fallen into each other's arms, as happens. Edwina Currie was a clever if somewhat bumptious Tory whose ministerial career came to an end over a non-sexual indiscretion. Maybe on the principle that she had more to lose, she kept the secret of her guilty liaison with Major to herself, though she teased the poor man by publishing a semi-salacious novel called *A Parliamentary Affair* in 1994, until the time came for her to kiss and tell (and collect the money).

All of these affairs of the heart ('and much more than the heart', as Anthony Blanche says) might seem irrelevant to great affairs of state. Gladstone's phrase about a politician not being a judge of faith and morals was as wise as ever. However ill-advised it was to speak of basics and core values, Major was not responsible for his colleagues' carryings-on, and even his own unfortunate escapade could be overlooked. But one name stained him and his party for ever after, and deserved to.

In 1992, at Major's instigation, Jeffrey Archer became Lord Archer of Weston-super-Mare. It was the most improper peerage for precisely seventy years. In the Birthday Honours of 1922, Lloyd George's last flourish, four names gazetted had caused something nearer rage than disquiet: they were war profiteers at best or swindlers at worst. Sir William Vestey had moved his meat business to the Argentine during the war to avoid British tax; the wartime record of Sir Archibald Williamson was, as Lord Curzon's private secretary minuted, 'putrid';

Sir Samuel Waring had carted investors earlier in his career; and Sir Joseph Robinson's skulduggery was notorious throughout South Africa. Archer was a worthy successor.

When the young Jeffrey Archer got married at Brasenose, the Oxford college with which he was very loosely associated, the Principal of the college had said good-naturedly that he must be the only principle Jeffrey had ever had, and if Archer did not actually pay for his peerage, that was one of the few things he had ever honestly acquired. His whole life was a web of fantasy and fraud, beginning with his false claim that his grandfather had been Lord Mayor of Bristol and his father a colonel in the Somerset Light Infantry. Archer's wife claimed that he had a 'gift for the inaccurate precis', which was one way of putting it. At one time or another he implied that, in his early life, he had been to Wellington, the famous public school in Berkshire, had a clutch of A levels, had graduated at Berkeley in California, had been an undergraduate at Oxford. All of that was false, but it set the tone. Turning to local government in London, he became known as 'Mr 10 Per Cent' after offering to help colleagues claim fake expenses in return for a cut.

In 1969 he entered parliament at a by-election despite a row about fiddling his expenses, this time at the United Nations Association where he had worked with Humphry Berkeley, he who had first pressed for the election of the Tory leader. When asked whether he thought Archer fit to be an MP, Berkeley said that he shouldn't be in parliament, 'he should be in a remand home'. Archer then made a fortune and lost it and had to leave the Commons in 1974 in the face of imminent bankruptcy. He now determined, in the manner of Sir Walter Scott if not with the same talent, to write himself out of debt, and did so with a string of novels which became best-sellers despite carping critics who said that 'the writing, especially the dialogue, is bad beyond belief'. It was true that he had a way with speech ('Frank, we have been friends for over fifty years. Equally importantly, as my legal adviser you have proved to be a shrewd advocate') that could never have issued from human lips.

He kept his enthusiastic connection with the Tory party, and his enthusiasm was reciprocated: hence his importance to this story. In 1985, astonishingly enough, he was made deputy party chairman by

Margaret Thatcher, who called him 'the extrovert's extrovert'. He threw himself into fund-raising and speaking on the 'rubber-chicken circuit' of local party evenings. But then, having climbed a ladder again, he stepped on a nasty snake in 1986 when the headline 'Tory boss Archer pays vice girl' appeared in a Sunday paper. He had indeed handed a prostitute £2,000 at Victoria Station and advised her to go abroad. The inference that he was paying her off after using her services was spelt out in another tabloid. Archer sued for libel and won what were then record damages of £500,000. His victory depended partly on the grotesquely tendentious conduct of this case by Mr Justice Caulfield, smitten by the 'fragrant' Mary Archer, partly on her own testimony that she enjoyed a 'full' life with her husband (and the judge's breathtakingly ignorant belief that no man who had an attractive wife to sleep with would ever be unfaithful to her), but most of all on an alibi for the night in question which Archer had concocted with his secretary and friends.

When the story broke, Archer had been obliged to leave his party post, but he continued to work for the Tories and still had his tongue hanging out for further reward and preferment. And he befriended John Major. Plenty of people in the party warned Major about Archer in the strongest terms. Michael Heseltine was no slouch when it came to making money, and no prude when it came to female companionship, but he was no fool either. He saw through Archer and kept clear of him. Mrs Thatcher's sometime aide Ferdinand Mount said that her promotion of Archer had been her 'most wince-provoking, hotmaking mistake'. When the idea of a peerage was first mooted, Archer had been quietly blackballed by the honours committee, while Willie Whitelaw said that Archer was 'an accident waiting to happen', and that he would enter the Lords over his dead body, although Whitelaw was still alive if not quite kicking in 1992. This dismal story shows what had happened to a once great party, not in terms of morality alone but of judgement. Major's elevation of Archer was not just wince-provoking but the most appalling of his errors, and it epitomized all that was by now wrong about the Tories.

It was not as though Major needed any more woes. The Europhobic right of the party had become his declared enemies, and they drove this apparently mild man to violent language. 'Where do you think most of the poison is coming from?' the prime minister asked Michael Brunson of ITN in July 1993, when they were off air, though the microphone was still recording. The poison was coming from disappointed colleagues who were going round making all sorts of trouble, Major said. All the same, and on Lyndon Johnson's on-the-inside principle, he was in no hurry to sack the malcontents in his Cabinet: 'Would you like three more of the bastards out there?' A year later at a dinner for the departure of Gus O'Donnell, Ingham's inoffensive replacement as the prime minister's press secretary, Major was talking to Brunson once more and told him 'I'm going to fucking crucify the right for what they've done.' And he was later overheard abusing them this time as 'Shits!', a word which the *Sunday Express*, in an ill-advised attempt to catch the spirit of the age, splashed on its front page. This catalogue of profanity was more evidence of his weak nerves, of a man 'in office but not in power', of a party which had lost its way.

Although Major pottered along, his government was rudderless and powerless, heeling and swaying this way and that. Its legislative record was undistinguished and largely damaging. The 1992 Further and Higher Education Act was most notable for allowing polytechnics to call themselves universities, a grave attack on the purpose of university education and maybe an act of revenge from a prime minister who had graduated with some difficulty from the University of Life. Then the privatization of the railways was a fine example of not knowing when to stop. The privatizations of the 1980s were always likely to be successful and popular, not least because the industries were capable of making a profit and did so; the selling off of British Rail was always likely to be unsuccessful and unpopular, not least because the railways could never run without a subsidy. This was a government which was going round in circles; in office but not in power; and merely postponing disaster.

11

It Was the *Telegraph* Wot Lost It

In December 1983 Alan Clark, as departmental minister, had attended for the government a parliamentary committee on employment. Labour had sent a tough team, he recorded, 'Little John Smith, rotund, bespectacled, Edinburgh lawyer. Been around for ages', as well as two men from the far left, a nasty young one 'and a nasty (the *nastiest*) old one – Mikardo. And two bright boys called Brown and Blair.' Within a little more than ten years, that lawyer and those bright boys would transform the fortunes of their own party, and thus the Conservatives' story also.

After Major's improbable victory in 1992, Neil Kinnock had resigned as Labour leader. An honest and likeable man as politicians go, he had been a few feet out of his depth for the nearly nine years he had led the party, and had been treated with unflagging contempt by the press, although he had in fact played a vital part in at least rescuing his party from oblivion: fewer than eight and a half million people had voted Labour in 1983, more than eleven and a half million did so in 1992. It was a mark of continuing malaise within the party that only two less than stellar candidates could be fielded to succeed him: Bryan Gould, an antipodean academic who had risen so far as to be shadow spokesman on national heritage, and that same rotund, bespectacled Edinburgh lawyer. The electoral college was reconvened and John Smith won an overwhelming, nine-to-one victory. Gould had previously written a book entitled *A Future for Socialism* but now decided that perhaps there was none after all, and took himself off to Waikato University in his native New Zealand where he wrote another book, a memoir with the unoriginal but unambiguous title *Goodbye to All That*. It might have intended goodbye to social democracy, to the Labour party as he had known it, and to any chance of defeating the Tories.

Although Smith was widely liked and his election widely welcomed, not everyone shared the elation. Tony Blair was already embarked on a remarkable political pilgrimage. He had no personal roots at all in the Labour movement and no interest in socialism as a creed. A barrister who had got religion at Oxford, he had been formed by successive elections. At the time of his own entry into parliament in 1983 he had undergone a kind of ritual ordeal in his constituency at the hands of the veteran left-winger Dennis Skinner, who said that someone else should have been the candidate, and Blair resolved that if ever he had the opportunity he would crush the left. By the 1987 election he had decided that Labour needed to be drastically reshaped if it were ever to recover. And in 1992, he was perhaps the only Labour MP who thought and said beforehand (not of course in public, but to trusted confidants) that Labour was going to lose. The culprit in his eyes was not Kinnock, for all his embarrassing performance at Sheffield, nor Roy Hattersley, the deputy leader, but Smith, the shadow Chancellor, who had gone into the election proposing higher public spending and higher income taxes to pay for it. From that moment Blair knew that if he should ever come to lead the party it would never in any circumstances be associated with high taxation. That would break the Tories' sharpest sword, and he might yet go even further to appropriate a large part of the Thatcher legacy.

'If he should ever' came sooner than anyone foresaw. While Major continued to flounder, Smith cut a genial if unelectrifying figure as leader of the opposition. His sudden death from a heart attack less than two years after he had become Labour leader was one of those random events which transform history. Had Smith lived, he would, given the disarray of the government and the national exhaustion with the Tories, doubtless have led his party to victory at the next election, but it would have just as certainly been a very different party from what it became, and the political landscape would not have been utterly transformed. As it was, Blair and Brown were the obvious candidates to succeed him and they should have fought a straight fight. But Blair always preferred the indirect approach; having neutralized Brown with vague promises which would still embitter their relations a decade later, he stood against two other, insignificant opponents, and won easily enough in July 1994.

Although that strictly belongs to the history of the Labour party, Blair's ascent was absolutely central to the demise of Tory England. This was far more than just a change of leader. Robert Harris put it nicely when he said that in 1994 something strange happened to British politics, as if in an old science fiction movie where 'a mad boffin throws a lever and the poles are reversed. Political matter suddenly became antimatter. Negatives became positives.' After many years of envenomed intestine warfare, not just in the noxious 1980s or the fractious 1950s but going back to the scission of 1931, the Labour party suddenly discovered the virtues of loyalty and unity. 'At the same time, someone switched the bottles and the Tories became reprogrammed with socialist DNA. Endlessly dreaming up implausible schemes, ever ready to denounce one another for a lack of ideological purity, they became, in a word, weird.'

In truth, the weirdness was only distilled by Blair's emergence; it had been bubbling up inside the party for years past, above all because of the question of Europe; and the viruses infecting the party long predated July 1994. The condition was aggravated by the manner of the prime minister's removal in 1990 which left a mephitic atmosphere in its wake. It was further deepened by Lady Thatcher herself, as she had become after leaving the Commons in 1992. And it was made much worse by a press which played a central part in the Tory collapse.

By the early summer of 1993 the atmosphere inside the parliamentary party was, if not openly mutinous, then widely contemptuous of Major. He had sacked Kenneth Baker as Home Secretary after the election, and within a couple of years Baker was muttering that Major was 'dead in the water'. Among the egregious Maastricht rebels, Anthony Marlow called for Major's departure, the European elections in June 1994 were bad (though not quite catastrophic) for the government, and in October Lamont 'came out' by giving a speech which for the first time openly, and quite lucidly, argued the case for British withdrawal from the European Union. That was what plenty of Tory MPs were by now longing to hear.

All of this was closely affected by the Tory party's relationship with the supposed Tory press; supposed, since its loyalty to the party and the government was by this point anything but certain. Almost as soon as Blair became Labour leader, he began cultivating newspaper proprietors and editors, notably Lord Rothermere and David English at the *Daily Mail*, but above all Rupert Murdoch. Blair travelled to Australia in 1995 to address Rupert Murdoch's corporate gathering, which he did in words still more remarkable than his mere presence as a guest of the Prince of Darkness:

During the sixties and seventies the left developed, almost in substitution for its economic prescriptions, which by then were failing, a type of social individualism that confused, at points at least, liberation from prejudice with a disregard for moral structures. It fought for racial and sexual equality, which was entirely right. It appeared indifferent to the family and individual responsibility, which was wrong.

There was a real danger, occasionally realized, that single-issue pressure groups moved into the vacuum. Women's groups wrote the women's policies. Environmental groups wrote the environmental policy, and so on. This was the same elsewhere. I remember a telling intervention of a speaker at the Republican convention of 1984 in the US asking rhetorically, 'When was the last time you heard a Democrat say no?' It was too close to the truth for comfort.

If a Labour leader was quoting American Republicans with approval (and if he could say such things unrebuked by his own party) then something truly remarkable was happening. Blair was using blatantly right-wing rhetoric and taking over the Tories' territory, in a way which would have catastrophic consequences for them.

The turn in Major's fortunes had already been illustrated by the *Sun*, the best-selling paper in the country and the flagship of Murdoch's London fleet. It was, of all things, the descendant of the old *Daily Herald*, once half-owned by the TUC and the one national paper specifically committed to Labour. The *Herald* had fallen on hard times, had desperately tried to relaunch itself as the *Sun* in 1964, with a promotional gimmick by which every pub in the country called the Sun offered a free pint at the paper's expense. Despite this handsome gesture towards the drinking classes, the new *Sun* continued to decline, and in 1969 it was bought by Rupert Murdoch, who very soon turned it into a paper of a kind which had not been seen before in England, not so much brash (as the *Mirror* had liked to call itself) but screechingly vulgar, brutal and obscene.

Its fortunes rose with Mrs Thatcher's. It was said that the Boer war had given the original cheap press the first chance to display its quality, and the Falklands war gave the *Sun* its own chance. There was the front page, 'Stick it up your junta! A *Sun* missile for Galtieri's gauchos', there was the leading article attacking the *Daily Mirror* and other critics of the war with the words 'There are traitors in our midst,'[1] and there was the headline 'Gotcha!' after an Argentine warship had been sunk with the loss of hundreds of lives. Throughout the Thatcher years the *Sun* was 'her' paper more than any other, even if the prime minister must sometimes have winced at its indecency. After her fall the paper remained loyal: up to and into the 1992 election it campaigned with astounding partisanship and unfairness, even by its own standards, culminating in a front page on election day, 'If Kinnock wins today, will the last person in Britain put out the lights?'

But if Major thought such a friend would always be true, he had not long to be disabused. On the night of Black Wednesday, Kelvin MacKenzie, the editor of the *Sun*, rang him, Her Majesty's First Lord of the Treasury, the heir of Walpole, Peel, Gladstone and Churchill, and told 'John' breezily, 'I'm holding a bucket of shit and tomorrow I'm going to empty it over your head.' The next morning's front page read 'Now We've All Been Screwed by the Cabinet', an allusion lost on no one while Mellor desperately hung on to his job. Not only did the editor regard himself and his proprietor as more important men than the prime minister – a view perhaps shared by Major – but the press coverage of those episodes, the prolonged involuntary departure of Mellor and then of Lamont, made them even more damaging than they need have been.

And yet that verbal violence did not necessarily mean that the press played an equally – or indeed any – constructive role, even in terms of winning elections, however much that was believed by some people, Alistair McAlpine among them. One of the more human members of

---

[1] To which the *Mirror* replied, in an echo of Baldwin (see p. 217) that the *Sun* was 'the harlot of Fleet Street'.

Mrs Thatcher's kitchen cabinet, he was an affable and epicurean scion of a family which had made its money in the building trade. Apart from entertaining lavishly at party conferences and in London, he had served as deputy chairman during her first governments and, even more effectively, as party treasurer throughout the whole of Mrs Thatcher's leadership. With the decline of the unions, the Tories enjoyed a still larger financial advantage over Labour (until Blair likewise took to raising money from the rich), and McAlpine ensured that the coffers were full before each election. He had ended his formal connection with the party in 1990 and later took up with the Europhobic fringe, but his most famous words were spoken after the 1992 election. The party had fought an unimpressive campaign, McAlpine said, and they owed their victory to the tabloid newspapers, a verdict gloatingly paraphrased and puffed by the most carnivorous of those tabloids on its front page: 'It Was the *Sun* Wot Won It.'

Was it? McAlpine and Blair were not the only ones who believed in the power of 'the Tory press'. That was a phrase which Lloyd George had used contemptuously, though also apprehensively, even before the Great War. Although some Tories despised journalism and journalists, successful politicians had always known how to use the press. Palmerston wrote leading articles in praise of his own policy, unsigned but quite unmistakable in manner, and Salisbury had a busy career in journalism before devoting himself to politics, after which the *Standard*[2] and the absurd Alfred Austin had been his mouthpieces. That was part of a flourishing political press which had sprung up thanks to the abolition of taxes on advertising in 1853, on newspapers in 1855, and on paper in 1861. Apart from *The Times*, in a class of its own not only because of its threepenny price, the 'penny newspapers' included the Liberal *Daily News* and *Daily Chronicle*, the High Tory *Morning Post*, and the *Daily Telegraph*, which then and ever after was the paper of the business class and the City.

In 1896 there was an explosion when Alfred Harmsworth founded the *Daily Mail*, distinguished not by size (the tabloid was a later arrival) but by price, half that of the others, and by sensational presentation of the news. The halfpenny *Mail* appalled polite society and

---

[2] A morning paper rather than the later *Evening Standard*.

high thinkers, soon far outstripped the penny papers in circulation, and had a devastating effect on them and on politics. But even when politicians disliked the press, they could not keep away from it. Odder still than Palmerston or Salisbury, Lloyd George seriously considered becoming editor of *The Times* after he had been prime minister, and Lady Soames has said that Churchill, her father, was a journalist first and foremost, who indeed helped himself through his years of opposition in the 1930s by writing any nonsense the *Daily Mail* asked for, on an enormous retainer.

For most of the twentieth century most national newspapers favoured the Conservatives and it appeared that this had given the party an unfair advantage up to and including the 1980s. In 1947 Beaverbrook saucily told the Royal Commission on the Press that he ran his papers 'purely for the purposes of propaganda'. Comically enough, this seemed to confirm what the American radical Dwight Macdonald called one of 'the main tenets of the liberal myth: that the main trouble with our press is ideological, i.e. that it reflects the reactionary views of its owners'. Orwell was one subscriber to that myth, and in his splendid essay on boys' comics he suggested that 'the antiquated, conservative tone of these stories is deliberately maintained by capitalist newspaper proprietors in the interest of the class structure of society': or that was his view as summarized in an otherwise admiring essay by Evelyn Waugh, who added sarcastically that 'A study of those noblemen's more important papers reveals a reckless disregard of any such obligation.'

In reality Beaverbrook had shown just how little power the press possessed. Every single cause he took up over half a century, from Empire Free Trade to blocking the postwar American loan to opposing British entry into the Common Market, was a failure. Rothermere had little more success, either with his support for Mosley and the Blackshirts or his more justified campaign to revise the borders imposed on Hungary by the Trianon treaty. When the two of them had tried to destroy Baldwin as Tory leader in 1930, he routed them with a single speech and a single phrase (donated to him by Kipling, his cousin): the press lords were aiming at 'power without responsibility, the prerogative of the harlot throughout the ages'. Never again through that period did the papers challenge a party leader. And newspapers were then on the face of it much more powerful than by the end of the century, since there were no competing media: radio and cinema were in their infancy (and entirely unpolitical), television was unborn. By 1945, the *Daily Mirror* had become the first paper which was the authentic voice of the working class, thereby winning the circulation war, and it was easy to suppose that it had also won that year's election for Labour. But in truth Labour's landslide and the *Mirror*'s circulation battle had been won from the same causes. And so it was when Mrs Thatcher won her elections and the *Sun* its own circulation wars, again from the same causes. The truth remained that, as A. J. P. Taylor said by way of seconding Waugh, 'The popular newspapers supplied news and, more often, entertainment; they did not direct opinion.'

There was nevertheless an intimate and most unsavoury relationship between Murdoch and the Tories. In 1981 he acquired the *The Times* and *Sunday Times*, an acquisition which breached the regulations about the number of national titles, or the total circulation, which could be held in one hand. To circumvent that, John Biffen, the responsible minister, combined sleight of hand with *suppressio veri* and declared that the rules could be suspended since the papers were not trading at a profit. Taking *The Times* alone, that was almost true – its travails with the unions had culminated in a long disastrous closure in 1979 – but taking the two titles together it was quite untrue, as the *Sunday Times*'s healthy profits more than carried its sickly sister. After that, Murdoch owed the government one, which he delivered during the Falklands war and at the next election.

While Mrs Thatcher and Major were careful to cultivate Murdoch, some Tories never liked him; and yet they also misunderstood him. One of his haughty critics in the fogey press called him the greatest hypocrite alive, which was most unfair. A billionaire international media magnate whose immediate and public reaction to the death of Princess Diana was to say that at least his tabloids would not have to pay stupid prices to the paparazzi for pictures of her any more might be called many things, but not a hypocrite. The left also misprized Murdoch, assuming that he was in business to wield influence rather than make money, and that he had any coherent political ideology. After Andrew Neil had spent years as editor of the *Sunday Times* he involuntarily left the paper and then said that Murdoch was 'much more right-wing' than anyone realized; and yet that was to attribute to Murdoch's career an ideological basis it did not possess.

What neither left nor Tories grasped was not only how fickle or ruthless Murdoch could be in his political attachments, but that his version of 'free enterprise' was not conservative at all. It was dynamic, demonic and destructive. This was one thing about capitalism that Marx had perceived correctly: 'All fixed, fast-frozen relations, with their train of ancient and venerable prejudices and opinions are swept away, all new-formed ones become antiquated before they can ossify. All that is solid melts into air, all that is holy is profaned.' If there had been room for them, those words could have stood on the masthead of the *Sun*.

Above all, while offering tactical support to the Conservatives for his own ends, Murdoch threatened everything Tory England should have stood for. Unlike Northcliffe, Murdoch was not uneducated – to the contrary, he had been at Worcester College, Oxford, where he kept a bust of Lenin in his room – but Sir Robert Ensor's description, written in 1935, of Northcliffe and his relations with the Tories in the first decades of the century applied with frightening exactness to Murdoch and his relations with the Tories in its last decades: 'He saw events and policies in terms of the headlines which would sell his papers; he was ignorant of history, indifferent to English political tradition; and yet he exerted over the party which ought to have conserved it a masterful sway, which the parliamentary leaders were at once too proud to confess and too weak to curb.'

To the extent that the press did exert any influence it was paradoxically almost in inverse ratio to sales. However obnoxious the 1960s advertising slogan 'Top people take *The Times*' had been (not to say that it showed the paper was already losing its nerve that it needed to say such a thing), it had once been quite true: and the fact was that the paper was much more influential at the beginning of the twentieth century than at the end, by which time its circulation was ten times larger. And as far as actual policy and conduct went, the Attlee government was far less influenced by the *Mirror* than by the weekly *New Statesman* with one-hundredth of its sales.

Similarly it had not been the *Sun* which adumbrated the serious nature of Thatcherism so much as the *Spectator*. This magazine had long been the voice of civilized Conservatism, and in the 1950s and 1960s when it was owned by Ian Gilmour it had been notable for its social and political liberalism. In the one black deed of his life, Gilmour sold it in 1967 to a disreputable businessman and it soon descended into a pit of rancorous vulgarity, even though its editor was George Gale, a history First from Peterhouse, Cambridge, and its literary editor was Maurice Cowling, a don of that college and one of the apostles of the new Cambridge right.

Then in 1975 it changed hands again when Henry Keswick, the Hong Kong magnate, bought it and appointed as editor the only journalist he knew, Alexander Chancellor, under whom its character once more changed. For years little happened in terms of circulation, but the magazine's renewed espousal of libertarianism was marked at the time of its hemiocentenary in 1978 by a long leading article in *The Times*, which began gratifyingly, 'The *Spectator*, having quite recently been a very bad magazine, is at present a very good one', and was headed, 'On the Side of Liberty'. Understandably weary of the losses he was incurring (and maybe peeved by the ingratitude of a Tory party which would not offer him a parliamentary seat), Keswick sold it in turn to J. G. Cluff, another entrepreneur. In 1984 the plot took a further twist when Cluff replaced Chancellor with Charles Moore, still in his twenties, a product of the Cambridge right who had been working for a few years for the *Daily Telegraph*.

The *Telegraph* was by now the only specifically Conservative survivor of those penny papers at the beginning of the century (its price had gone up). It was originally founded as a 'single-issue' paper of the most unlikely character, to campaign against the autocratic rule of the Duke of Cambridge as commander-in-chief of the British army, but it survived and prospered to become one of the most successful of all London papers. It was owned by the Lawson family, formerly Levy-Lawson, until 1927 when they sold it to the Berry family, and it was mildly strengthened in 1937 when the ailing *Morning Post* finally succumbed and was folded into it. One of the *Morning Post*'s young reporters in its last years was the young W. F. Deedes, who joined the paper in 1931 when Baldwin led the Tories, served with distinction as a rifleman in the war, sat for years as a Tory MP, was briefly a minister under Macmillan, edited the *Daily Telegraph* in the 1970s, and was still writing for it in his nineties when Michael Howard led the party in 2005.

Under the ownership of the Berrys, the *Telegraph* grew stronger after 1945 until it was something unique, a middle-class broadsheet selling more than a million copies daily. Its politics were bluffly Conservative but thoroughly unideological, offering critical support to the Tories in a spirit perfectly expressed in a leader at the beginning of 1956 (written by the deputy editor, Donald McLachlan), which said that most Conservatives 'are waiting to feel the smack of firm government'. The phrase might have had a slightly kinky flagellant flavour to it, and it was believed by some to have impelled Eden towards the disastrous Suez adventure, but it was what many Tories wanted to hear: common sense and no fancy highflown ideas. In moments of crisis, one of the last of the old school of Tory backbenchers, Rear-Admiral Morgan Giles, used to tell the 1922 Committee, '*Pro bono publico*, no bloody panico', and that was the *Telegraph*'s watchword also, until the later years of the century.

In the 1970s there was a not entirely creative tension between Deedes and his deputy editor, the attractive, clever, bibulous lost soul Colin Welch. Welch was a Tory of sorts but even more a free-marketeer. Under his guidance, and that of T. E. Utley, the paper took on a more doctrinaire tinge. It was sharply critical of the Heath government's shifts and compromises, and became a home of 'premature Thatcherism'. As Enoch Powell said of Utley, 'In some degree he paved the way intellectually for the changes in the direction of Conservative policy which she initiated and implemented,' and intellectually was the word.

'Why is it always the intelligent people who are socialists?' the Headmaster asks in *Forty Years On*. If it had always been so, by the 1980s it was true no more. Instead, the *Telegraph* as well as the Cambridge right illustrated a most fascinating and little remarked development. In a famous phrase, John Stuart Mill called the Conservatives 'the stupid party', and a hundred years later this was glossed by A. J. P. Taylor when he said Mill's words were not unfair: 'to be stupid and sensible are not far apart. The Progressive party, Radical and Socialist, is clever, but silly.' What happened in the later years of the twentieth century was the emergence of a right which was clever, but silly.

This was far from a purely English development, and a quasi-intellectual 'new right' could be seen in one guise or another in many countries. Successive waves of men and women who had been captivated by the Communist dream were disillusioned and became anti-Communists, sometimes of a most zealous character. John Biggs-Davison was one of the more attractive Tory MPs of the 1970s and 1980s on the romantic right of the party, but he had begun political life as a comrade of Denis Healey in the Oxford Communist party (as Healey liked maliciously to point out). In France, this disillusionment took longer and it was not until the 1970s that a generation of *intellos* discovered by reading Solzhenitsyn that Soviet Communism had not been entirely benevolent after all.

In America there was another development again. Writing in 1952 about the early career of William F. Buckley, Dwight Macdonald mentioned 'the neo-conservative tendency that has arisen among the younger intellectuals', perhaps the first sighting of that potent word. He intended people who had reacted against the progressive pieties of the New Deal era. It was not until the 1960s that the term gained wide currency, at that time describing a group of rightwards defectors who had been liberals and Democrats, and some of whom had once been much further to the left, as Communists or more often Trotskyists. They had now been 'mugged by reality' in various ways, but more than anything because of the bitterly divisive question of Israel and Zionism.

In England there was no such contemporary neo-con movement, although here also there were in every generation men and women who moved to the right as they moved into middle age. George V had said that any man who is not a socialist before he is thirty has no heart, and any man who is a socialist after thirty has no head, an aperçu, such as it was, which Tories capitalized on. The great historian of Soviet despotism Robert Conquest (himself another Comm-turned-anti-Comm) made a better point by saying that everyone tends to be more 'right-wing' on any particular question the more he actually knows about it. But the American poet Robert Frost may have made the best point of all when he said he was so glad he had not been a revolutionist when he was young, since it meant he did not have to become a reactionary when he was old.

No doubt 'the stupid party' had always needed to be qualified. Hume and Burke were not stupid, nor were Disraeli and Salisbury. Both of the latter had indeed, in their quite different ways, a touch of clever-but-silly about them, but Baldwin was more in tune with his party's mood when he played the plain man. He used to say that at Cambridge he had been taught Sir Henry Maine's thesis that the great change in English history was from status to contract – 'or was it the other way round?' Quintin Hailsham was one more clever man who had acclaimed a Tory tradition in which the wiser had devoted their time to religion and the simpler to fox-hunting.

Even in Baldwin's day there were already a few 'clever-silly Conservatives', the very phrase Orwell used for a group he particularly disliked, 'people like Sir Alan Herbert, Professor G. M. Young, Lord Elton, the Tory Reform Group or the long line of Catholic apologists from W. H. Mallock onwards'. But he added that they were people 'who specialise in cracking neat jokes at the expense of whatever is "modern" and "progressive" and whose opinions are often all the more extreme because they know that they cannot influence the actual drift of events'. The difference was that by the 1980s the clever-but-silly right was very much in a position to influence events, though by no means necessarily to the Tories' ultimate advantage.

For all their premature Thatcherism, the *Daily Telegraph*, and its sister the *Sunday Telegraph*, had run into grave financial trouble by the mid-1980s. That was in itself an appalling reflection of the state of industrial relations in Fleet Street: but for rapacious unions and feeble management, the daily in particular should have been making a handsome profit. But in a sadly ironical twist, the Berrys did not survive at their papers to benefit from the Thatcher–Murdoch revolution in newspaper production. Looking desperately for support, Lord Hartwell, formerly Michael Berry, turned to a shadowy Canadian businessman called Conrad Black, who managed quickly to acquire control of the papers, and who in 1986 appointed two very different men as editors, Max Hastings at the *Daily Telegraph* and Peregrine Worsthorne at the *Sunday*. Hastings had made his name as a war correspondent and an outstanding military historian, Worsthorne had been at the *Telegraph* for more than thirty years but had been kept from the editor's chair (as had his friend Welch) by Hartwell with his suspicion of bohemian, clever, 'viewy' journalists.

For the next four years the papers were quietly reformed and, when they followed the other London papers out of Fleet Street, saying goodbye to the print unions, Black was soon making the money that had eluded the Berrys, a fine display of the Tory principle that life is not fair. There was also a power struggle within the group, which was decisively won by Hastings. The editor of the *Sunday Telegraph* was first of all kicked upstairs in 1989 to run the comment section only, 'Worsthorne College' as someone fatuously named it, and was then removed altogether in 1991. This was more a clash of personalities than an ideological division: Hastings had no large political beliefs, merely an attachment to good government and low income tax. He was never any kind of zealous supporter of Mrs Thatcher, he wanted Heseltine to succeed her, and he would later transfer his allegiance smoothly to Tony Blair. Worsthorne was a romantic High Tory – though likewise without the doctrinaire zealotry of younger neo-cons – who unwisely used the paper to start his own hares and pursue his own vendettas. One was against Heseltine, and the clash boiled over in November 1990 when Worsthorne wrote a leader saying that there was too much 'tittle-tattle' surrounding Heseltine, although as his colleagues loyally pointed out, Perry was a fine one to talk. Hastings tried to have the leader spiked; it was published, but bizarrely with the offending initials 'PW' appended; Worsthorne was doomed. After a short interregnum, the musical chairs resumed, and Charles Moore took over at the *Sunday Telegraph* to be succeeded at the *Spectator* by Dominic Lawson, son of Nigel, the former Chancellor and indeed former *Spectator* editor.

In his seven years at the *Spectator*, Moore had already given right-wing journalism a distinctive flavour. Part of it was tone of voice, with a strongly fogeyish[3] or tweedy flavour, sometimes taken to the point of parody. Moore was at the time a pious high churchman but distressed by the changes in the Church of England, above all the

[3] It was in fact in a *Spectator* column that Alan Watkins coined, or at least revived, the phrase 'young fogey', which became a nine days' wonder.

prospect of women priests, and wrote in anguish that he had supposed Christ handed Peter the keys of the Kingdom, including one cut which opened the 'mystery of the English heart'. When the *Spectator* was later obsessed by the fact that Ferdinand Mount – or rather a journal- ist, as yet unnamed – had inherited a baronetcy but chosen not to use it, Moore affected not to know who this was: 'For all I know, this missing baronet might live a mere 200 yards from our door . . . Just think! The woman who does not wish to be known as Lady That could be our son's godmother. Mere idle day-dreaming, I know.' As Hermione Gingold might have said, the Admiralty couldn't be more Arch.

There was a curious contradiction in this fogey right which now flourished at the *Telegraph* group (Black having acquired the *Spectator* also). Most of these tweedy chaps were ardent admirers of free-market capitalism on the American model, Moore pre-eminently. He did not appear to see any contradiction between his Church-and-Crown Toryism and the rampant market-place which swept away ancient and venerable prejudices and opinions. There was an even more specific contradiction. In protest against those priestesses, Moore finally acceded to Roman Catholicism ('an excellent religion for peasants and women', as Salisbury had called it), thereby joining a number of others who combined papistry with Thatcherism, in parliament like the Maastricht rebel Bill Cash or in the press like Paul Johnson and William Rees-Mogg. Were these Catholic laissez-fairies really unaware that Manchester School liberalism was about the only social and economic doctrine to have been regularly and unequivocally con- demned by the Vatican from the 1891 encyclical 'Rerum Novarum' onwards?

Long and dark over this lay the shadow of one man. On one measure Enoch Powell was an interesting but distinctly minor politician, who held Cabinet office for all of fifteen months in his life, who attracted the votes of one in twenty of his parliamentary colleagues on the only occasion when he stood for leader, and who then did what he could to wreck the party. And yet the cult of Enoch could scarcely be exaggerated. Powell himself was not a social reactionary: his young acolytes liked to overlook his opposition to capital punishment, just as they forgot (if they ever knew) what life was actually like in the bad old days. On the occasion of his eightieth birthday in 1992, the *Spectator* published an adulatory profile by the high priest of the cult, Simon Heffer, later the author of a admired biography of Powell.

In the course of the interview Powell said, not for the first time, that his greatest regret was that he had not been killed in the war, a claim of which it might charitably be said that it was either neurotic or false. For emphasis, Powell histrionically declaimed:

> Shot? So quick, so clean an ending?

It was an example of his self-dramatization, and his gift for selective quotation, that neither he nor Heffer seemed aware that this line from 'A Shropshire Lad' had nothing to do with battlefields but had a quite different inspiration in real life. There had been a homosexual scandal at Woolwich Military Academy, ending in the suicide of a young officer cadet. Living in the shadow of the same stupid and cruel law, Housman had been deeply affected by this:

> Oh that was right, lad, that was brave.
> Yours was not an ill for mending.
> Best to take it to the grave.

There was now a generation of zealous right-wingers obsessed by the evil changes of the 1960s, who did not even remember what life had been like before then.

Meantime Major was beset by this clamant and cantankerous press, and the government's fortunes fell ever lower. The Gallup rating had dropped below 30 per cent in the spring of 1993 and, with the odd illusory blip, remained there (except occasionally to fall even further). In December 1994, the figure was only just above 20 per cent; otherwise the Tories flat-lined, in the grim phrase of hospital practice when a patient's chart shows no signs of recovery. There was little poor Major could do except hang on for dear life, but by the summer of 1995 he could bear no longer the slings of the 'bastards' in his party and the arrows of the press. Other Tories had their own troubles with the media. Scandals continued to erupt, with Neil Hamilton among other MPs being accused of asking parliamentary questions in return for cash. Then in April Aitken resigned from the Cabinet to fight a libel action against the *Guardian* and a television company which had

1. Iain Macleod, and Sir Alec Douglas-Home, 1964

2. Edward Heath, Alec Home and Harold Macmillan, *c.* 1972

. . . AND TWO UNEASIER

3. Heath and Margaret Thatcher, 1998

4. The prophet perplexed: Sir Keith Joseph, 1979

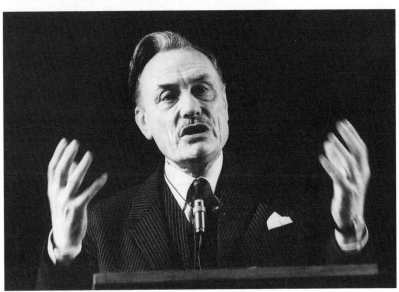

5. The prophet exalted: Enoch Powell 1978

'Rejoice!'

6. Mrs Thatcher, 1987

7. Margaret Thatcher and Sir Geoffrey Howe, 1983

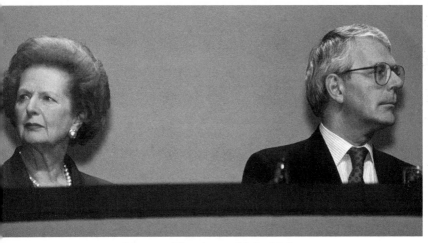

8. Margaret Thatcher and John Major

9. 'His hair's too long': Mrs Thatcher inspecting Michael Heseltine, 1981

10. Who dares grins: Michael Portillo, 2001

11. 'Come with me to the Rother Valley': William Hague, 2001

12. 'The quiet man is here to stay', he thought: Iain Duncan Smith, 2003

13. 'A theatrical party in Maidenhead'? John Redwood and supporters, 1995

14. Somethings of the night: Michael Howard and David Davis, 2004

accused him of dodgy arms dealings with Arabs. He did this with the grandiose and hubristic words: 'If it falls to me to cut out the cancer of bent and twisted journalism in our country with the simple sword of truth and the trusty shield of British fair play, so be it. I am ready for the fight.' Another fuse was lit under the Tories.

In his own way, Major also hoped to wield the shield of fair play. The most dastardly bastards were the Maastricht rebels, eight of whom had for a time been deprived of the Tory whip, and who had continued to vote against the government over VAT and fisheries. By that summer, Major could not address a backbench meeting without being treated, as Alan Watkins wrote, 'as a guest speaker of dubious credentials', rather than head of government. And the treacherous rumblings when he went off to a summit in Canada were so loud that he felt like an African leader who could barely leave the country for fear of being deposed.

He always liked to proclaim his love of cricket and had sycophantically been made a member of the MCC, without the usual waiting period, soon after he became prime minister. But the fact that a Test match was being played at Lord's that June did not prevent him from springing the most bizarre surprise of his prime ministership. Some unfortunate journalists were dragged away from the pavilion when Major announced that he was resigning the party leadership to stand again for election, so as to take on 'a small minority in our party' who had been doing everything they could to undermine him: 'I am not prepared to see the party I care for laid out on the rack like this any longer.' Despite Lloyd George, who had been 'a prime minister without a party', or Churchill, who for five months in 1940 had been prime minister but not Tory leader, this was quite unprecedented, and Powell queried the constitutional propriety of such a strange *coup de théâtre*.

This self-inflicted coup was also patently designed to smoke out the disloyal elements in his Cabinet – or silence them. For a moment it looked as though there would be no challenger, and Major taunted his own colleagues, 'Put up or shut up.' Michael Portillo had done everything to turn himself into the man of the right who would succeed Major. He had roused the rabble at the Tory conference by quoting the SAS motto, 'Who dares, wins', thereby repelling those who had actually worn uniform and seen action, but now he did not quite dare.

John Redwood did, and resigned the Welsh Secretaryship to stand against the prime minister.

A clever, cold, ambitious Tory with a regrettably sinister mien, he had made his way from a modest background to Oxford and an All Souls fellowship, had written an academic work on *Reason, Ridicule and Religion* before going into the City and then serving in Mrs Thatcher's private office as an adviser. His latest office was one which no one could blame him for laying down. Until 1964, Wales had been the responsibility of a parliamentary under-secretary at the Home Office, but Harold Wilson created the Secretaryship of State and a department to go with it as an act of kindness to Jim Griffiths, a much-loved master of windy Cymric rhetoric. Poor Redwood had not enjoyed himself in the principality – he was filmed singing or attempting to sing 'Hen Wlad fy Nhadau' ('Land of my Fathers') when he clearly did not know the words – and had good reasons for his pique.

While Major skilfully pressed several colleagues to demonstrate their loyalty by running his campaign, Redwood enlisted a gruesome collection of supporters from the ranks of the Maastricht bastards. They were unforgettably photographed at Westminster, among them Teresa Gorman dressed to kill and Anthony Marlow grinning dementedly from above an Old Wellingtonian blazer, and altogether deserving of the rebuke from Charles's cousin Jasper in *Brideshead Revisited*: 'Your present get-up seems an unhappy compromise be-tween the correct wear for a theatrical party at Maidenhead and a glee-singing competition in a garden suburb.'

At least Redwood had shown some nerve. As happened twenty years earlier when Mrs Thatcher had stood against Heath, others awaited the vote, willing to wound but afraid to strike, and hoping that the prime minister would be winged and that there would be another ballot. Portillo was notably reticent in his expressions of enthusiasm for his chief, and it was then learned that he had had a bank of telephones installed in a house near parliament for just that eventuality. Loyalty was no longer this party's secret weapon, if it ever had been.

Since the general election, the Tories had lost five by-elections, one to Labour, one to the Scottish Nationalists and three to the Liberal

Democrats. From those depleted ranks, 89 MPs voted for Redwood and 218 for Major with 22 abstentions. Although the prime minister was confirmed in office, the disaffection of some of his closest colleagues was also confirmed, and with no more than two-thirds of his MPs voting for him, the prime minister was more than ever in office and not in power.

But nothing was more astonishing about this episode than the fact that both the *Daily Telegraph* and *Sunday Telegraph* actually backed Redwood. Moore at the *Sunday* did so out of ideological zeal. Although Hastings at the *Daily* was no doctrinaire, he was a man in conversation with whom few people had ever been allowed to finish a sentence, and his sheer impatience with the inept Major and his scandal-ridden and incompetent government, as well as a certain amount of egging on from Heffer, the deputy editor, tipped the scales. This was the decisive moment at which the Tory press and even the party lost contact with reality. However bad Major was, the idea that Redwood was the man to inspire the country was so obviously risible, and the appearance and character of his followers so obviously grotesque, that those supporting him might have been motivated by an unconscious desire to damage the party.

By coincidence, there was another round of newspaper musical chairs months after that midsummer madness. David English, creator of the *Daily Mail* in its latest guise, lured Hastings back to the *Evening Standard* where he had begun his working life, and which now belonged to Associated Newspapers, the *Mail* group. There, Hastings followed the logic of his position and endorsed Blair at the coming election. He was succeeded at the *Daily Telegraph* by Moore, who followed some logic of his own, whatever it would do to the party.

One small example of the destructive success of the right came with the election in May 1997, postponed by Major as long as he could. In the Islington constituency where, as it happened, Charles Moore and Ferdinand Mount both lived, the Tory candidate published an election address near to the new *Telegraph* editor's heart. There were only three questions of vital concern to him: ruling out membership of the single currency in the life of the next parliament, reducing the permissible interval for abortion, and lowering local taxes. Mount accounted himself a lifelong Conservative, supposed that he would remain a Conservative, and had imagined that he would be writing a column to say why he was voting Conservative again. Instead he explained that he – Lady Thatcher's former political valet (his own phrase) and the author of the 1983 manifesto – had read this candidate's testament, so utterly wrong on all three counts, and had decided to vote Lib. Dem. instead.

And one other vignette serves as a droll postscript to 'the power of the press'. On the night of 1–2 May 1997 the sheer scale of the Labour triumph became clear. Sitting in his headquarters in his Sedgefield constituency, Tony Blair looked more and more pensive, since the scale of the landslide was not in truth welcome to him. Meanwhile in the offices of the *Daily Mail*, the visage of the editor grew not merely pensive but blacker as events unfolded. Then in the small hours Finchley fell from Tory to Labour: Finchley, the heart of suburbia and the seat which Margaret Thatcher had represented for more than thirty years. As that 'Labour gain' was announced, Paul Dacre shouted at the newsroom television, 'What the fuck's going on? These are fucking *Mail* readers!' So they were, but the *Mail*'s beloved Middle England had deserted the Tories at last.

12

Things Fall Apart

Plenty of others besides the editor of the *Daily Mail* were stunned that early May morning as the sheer scale of the Tory rout became clear. There had been only two elections like it in the past century – in 1906 when the Liberals won 400 seats and reduced the Tories to a rump of 157, and 1945 when Labour won 393 and reduced the Tories to 213. This time Labour won 419 seats, more than Campbell-Bannerman or Attlee had, and had an absolute majority over all other parties of 159. The Tories were once more a rump, at 165 MPs, fewer even than in 1945. During the campaign, 'the "l" word' – landslide – had been superstitiously banned at the Labour headquarters in Millbank. They were not permitted to mention it as a possibility – and Blair himself suppressed the thought of what was in reality a problematic outcome in terms of his own intentions.

The 'project' his acolytes had talked about more than they had explained it meant a realignment of the political structure, with a classless coalition of supposedly centre-left parties, New Labour and Liberal Democrats, presumably if not explicitly leading to their amalgamation, and at last ending the political 'cleavage of classes' of Harcourt's phrase. Before the election Blair had made approaches to the Liberal Democrat leader Jeremy 'Paddy' Ashdown, and offered him a Cabinet seat when he formed his government, or so Ashdown clearly understood. But that was impossible to sell to Labour MPs once the party had triumphed and had no need of any allies.

Another centrist whom Blair had befriended was Roy Jenkins, the veteran Labour politician turned Social Democrat and then Lib Dem. He liked Blair and saw him as a man who could reshape the Labour party much as Jenkins had once wanted to, and would lead his country toward a deeper integration in Europe, first of all by joining the single currency. Jenkins was given to understand that Blair favoured electoral reform, the proportional representation which was still the Liberal Democrats' Holy Grail, which made sense in terms of 'the project', but which needless to say most of the Labour party wanted less than ever after the election. When a politician gives an undertaking to others of the kind Blair was now in the regular habit of giving, and quietly forgets about it, then those others are, in the hallowed phrase of Irish politics, left with their arses hanging out of the window. Ashdown and Jenkins were only the first two of a long line who dealt with Blair and who would find themselves in that undignified posture.

No one was more shell-shocked than John Major – or maybe demob happy. The alacrity with which he resigned the Tory leadership on the morrow of defeat, before the last results were even in, was frankly irresponsible. John Biffen was standing down as Member for Oswestry after an eventful parliamentary career, and had said during the election that in the event of a defeat Major should stay on for at least a few months to allow passions to subside. It would unquestionably have been better if the party had been given time to make a considered choice, as indeed it would have been in 1990 and would be again in 2001. But it was hard to blame Major. The country had had enough of the Tories and so had he, of trying to hold together an impossibly fractious and disloyal party, enough of the frantic abuse of the newspapers. He celebrated his new freedom on 2 May by sauntering off to the place he chose on 'Desert Island Discs' as the 'one luxury' he would take to his tropical isle, the Oval cricket ground.

As the parliamentary party convened to choose his successor, its character was striking, apart from its exiguous numbers. Its centre of gravity had shifted further to the right, and the Maastricht rebels had won a kind of destructive victory. Meantime the eclipse of Macmillan's 'old governing class' continued apace. In the nineteenth century the Commons had been littered with titles, on the Treasury Bench as well as the backbenches, Irish peers like Viscount Palmerston, elder sons of peers like the Marquess of Hartington, younger sons like Lord John Russell, and enough Sirs to give their name to 'the baronets' bench'. In the parliament elected in 1992 there had been just two such aristocrats, sitting for adjacent constituencies in Wiltshire, and it was a mark of the times that each concealed his title. The Earl of Kilmorey – an Irish peer who had once, as a minister, been overheard speaking of Mrs Thatcher as a 'cow' – called himself Richard Needham, and the Earl of Ancram, son of the Marquess of Lothian, called himself Michael Ancram or Mr Ancram (which he was not). By 1997 he was the only one left. And for the first time in three centuries the House of Commons contained no Old Harrovian, not a single man educated at the school which had produced Palmerston, Aberdeen and Churchill as well as Baldwin, he who had said on becoming prime minister that he wanted a Cabinet Harrow would be proud of. The social revolution Macleod had begun with his attack on the magic circle had reached its climax. A year before his resignation, Macmillan had appointed to an under-secretaryship his nephew by marriage, the Duke of Devonshire, who himself called it the most outrageous act of nepotism of the age; now Andrew Devonshire himself admitted that 'the aristocracy is a spent force'.

As to the Celtic fringes, the Tories were not eclipsed but obliterated. Only four decades earlier, after the 1955 election, they had held a majority of Scottish seats; in 1997 not a single Tory MP was elected in Scotland, or in Wales either. Such Scottish Conservatives as survived in the Commons had prudently decamped to the south, like Ancram, in his case from the Borders by way of Edinburgh to Wiltshire. The Caledonian wipe-out meant that Malcolm Rifkind, since 1974 the member for an Edinburgh seat, a very capable Defence Secretary and then Foreign Secretary under Major and far from a remote outsider for the succession to the leadership, was scratched from the runners. It meant also that the Tories had become an English party. Or indeed, still holding 95 out of 165 seats in southern England outside London, they were a regional party, unhappily similar to the Bavarian Christian Social Union or the Northern League in Italy.

Although the 1997 election was not as puzzling as its predecessor, it was widely misunderstood. The mood of expectation beforehand, when a shrewd observer could say, quite wrongly, 'These are revolutionary times', and the unmistakable elation of the first week of May, when even apolitical people felt a different tang in the air, were misleading. The truth was that there had been plenty of good reasons for voting Labour, but that most of them were negative. At its simplest, the British did not want to become a one-party democracy, like Italy ruled for decades by the Christian Democrats, or Japan under the Liberal Democrats, or Mexico ruled for more than half a century by the exquisitely named Party of Institutional Revolution. 'Time for a change' was a perfectly sensible instinct. For a party to be in office for eighteen years was simply too long. Any historic mission of Thatcherism had long since been fulfilled. The Tories were worn-out, shop-soiled and shabby, the country was fed up with them, and they were fed up with themselves, almost longing to be put out of their misery. It was bad enough that they were unpopular; far worse, they were simply unneeded.

And yet there was an element of fantasy about the claims made at the time by more dewy-eyed figures on the left, many of whom had opportunity to repent at leisure their raptures that May. On one level there is no arguing with what Bagehot called the brute force of a parliamentary majority; but Blair's landslide was a function of technical causes. To be sure, the Tory vote had collapsed, from just over 14 million to just under 10 million, the lowest since 1945 and, as a proportion, easily the lowest the Tories had polled in the twentieth century. The electorate had pronounced something close to a true death sentence. It was wrong to conclude that this unmistakable vote of no confidence in the Tories was a positive vote of confidence in New Labour. For one thing, the British had learned the art of tactical voting for the first time since the 1920s. That this is not surmise was proved by the statistically quaint result that, whereas in 1992 the Liberal Democrats had polled fractionally under six million votes and won twenty seats, five years later they polled a distinctly smaller 5.2 million, but won forty-six seats. And the first-past-the-post system produced its usual startlingly exaggerated effect: many leaders in countries with proportional representation, from Italy to Israel, must have wished they could achieve so much as a parliamentary majority, let alone 63 per cent of legislative seats, with the 43 per cent of votes cast, as Blair did.[1]

Looking closer still, that 43 per cent was no more than the pro-

---

[1] Labour: 13.5 million votes, 43.2 per cent, 419 seats; Tories: 9.6 million, 30.7 per cent, 165 seats; Liberal Democrats: 5.2 million, 16.8 per cent, 46 seats; Others: 29 seats.

portion of the popular vote the Tories won in 1992, and Blair won fewer votes cast than the Tories had at three out of the four preceding elections, including of course Major's record-breaking achievement in 1992. More remarkably, it was less than the number of people who voted Labour as far back as 1951. But the most significant – and ominous – fact about the election of 1997 was that it saw the lowest turnout since 1935, less than 72 per cent. This was 12 percentage points below the 84 per cent turnout of 1950. Less than one adult citizen in three had voted Labour, and many people were as disenchanted with politicians as they were bored by politics. The electors, so nervous about Labour that they had even returned the Tories when they were led by Major during a severe economic slump, had waited until they could safely vote Labour without the smallest chance of any revolutionary effect at all. Tory England had suffered a grave or maybe even mortal blow, but it was entirely wrong to suppose that anything which could be called 'the left' had triumphed.

One other factor insufficiently emphasized at the time was the effect of the Europhobic vote. In 1995 the Referendum party had been founded by Sir James Goldsmith. In many ways it was a risible affair, noisily supported at one glitzy gathering after another by such notabilities as the actor Edward Fox, Carla Powell, the vivacious socialite wife of Lady Thatcher's sometime aide Sir Charles, now Lord, Powell, Woodrow Wyatt's daughter Petronella, half the Sloane Rangers in London, and altogether a fine cross-section of rich white trash; there had been nothing like it since the flapper in *Vile Bodies* complained, 'The Independent Labour Party? Why haven't I been asked?'

A more than faintly demonic figure, Goldsmith had been both a very successful businessman and a prominent figure in the dubious international *gratin* of money and power. In the wake of the Lucan affair[2] he had conducted a ferocious vendetta against *Private Eye* and then tried without success to become a press mogul himself. He was bullying and indeed frightening, although also faintly ridiculous. During the interminable litigation with *Private Eye*, Alexander Chancellor, the editor of the *Spectator*, and I, his literary editor, had

[2] When Lord Lucan, a decayed gambler and drunkard, had killed his children's nanny mistaking her for his wife, and then disappeared.

gone appropriately as spectators to the High Court, where we had bumped into Taki Theodorocopulos, the magazine's society columnist, and with him John Aspinall, the playboy who was the central figure of the set to which Goldsmith, Taki and Lucan had belonged. Aspinall offered us a lift in his very large motor-car, on our way to which Goldsmith spotted us and, not quite wrongly associating the *Spectator* with the *Eye*, screamed, 'Aspers! Keep away from those people! They are pus!' This was the man who was about to play an important role in the Tories' decline.

Like so many brilliant entrepreneurs, from Rhodes and Ford onward, he was an obsessive, and like them he was a child in politics. But when he took up the anti-European cause it was no child's play. He put twenty million pounds of his own money into the party, whose single issue was to demand a referendum on continued British membership of the European Union, and he was able to run all of 547 candidates at the election. Goldsmith himself stood against Mellor in his Putney seat and, although Goldsmith did not win, Mellor lost. On election night even those who abhorred Mellor were disquieted by the sight of Goldsmith at the count screeching 'Out! Out!' through what looked like foam-flecked lips. He died only months later, but he had finally made an impact on British politics, albeit negative: 505 of his candidates lost their deposits, but they also took on average 3.1 per cent of the poll, and the party nationally won 811,827 votes. More than half a million electors voted for other fringe parties, including the United Kingdom Independence Party: it was no small problem for the Tories that a tenth of their remaining vote had defected to Europhobic parties of the right. And it was both a largely self-inflicted difficulty and one to which they had no answer. Labour had been divided in the past, over the 1931 crisis or over unilateralism, but now wore a smile of unity. It was the Tories who were riven. Foes of Michael Heseltine and Kenneth Clarke said correctly that their enthusiasm for joining the single currency sooner rather than later implied consent to broader economic and political union, but the party now contained a fair number of people whose own position implied withdrawal from the European Union, and who were the more frustrated because they were not able to say this as candidly as Goldsmith's crew.

Several months before the election, David Heathcoat-Amory, himself an intelligent MP on the Eurosceptic right who had been a whip and a junior minister, had predicted that 'the whole course of history of both the party and the country would be decided in conclave after the election by who backed whom for the leadership.' To say 'and the country' assumed that the Tories might return to power in the foreseeable future; what was true was that the party was due for prolonged internal bleeding. While the candidates to succeed Major started jostling, the field had been thinned out. Rifkind and Mellor apart, the carnage included other notable casualties, including Lamont in the North Riding and Waldegrave in Bristol, who left with philosophical dignity, saying that there was life after politics. As for him who would dare and win, one gloating book about the election was called *Were you up for Portillo?*, which is to say up in the small hours when the Defence Secretary lost his Enfield seat. Like Benn in 1982, he was ruled out of the coming contest, when he would have been a serious candidate, presumably of the right, although he was now repositioning himself again.

The obvious candidate of the left in his own eyes was Heseltine, but fate took a hand here also when, a few days after the election, he was struck down with a heart illness and rushed to hospital. At the urging of his wife more than his doctors, he now withdrew from the field. Plenty of Tories (to the extent that 'plenty' could be used of the surviving rump) had wanted a straight fight between right and left, Europhobe and Europhile, laissez-fairy and corporatist, young and old: at the time of the general election, Portillo was forty-three to Heseltine's sixty-four.

Maybe such a duel would have cleared the air if it could have taken place; as it was, the atmosphere within the party was as noxious as ever. The party could not even decide on the method for electing a new leader. The Liberal Democrats had moved to one member, one vote, and Labour had chosen its leader with a modified form of the electoral college. Since the Liberal Democrats had enjoyed unwonted, and Labour astounding, success, some Tories thought that election by party members might be their sovereign remedy too. One problem was what 'the members' meant. An arcane argument cropped up that the party had no legal existence; more to the point, its membership had shrunk far more drastically even than the party's parliamentary representation. The Conservative party had never published accurate figures, but there was reason to think that in 1953 its membership had reached an astonishing 2.8 million – and reason to think also that by 1997 this was down to about a quarter of a million. Whatever the figure, Tory apparatchiks confidently stated that a full party ballot would take at least two years to organize, and the contest was thus conducted on the same lines as before, although to help (or perhaps confuse) matters further, the chairmen of Conservative constituency associations as well as Tory peers were asked for their choices.

In the diminished field the first front-runner was Clarke, who said that there should be a review of the electoral procedure, but only after a new leader – meaning himself – was chosen. Another candidate, the comparatively youthful William Hague, also said that there might be a new system, but only after the next leader was 'chosen by the people who knew the leadership candidates the best', under a proceeding which 'had stood test of time', which was, even by the standards of invented tradition, an odd description of a system a little over thirty years old.

In the event, there were five candidates when the first ballot was held a little less than six weeks after the debacle, Clarke, Hague, Redwood, Peter Lilley and Michael Howard. Clarke was a genial soul, one more of the new Tories who had come from grammar school, in Nottingham in his case, to Cambridge and the Bar. He had ascended steadily during the 1980s despite Mrs Thatcher, who never liked or trusted him, although he had in fact, as health and then as education minister, been almost more Thatcherite than the lady in his contemptuous attitude to vested professional interests. After Lamont's final departure from the Treasury, Clarke had replaced him, and his four years as Chancellor from 1993 to 1997 had been, economic historians would judge, notably successful, laying down that base of low inflation and interest rates, declining unemployment and steadily increasing growth, on which Gordon Brown would build. Clarke's reward from the electorate showed that yet again life isn't fair, and that it's not the economy, stupid. In person he looked like a man who enjoyed himself: not even as Health Secretary had he stopped drinking beer or puffing cheroots, and when he chose his eight records on the ever-revealing 'Desert Island Discs' he picked one Little Richard number to remind himself of his distant youth, and then all the others from his great love, modern jazz, displaying a real connoisseur's discernment.

Although the Conservative constituency associations of the land may not have been *au courant* with Dizzy Gillespie or Thelonius Monk, they recognized Clarke's affability and popular touch, more so than anyone had guessed. It was not so surprising that he won overwhelmingly in the poll of the predominantly Europhile peers (Clarke 177, Hague 45, Lilley 37, Redwood 13 and Howard 10), but it was very surprising indeed that he should also have won so easily with what everyone had supposed were the Europhobic constituencies (Clarke 322, Hague 188, Redwood 25, Lilley 24, Howard 23). Neither of those mattered. The rump of Tory MPs also voted for Clarke, though only narrowly, on the first ballot: Clarke 49, Hague 41, Redwood 27, Lilley 24, Howard 23. Under the foolish rules, the ballot was not exhaustive, and all the runners could stand again and again as long as they wished, and anyone else could join in; in the event, Lilley and Howard withdrew, and both urged their supporters to vote for Hague.

This was a slap for Redwood, who had presented himself as the remaining standard-bearer of the right, but even then it did not work. In the next ballot a week later, Clarke was still ahead with 64 to Hague's 62 and Redwood's 38. Redwood's immediate reaction was to offer himself to the higher bidder, which meant Clarke because he had 'got in first' with an offer and he was 'better organized than William Hague', Redwood said, and had also promised to make him shadow Chancellor. Maybe there was nothing inherently strange about a left–right balancing act. Such had been practised by the Liberals in the late nineteenth century when they ran Whig and radicals in harness, or by Labour when Tribunites and revisionists were juggled in the shadow cabinet, but there was an unusually cynical flavour to the Clarke–Redwood alliance. It was immediately compared to the Molotov–Ribbentrop pact of 1939, and, in scarcely less hyperbolic terms, the veteran MP Sir Peter Tapsell said that Redwood's behaviour was 'one of the most contemptible and discreditable actions by a senior British politician I can recall during my thirty-eight

years in the Commons'. It did not even work. In the third and mercifully final ballot, Hague beat Clarke by 92 to 70.

For all Clarke's wider national popularity, the balance had been
tilted in the end, partly because of revulsion among some MPs at the
pact, partly because of lingering doubts about Clarke's Europeanism,
crystallized in his refusal before the election to let Major rule out
joining the single currency during the life of the next parliament, and
partly because of Lady Thatcher. Like Erda in the *Ring*, she had risen
from her slumber, with a thunderous warning against 'an incredible
alliance of opposites', and then, in her best manner of a schoolmistress
addressing a class of 'special needs' pupils, she said, 'The name is
Hague. Have you got that? Hague.'

Apart from her loathing of Clarke, she had had a soft spot for
Hague since he spoke as a schoolboy at the Tory conference in 1977,
although not everyone had been overjoyed by that gruesomely pre-
cocious performance, in which he addressed the conference veterans
with the charmless words, 'Half of you may not be here in 30 or 40
years' time, but I will be and I want to be free.' Norman St John Stevas
was heard murmuring, 'Where do they find them? Euston station?'
(an allusion to a scandal of the time in which a paedophile calling
himself the 'Bishop of Medway' had picked up unsuspecting boys
at railway stations). Wherever found, William Jefferson Hague had
prospered, going from Wath-in-Dearne comprehensive in Yorkshire
to Oxford, where he was president of the Union, and then to work for
McKinsey, the dreaded management consultants, the mere prospect of
visitations from whom shook up the most torpid company. He had
stood unsuccessfully at the 1987 election, and then won Richmond in
the North Riding at a by-election in 1989, so that he had been in the
Commons for little more than eight years, and a Cabinet minister for
all of two, when he became Tory leader: he had succeeded Redwood
as Welsh Secretary after the 1995 midsummer madness. After he took
over there was a lull, as the party exhaled and curled up for a moment
during the summer recess, worn out by events. Then within seven
weeks Hague's first test came all unforeseen, with a tragedy which
was indirectly a calamity for his party.

For Tory England the darkest time of 1997 was not the first week
of May with the electoral rout, but the first week of September, 'Diana

Week'. On the night of 31 August, Diana, Princess of Wales, the former wife of the heir to the throne, was killed in a motor crash in Paris. This was a shocking event in itself, but just as shocking was the effect it had on the British people, and the torrent of nonsense which flowed when the news broke. On that day, Blair wrong-footed and routed the Tories and their new leader with that brilliant cynical sincerity which had become his trademark. Speaking with a choke in his voice, the prime minister said: 'She was the People's Princess. And that is how she will stay, how she will remain in our hearts and memories – for ever.' The phrase 'People's Princess' was borrowed by Blair – or Alastair Campbell, his Mephistophelean press officer – from the overwrought columnist Julie Burchill, and it might seem odd that, at the end of the twentieth century, anyone could be so tone-deaf to all the overtones of that adjectival 'people's': People's Courts, People's Democracies, People's Commissariat of Internal Affairs (NKVD), People's Police (Vopos). But for the moment Blair was in command, giving another performance worthy of Sir Henry Irving when he read the lesson at the princess's funeral (as no other politician had ever done before at any royal funeral). Poor Hague was left floundering. He looked bewildered, and could only offer the limply bathetic suggestion that Heathrow should be renamed Princess Diana airport.

What made it far worse was the broader reaction, which suggested more vividly that everything Tory tradition had stood for – not least restraint and common sense – had vanished. For the week between Diana's death and her funeral, London experienced something close to mass hysteria. The queen was bullied by the Murdoch press into making an embarrassed speech of regret on television, the Mall was carpeted with flowers, and the capital was swept by a great flood of inchoate sentiment, self-pity, and what Boris Johnson called Latin American peasant hagiolatry.

Merely the written effusions from the lumpenintelligentsia were terrifying. In 1876 when Gladstone sent Disraeli a copy of his pamphlet on the Bulgarian horrors, the massacre of Bulgars by Ottoman forces, Disraeli characteristically told a colleague that Gladstone's polemic was 'of all the Bulgarian horrors the worst'. It would be hard to say which of the threnodies for Diana was the most dismaying. Clive James lamented that 'The more you know she was never perfect, the less you, who are not perfect either, are able to detach the loss of yourself, and so have gone with her, down that Acherontic tunnel by the Pont de l'Alma and into the Halls of Dis . . .', while Tina Brown expressed her shock that Diana had even been in Paris in August: 'Dinner at the Ritz, weeks before *la rentrée*? The fact that she was there at all was discordant . . .' (or, as Nick Cohen put it, 'Diana died because she made the social error of visiting Paris out of season').

But nothing was as striking as the reactions of supposed men of the left. Anthony Barnett claimed that 'the year 1997 has altered Britain for good: politically, institutionally and emotionally', and he consciously linked the Labour landslide with Diana Week. The playwright David Edgar thought that:

the reason why so many people found that 6 September echoed 1 May was not just the roses and the sunshine (and David Dimbleby); it was that the demand was an echo of the demand of the British people at the general election that the brute, metallic logic of the market be constrained by a sense of moral responsibility. This time there wasn't a ballot box in which to put that message, but it was posted nonetheless.

Although this might seem sorry piffle, it was significant piffle. The old rational left was dead, and had been replaced by sickly sentimentality. Feeling had taken over from thought. In observable fact, the 'brute, metallic logic of the market' had triumphed politically and economically, as the Blair government would demonstrate beyond doubt, but the left (or a version of it) had won culturally.

Well before that September, the Prince and Princess of Wales had both demonstrated how much the old values had faded when they were separately interviewed on television to talk about their failed marriage, just like any Hollywood celebrities, and in the process illustrated W. H. Auden's phrase: the trouble with nowadays is that people have forgotten the difference between their friends and strangers. Love and sex, adultery and divorce, were things which normal people in civilized societies had always discussed with relish, but in private. But it was also Auden who presciently explained Diana Week. In a bravura, haunting vision written fifty years earlier, he foresaw with frightening acuity the coming age in which

Reason will be replaced by Revelation . . . Knowledge will degenerate into a riot of subjective visions – feelings in the solar plexus induced by undernourishment, angelic images generated by fever or drugs, dream warnings inspired by the sound of falling water. Whole cosmogonies will be created out of some forgotten personal resentment, complete epics written in private languages, the daubs of schoolchildren ranked above the greatest masterpieces . . .

Idealism will be replaced by Materialism . . . Diverted from its normal outlet in patriotism and civic or family pride, the need of the masses for some visible Idol to worship will be driven into totally unsociable channels where no education can reach it. Divine honours will be paid to shallow depressions in the earth, domestic pets, ruined windmills, or malignant tumours . . .

Justice will be replaced by Pity as the cardinal human virtue . . . The New Aristocracy will consist exclusively of hermits, bums and permanent invalids. The Rough Diamond, the Consumptive Whore, the bandit who is good to his mother, the epileptic girl who has a way with animals will be the heroes and heroines of the New Tragedy, when the general, the statesman and the philosopher will have become the butt of every farce and satire.

That was precisely England in September 1997, and it was a country the Tories could no longer cope with or even understand.

A month later, the Labour conference was a triumphal parade. MPs and party members who had long distrusted or disliked Blair and what he was doing to their party had to swallow their pride and principles. Nothing succeeds like success, and the brute fact of a parliamentary majority meant that more than 400 men and women of varying ability or none had found billets on the Labour benches. By contrast, the Tories gathered in Blackpool in October not only in black despair but in vengeful mood. At the lowest point of Labour's fortunes in 1981, the MPs had been corralled in a kind of pen at the party conference to be heckled and humiliated. So now, without the refinement of caging them in, the Tory MPs were paraded to be abused. One more businessman turned politician, Archie Norman, presented a 'green paper' for discussion about the party's future and Hague, gluttonous for punishment, foolhardily asked the conference to be as critical as it liked.

The representatives did not need prompting. It was not reasoned discussion they wanted, it was blood. Labour had abandoned the old system of choosing its party leader, had chosen Tony Blair under its new electoral college, and had won a landslide. The superstitious or imitative Tories thought they should do the same, and angrily demanded their own college, with constituency associations holding half the votes. The logic of this was not entirely clear. After Labour had first adopted the electoral college it had chosen Neil Kinnock and lost two elections. If the constituencies had decided, only months before the conference, Clarke would be leading the party, and to say that this was the answer was a funny way of supporting Hague. As much to the point, Sir Archie Hamilton, the new and unusually haughty chairman of the 1922 Committee, pointed out that if the constituencies had been the decisive voice in 1975, Heath would have been retained instead of Mrs Thatcher. But his recognition of the truth cut no ice and he was howled down by the mob.

And who was whipping up this frenzy? What tribune of the people led the charge and insisted that the national party should take over from MPs, who were to blame for the defeat? It was that man of iron principle, Lord Archer of Weston-super-Mare. His harangue at that conference epitomized the depths to which the Tories had fallen.

For the next three years and more almost nothing went right for Hague, and when things went right they went wrong, for reasons which both could or could not be blamed on him. Personable in private as well as intelligent, he had a jarring public manner. In an age of appearances his own did not help, part foetus and part death's head, apparently without having gone through the usual intervening phase of human life. That was bad luck. His knack of making ham-fisted gestures was his own fault. At that first conference, he let it be known that he and his fiancée Ffion were sharing a hotel bedroom, to show that they were an up-to-date couple, and perhaps rebut any unlikely charges of excessive chastity against the party, but he thereby annoyed old-fashioned people (including Lady Thatcher) without greatly impressing swinging youth. Altogether he regularly managed to get it wrong both ways. At one moment Hague would put on a baseball cap or play the cool dude at the Notting Hill carnival. At the next he damned the 'liberal elite' and asked the British people to 'come with me to the Rother Valley', an invitation they did not appear inclined to accept.

And all along the Tories continued to flat-line, never nosing much above 30 per cent in the polls, with nothing they could do seeming to make any difference. Nor for that matter anything the government could do: it soon turned out that New Labour had nothing to learn from any other party about corruption. A series of sordid episodes, from Ecclestone to Mittal, showed that the government could be bought, and yet Blair always rebounded. In the autumn of 2000 the country was shaken by the petrol protests, when lorry drivers brought motorways to a standstill, angered by the duty on their fuel. Even then, Hague was in a quandary. Should he exploit an illegal protest of doubtful moral validity for temporary advantage? And would it make any difference in any case? The following spring a foot and mouth epidemic devastated large parts of rural England. It was handled with the greatest possible incompetence by the government, and the election had to be slightly postponed, but even then the result was in no way affected. There was no recourse for the Tories, and no escape from further electoral disaster.

Nor could they exorcize the ghosts of the past, which to the contrary kept popping up to haunt them as in a funfair ride of horrors. Alan Clark had returned to the Commons after various antics, as politically and personally exotic as ever. While much of the world was convulsed by the Balkans, and Blair sent British aircraft to bomb Belgrade, Clark was 'hugely depressed about Kosovo. Those loathsome, verminous gypsies; and the poor brave Serbs.' Less controversially, he recorded a little less than three years after Blair's first election victory: 'Party absolutely no idea what it's doing or where it is going.' That verdict remained true up to Clark's death from cancer in September 1999.

A matter of months before he died, another Tory learned where *he* was going. Jonathan Aitken's hubristic challenge was followed by the harshest nemesis. The sword of truth was turned back on him when it was revealed in the course of his libel actions that he had perjured himself, and had induced his wife and daughter to do so as well. When his case collapsed, he was prosecuted for perjury, convicted and imprisoned. At this point, another election was less than a year away. All the Tories now needed was another performance from Jeffrey Archer, and that was just what they were about to get. Like Aitken, he too had brought a libel action on perjured evidence. Another prosecution was brought for perjury and was shortly to be tried when Blair called another election. The past was about to catch up with Archer, and with the Tories.

EPILOGUE

Full Circle

Just forty years after the magic circle of Iain Macleod's deadly phrase had intrigued to replace Macmillan with Home, and after the successive elections in which the party had chosen Heath, Thatcher, Major, Hague and Duncan Smith, the Tories reverted to type. In the autumn of 2003, another magic circle intrigued to oust the last of those and replace him with a successor as surprising to much of the nation as Home had been. But first the fortunes of the party had sunk very low. Not long before his death, Alan Clark had despairingly said that 'Little Hague continues to make a complete hash of things,' and he went on making a hash until the early summer of 2001.

To be fair to Hague (not that many were), no combination of Disraeli, Salisbury and Baldwin could have won that election, which approached with a dull inevitability. The four years of the first Blair government had been largely uneventful in domestic politics and barren of original achievement, as Blair himself later ruefully admitted. He held fast to his determination never to increase direct taxation, and paid the Tories the highest form of flattery by imitating many of their policies, throwing in a few reforms at the margins. Brown took the crucial but inherently passive decision to relinquish control of interest rates to an independent Bank of England, as essential a monetarist step as ending exchange controls had been, and otherwise built on Kenneth Clarke's achievement.

Inflation, unemployment and interest rates held steady or fell. Growth was vigorous, and prosperity increased, though not evenly: the mass of the people became steadily better off, the poor became poorer, relatively and in some cases absolutely, the rich became much richer. All in all, New Labour in office looked more and more like a moderately competent party of government untainted by radicalism, and for all the verbal violence between Blair and Hague, their parties often seemed like the Tories and Whigs of the 1820s in Hazlitt's words, splashing each other with mud but heading on the same road to the same destination.

For the Tories this was the ultimate 'problem of success'. They writhed in impotent vexation, unable to land any blows on the government even when a succession of scandals might have taken the shine off Blair's lustre, enraged at the way they had been outplayed and their inheritance stolen. It was Disraeli in 1845 who gave politics one of its most familiar images when he said that Peel had 'caught the Whigs bathing, and walked away with their clothes', but never had a whole wardrobe been purloined in this manner. By the turn of the century it might have seemed that the Tory party was Margaret Thatcher's greatest failure, and New Labour her greatest success. At the time I was talking about the Tories' dire condition to someone close to Downing Street, who said with a pretence of sympathy and an almost straight face, 'Of course, you can see poor Hague's problem. There's only room for one conservative party in this country.' That was part of the answer, but only part.

Since Blair became leader, his party had been distinguished by a new ruthlessness and will to win, displayed for one good example in the way that Labour had for the first time completely outsmarted the Tories when they challenged the redrawing of parliamentary boundaries and altered the electoral map to their own advantage. Rarely had that ruthless cynicism been so vividly on display as when the election was called for June 2001. In an outrageous break with convention, the date of polling day was leaked to the *Sun* before the queen as head of state had been informed (there was scarcely any pretence that she had been 'asked for a dissolution'). Blair announced the election publicly at a gruesome gathering held for no obvious reason at a girls' school in south London, where he stood with a refulgent halo-glow from a window behind him and talked in his most parsonical way about 'foundations laid for a brighter future . . . real progress . . . beacons lit showing us a better way.'

As they faced the election, the Tories kept upper lips as stiff as they could manage, but they were a forlorn hope, and if there was any unity at all among them it was reminiscent of the masters at the prep school where Evelyn Waugh taught (and which he immortalized as Llanabba Castle), 'a rum lot united like defeated soldiers in the recognition of our common base fate'. Most Tories at least stayed at their posts to the bitter end, but some thought discretion the better part of valour.

A Bristol grammar-school boy who did well at Cambridge, Shaun Woodward had worked as a lobbyist, besides a spell as the Tories' grandiosely named Director of Communications, before he did even better by marrying a very rich woman, the daughter of Sir Timothy Sainsbury MP. Then on the old Hollywood principle 'The Son-in-Law Also Rises', Sainsbury left parliament in 1997 and Woodward entered it, still a Tory, but not for long: before the next election he had crossed the floor, deserting his comrades for the victorious forces opposite.

Some men are born to give the world a phrase, and on the election night of 7 June 2001 Woodward uttered the wondrous definition that New Labour was 'a party for everyone, not of any particular class or any particular view'. That took the idea of the Blairite 'big tent' to its logical conclusion. Blair himself had attacked 'the forces of conservatism' in his speech at the 1999 Labour conference, a phrase which thrilled some of his more credulous followers, although those forces turned out on examination to be anyone, from honourable Tories to principled socialists, who hesitated to enter the big tent. But anybody else could come on in: this was a party for people of all political beliefs or none. In that same conference speech, after all, Blair had said that New Labour was 'the political wing of the British people', in which case there was plainly no need of any other parties at all.

Although the result was a foregone conclusion, not even the smartest political punter could have guessed that the election would almost exactly replicate the result of four years earlier, Labour with 413 seats to the Tories' 166.[1] The whole election was almost a paranormal reprise of the last, except for one quite extraordinary difference; the same parliamentary outcome had resulted from a far smaller poll, after much the sharpest drop in turnout ever recorded. Most political

[1] Labour: 10.7 million votes, 42 per cent, 413 seats; Tories: 8.4 million, 32 per cent, 166 seats; Liberal Democrats: 4.8 million, 19 per cent, 52 seats; Others: 28 seats.

observers had foreseen that turnout would fall from 72 per cent to below 70 or even 65 per cent, but almost no one guessed that it would collapse to 59 per cent. And this happened in a country were voting had once been a passion. At the 1950 election, 84 per cent of British citizens went to the polls. That was the year of the famous Tory vintage, with the arrival in parliament of Heath, Macleod, Powell, and of Maudling, in whose Barnet constituency 87.4 per cent of electors voted that year, a figure as high as in almost any free country at any time.

One plausible explanation for high turnout at earlier elections was that they were real contests, with not only serious ideological differences between parties but a genuine uncertainty as to the result. But that does not explain a turnout of 76.7 per cent in 1955, when the Tories were certainly going to win, or 75.8 per cent in 1966, when Labour was. A more sombre explanation was that people were no longer voting because politics no longer meant anything to them. At any rate, the moral validity of Blair's second victory was very questionable, with a much smaller numerical Labour vote even than when the party had lost in 1970 or 1979.

In 1997 fewer people voted for Blair than had voted for Major in 1992; in 2001, fewer people voted for Blair than had voted for Kinnock in 1992. It was a fact that Blair had won two huge Commons majorities; it was also a fact that at his first victory less than a third of the electorate had voted for him and his party, and that at his second, less than a quarter had. For the first time in British history those voting for the largest party were now outnumbered by those who did not vote at all. This collapse in voting might even be seen as Blair's greatest achievement. He was both cause and effect of the steady depoliticization of society; had come to dominate the land by voiding politics of its content, or by taking the politics out of politics; the electorate were only following his lead when they did not vote at all.

Before the polls closed, one Tory party worker said to a senior frontbencher that whatever the result, 'Just tell William not to go to the cricket on Friday.' Hague did not follow Major's footsteps to the Oval, but he followed his unhappy example in resigning immediately, with the morose words, 'Despite that stronger base and the diminishing enthusiasm for New Labour, we have not been able to persuade a majority or anything approaching a majority, that we are yet the alternative government that they need.' A leadership contest was soon wearily under way, but with new rules.

A theme of this story has been the way that the Tories were never at ease when they came to elect leaders and never properly understood the voting systems they were using. A wise party would have turned to as simple a method as possible for choosing a leader, which is to say the good old Labour method of a plain exhaustive ballot among the parliamentary party, but the Tories were beyond wisdom now. So far from simplification, they had used their period of miserable opposition to concoct a still more exotic means of finding a leader. The MPs would vote among themselves to choose not one name but two, which would then go forward to the party membership in the country who would decide between them.

Once again the saying about failure being an orphan applied, and few now want to claim paternity for this half-baked idea. It had almost every conceivable drawback. There was nothing especially democratic about the party membership choosing a leader. The American system of primaries has the justification that anyone can register as a Democrat or Republican without even joining the party, and that these electorates are thus far larger and more representative. It might have been sensible to hand the Tory election to party members when there were more than two and a half million of them; it was fatuous to do so when numbers had shrunk to below 300,000, a membership much older and more right-wing than most people who voted Conservative, let alone than of the general population.

There is a very good case for saying that party leaders should be chosen by those who know them best, their fellow MPs. Under parliamentary government, the head of government at any moment is whoever can command a majority in the primary, which is the lower, house of the legislature, and it is entirely logical and equitable that this prime minister should be whoever initially commands a majority of his own MPs. Instead, thanks to the new system, it was now perfectly possible in theory for a Tory leader to begin his tenure in the public knowledge that he enjoyed the confidence of only a quite small minority of Tory MPs; and that was exactly what was about to happen in practice.

One of the indirect begetters of this scheme was no longer around. More than three years after he had harangued the MPs at the 1997 conference, Jeffrey Archer came to trial for perjury, defended to the last by senior Tories with the same lack of judgement they had earlier shown in bestowing favour on him. Apart from everything publicly known by now, Hague was given more detailed private warnings by Michael Crick, an Oxford friend of his who had written an entertaining and devastating biography of Archer, but with a kind of perverse obstinacy Hague persisted in praising Archer's 'probity and integrity' just as his total lack of those qualities was about to be demonstrated in the most conclusive way. In July, a matter of weeks after the election, Archer was convicted and sentenced to four years' imprisonment. The prime minister who had awarded Archer his peerage might also have found this a good opportunity for keeping quiet, but instead Major said mawkishly, 'I am deeply, deeply sorry at the outcome. I hope at this difficult time everyone will also remember the many kind and generous things Jeffrey has done,' which was not what most people were remembering at that moment.

When hats were thrown in the ring to succeed Hague, they did not include those of Michael Howard or Ann Widdecombe, his sometime colleague and then critic, although she threatened for a moment to stand. MPs began balloting in the second week of July, with five candidates taking the field, Michael Portillo, Iain Duncan Smith, Kenneth Clarke, David Davis and Michael Ancram. Portillo was able to stand because of the death of Alan Clark, whose seat he had won at the subsequent by-election. He had not only come back but come out, to the extent of admitting that he had once gone through a homosexual phase. The Tories had been making noises about modernization and a new mood of liberalism, but that had not reached Norman Tebbit, who bestowed his blessing on Duncan Smith by saying that he was a 'normal, family man with children', a gibe plainly aimed at Portillo, and a particularly cruel one since he and his wife were childless. Asked whether he thought that Portillo had got cold feet, Tebbit added that he didn't know: 'I've never been to bed with him.'

Despite that, Portillo went into the election with the support of a solid centre of MPs who thought him the one candidate who could unite the factions still warring over Europe. He was the natural choice according to the conventional wisdom, just like Maudling, Whitelaw, Hurd and Clarke before him. Once again conventional wisdom was confounded. A succession not so much of exhaustive as exhausting ballots followed, the first of which did not even eliminate any of the runners, all of whom forthwith stood again, with only slight changes in the outcome: Portillo won 49 votes then 50, Duncan Smith 39 then 42, Clarke 36 then 39, Davis 21 then 18, Ancram 21 then 17. The last two withdrew rather than prolong the agony, to allow a third ballot the following week, in which Clarke won 59 to Duncan Smith's 54 and Portillo's 53. A single vote having ended his political career, Portillo departed sorrowfully to devote himself to Wagner and other higher things. The remaining two names went forward to the party members, who were thus allowed a straight left–right, Europhile–Europhobe choice – or 'the physical incarnation of the split that has poisoned our party', in the grimly accurate words of Nicholas Soames, Christopher's son and Churchill's grandson, an MP who had supported Portillo.

Even those who liked Clarke's air of not giving a damn had been taken aback to learn that he had spent his years in opposition working for a tobacco company which sold cigarettes in the Far East, following the example, it should be said, of Lady Thatcher, who had become chairman of BAT. One of the best and brightest of younger Tory journalists, Boris Johnson had just entered parliament as the Member for Henley in succession to Heseltine. Johnson did not share Heseltine's 'federast' proclivities – a stint as a correspondent covering Brussels and the follies of its officialdom had increased his innate Euroscepticism – but he declared himself a Clarke supporter. Rather than directly defend his man for trying to control the Asian population explosion, Johnson breezily insisted that the cigarettes were neither here nor there: 'Ken Clarke can go and sell tobacco to the Vietnamese. Tobacco is legally sold in this country; it is legally sold in Vietnam.' It seemed a long time since the days when many people, even some Tories, recognized the difference between that which is actually illegal and that which is merely reprehensible.

During these turmoils, the Tory press tied itself in knots. Like Johnson, the *Daily Mail* swallowed its pride and backed Clarke. The paper did not like much of what he stood for on Europe but might have echoed what Macleod once said of Butler: Clarke had the priceless quality 'of attracting to himself wide understanding support from many people outside the Tory party'. The *Daily Telegraph* saw it differently, and surpassed itself. As soon as Hague resigned, Charles Moore had said that in his own view the best man to lead the Tories was David Trimble, the leader of the Ulster Unionists (which astonished no one more than Mrs Trimble: 'I was in the car listening to him on the radio, and I nearly drove off the road'), but in his absence the paper enthusiastically backed 'IDS' the former Guards officer: 'There is often a moment on the television news – in Kosovo, perhaps, or in the foot and mouth crisis – when the chattering politicians briefly give way, and the British soldier on the spot comes on. When he speaks, you believe him. Mr Duncan Smith, both in character and in experience of life, is the nearest a politician can get to that soldier.' That claim would soon be put to the test.

Even now a malign Providence was jinxing the party. In 1997, 'Diana week' made Hague look hapless, and left the Tories baffled. Four years later the party named Wednesday 12 September as the day on which the result of the ballot of national members would be announced. Osama bin Laden and his comrades were not thinking about the fate of the Conservative and Unionist Party of Great Britain when they made other plans for the previous day, but by the afternoon of 11 September no one in London or anywhere else cared less who became Tory leader.

An announcement of the result was postponed for a day out of respect for the dead of New York, but as a small repercussion among many greater ones of that dreadful day, the Tories' election looked quite insignificant. When the result was belatedly announced, Duncan Smith won easily, by 61 to 39 per cent, 155,933 votes to Clarke's 100,864, although the most ominous figure was the total, a paltry 256,797. Now Blair played the new Churchill, a national hero in America when he expressed solidarity and determination in more eloquent terms than Bush himself, while Duncan Smith could only trail in his wake, as he ineffectually did for months to come.

The country had changed, and the Tories had changed, but unfortunately they had not changed in the same direction. If the Tories had been making a statement, in the modish phase, it was a curious one.

Having gone down to another disastrous defeat under an old-fashioned, balding, right-wing leader, they had now chosen a man who was more old-fashioned, even balder, and still further to the right. Duncan Smith's background was not quite as obscure as Major's, but it was shadowy. Only during the leadership election did the interesting fact emerge that he had a Japanese great-grandmother. More to the point, his mother was Irish and he was the first Roman Catholic ever to lead the party.

He had been educated at a private naval academy which was some way above a reformatory but some way below Dartmouth. IDS was no Jeffrey Archer in terms of a 'gift for inaccurate précis', but his potted biography had an element of suggestio falsi: 'University of Perugia' meant that he had spent a brief spell there as a foreign-language student, before Sandhurst and the Scots Guards. He had entered the Commons in 1992, just in time to join the Maastricht rebellion.

'From Iain to Iain' makes a poignant tale. Duncan Smith's views on almost every subject would have dismayed Macleod. 'The Tory party for the first time since Bonar Law is now being led from right of centre,' he had written after Home's succession; it was now being led from further to the right than ever. Oddly enough, IDS was out of step even when it came to nomenclature and tradition: Macleod always preferred the romantic label 'Tory' to the dull 'Conservative', but Duncan Smith disliked to be called a Tory (and some in the party even talked despairingly of discarding both names, perhaps for 'Democrats'). More than that, IDS seemed a throwback culturally. Blair could be tiresome when he twanged a guitar and talked about rock music, but Duncan Smith gave the impression that he had never worn a pair of jeans in his life. Not that this bothered some admirers. When a *Telegraph* writer said that he seemed all right, 'but isn't he a bit 1950s?' the editor replied, 'What's wrong with the 1950s?'

Whatever hopes some Tories had were soon dashed. As party leader, Duncan Smith was inept and petulant, not quite the officer-like qualities which the *Telegraph* thought it had discerned. He suspected the absolute loyalty of David Davis as party chairman, maybe not without reason, but he sacked him in a way that looked vindictive. With Ancram dutifully sticking at his post, but with Clarke and Portillo both gone in pursuit of fame and fortune, or at least fortune, that meant tellingly that only two of the five candidates for the leadership in July 2001 were left on the front bench.

Throughout 2001–2003 the country moved steadily towards war with Iraq, although this was not as clear at the time as it might have been, since Blair was very far from candid about his motives and what commitments he had made to President George Bush the Younger. A year after the 11 September attacks, he overawed parliament and made the nation's flesh creep with his wilfully exaggerated claims about alleged weapons of mass destruction which Saddam Hussein could deploy in forty-five minutes, and with what, in an infamous phrase, he called the 'serious and current' threat Iraq represented to British interests.

These claims would come to be seen as false by most British people, but the greater falsity of Blair's position was grasped by few at the time or even later, least of all by the Tories. Although some people wondered that autumn whether Saddam really possessed 'WMD', to ask that would allow the prime minister even afterwards, when no evidence of biological or atomic weapons came to light, to enter a plea of error in good faith. The question should have been not, 'What weaponry does Saddam possess?' but, 'Is Saddam's weaponry, whatever it might be, the real reason for the war on which this country is plainly about to embark, or is it a pretext after Blair has already committed the country to war?' And the most crucial question of all was thus when the decision for war was taken by Blair.

He had certainly done so no later than his visit to see Bush in Texas in April, months before he made his case in parliament. Americans would come fretfully to wonder whether Iraq was Vietnam revisited, which it was clearly not. To English eyes there is a much better parallel. Iraq was not another Vietnam, it was another Suez: a war fought to destroy an Arab dictator by western governments which could not, however, avow their motives and actions and had to resort to conspiracy and deceit. But whereas Labour MPs and liberal newspapers had once clamorously denounced Eden's conspiracy, there was now nobody in the Tory press, or on the opposition front bench, to echo David Astor's *Observer* in 1956: 'We had not realized that our government was capable of such folly and crookedness.'

It was often said at this time that the Tories in parliament were inert and that the press, from the *Daily Mail* to the *Guardian*, provided the only effective opposition to Blair. But on the question of the war, no one was more zealous in support of Blair than the Tory party's own newspaper. Before the prime minister went to Texas, the editor of the *Daily Telegraph* had just preceded him across the Atlantic. In Washington that March, Charles Moore fell into the kind of raptures once heard from doting fellow-travellers in Moscow.

At the Pentagon he found himself in the presence of greatness. Donald Rumsfeld 'looks like a fit, recently retired professor of science from an Ivy League university,' Moore wrote. 'He talks with a don's intellectual interest, but an executive's concern for clarity and action. He answers a question precisely, e.g. "How confident are you that bin Laden will eventually be caught?" "I don't know that it matters how confident I am. He either will be or he won't. He'll either live or he'll die."' Rumsfeld was 'a phenomenon for which the American system makes better provision than our own – a public servant who is also a political leader.'

And Moore added that 'Rumsfeld is better at soundbites than any Clintonian.' That was certainly true. 'He'll either live or he'll die' was only one example of the Defense Secretary's epigrammatic gift. He later repeated that insight, saying of bin Laden that 'We do know of certain knowledge that he is either in Afghanistan, or in some other country, or dead,' and he would be remembered besides for other professorial apothegms: 'As we know, there are known knowns; there are things we know we know. We also know there are known unknowns; that is to say we know there are some things we do not know.' 'Death has a tendency to encourage a depressing view of war.' 'Stuff happens.'

Stuff was happening during Duncan Smith's brief reign as Tory leader. War drums rolled, diplomatic manoeuvres continued at the United Nations, and Blair claimed still more absurdly that he was doing everything he could to work for peace, when it was perfectly clear that he was doing everything he could to work for war, acting as what an Arab newspaper sharply but not unreasonably called 'Washington's international gofer'. But for all Blair's eloquence, and sinuous misrepresentation, his party was split; in the crucial division on the war in March 2003, 139 Labour MPs voted against the government, much the largest such rebellion since the Liberal scission over Home Rule in 1886. If a majority of his own MPs had voted against him, Blair could scarcely have survived, although even then he would have won the vote itself since the official opposition tamely accepted the prime minister's arguments, with Duncan Smith even keener to demonstrate uncritical loyalty to Washington.

And yet the Tories also were divided, moreover in a most fascinating way: not right or left, wet or dry, One Nation or monetarist, but as much as anything a clash of generations. It was most noticeable that many of the veterans of the last Tory administrations (leaving aside Lady Thatcher herself, who had at last withdrawn from the public fray) were sceptical about the war, or openly opposed to it. Since so few of the old guard remained in the shadow cabinet, these dissenting voices were heard from the backbenches, like Clarke, or from the Lords, like Hurd, or from outside parliament, like Sir Malcolm Rifkind who had quixotically stuck with his old Edinburgh constituency after losing it in 1997 and condemned himself to further exile from the Commons after the next election.

A lucid analysis by Clarke of the unwisdom of the war, and of its unhappy likely consequences, was seconded by Douglas Hogg. Son of Hailsham, and inheriting something of his father's pomposity as well as his intellect, an Oxford contemporary of Chris Patten, William Waldegrave and Michael Ancram, he had spent years in parliament and junior office, entering the Cabinet as agriculture minister towards the end of Major's government. But his finest hour was his critique of the Iraq adventure. 'The British people instinctively know that adding another war to the Middle East – where there are already quite enough wars – does not seem a sensible idea,' Hogg said. 'I do not think the threat that we face is either sufficiently grave or imminent as to provide the moral basis for war.'

His words were unheeded, and the Tories were impaled on the war when it began. This was their come-uppance after years of bitterness over Europe, of the transatlantic rift which had been highlighted by the Westland episode, of the disloyalty of the Maastricht rebels, notably the man who was now leading the party. There was more to it than a generation gap, more even than the Continental divide. The

Europhobes in the party had won, at least for the time being. It was now Tory policy to rule out membership of the single European currency for the life of the next parliament, although given Blair's own serpentine feints and reversals on this question (betraying many who had devotedly followed him), and given the vigour of the British economy compared with its neighbours in Europe, this looked like a question which had answered itself anyway, and one over which the Tories need never have torn themselves apart.

But there was a weird paradox when Tory anti-Europeans spoke in Enoch Powell's language of sovereignty, without following the logic of his position where the United States was concerned. In every other European country there is a rightist or conservative party whose fundamental principle is patriotism and the national interest, of that country. Only England now had a Conservative party whose leaders, and whose cheerleaders in the press, thought their first duty was to support the national interest – of another country. Men obsessed by any loss of sovereignty to a handful of irritating bureaucrats in Brussels were quite happy for England to become a client state of Washington, and for the British army to serve as the American Foreign Legion.

What made this all the stranger was that so few ordinary British Conservatives shared such an enthusiasm for automatically supporting every American action. Opinion polls regularly confirmed what everyday observation already suggested, that the Iraq war was markedly more unpopular among Tory than among Labour voters. When Bush was invited to London on a state visit in the autumn of 2003 (in decidedly premature celebration of a peaceful outcome in Iraq), polls demonstrated his unpopularity with Tories. Another poll in June 2004 found that 52 per cent of Tories thought the Iraq war unjustified, compared to 39 per cent of Labour supporters; in one more poll at the time of the subsequent presidential election, only 19 per cent of Conservative voters said they would vote for George Bush, and Senator John Kerry was more liked by Tories than by Labour supporters. Johnson has admitted that, in his Henley constituency, more than half of his party committee had opposed the war; another MP with what is for nowadays still a large Conservative constituency membership says privately that his members had been two to one against.

This instinctive Tory dislike of the war, and even suspicion of America, has been little remarked but is not so surprising. Why would ordinary patriotic Englishmen relish becoming an American dependency? But then how had the party leadership grown so out of touch with their voters, and even so devoid of an elemental sense of nationhood?

Adulation of America was not confined to the pages of the *Daily Telegraph*. In *The Times*, Michael Gove not only confessed 'I can't fight my feelings any more: I love Tony . . . as a right-wing polemicist, all I can say looking at Mr Blair now is, what's not to like?' but he also passionately believed that 'America is there to be supported', regardless of the merits of the case, and that Bush was a leader of the same stature as Churchill: 'It's one word. Will.' Gove also said that one 'hero to conservatives like me' was Rudolph Giuliani – the former mayor of New York who had praised the IRA as brave freedom fighters. At that point 'support for America' had become positively masochistic. Still, at least some Tories appeared to agree, since Gove became a Tory MP in 2005.

But the *Daily Telegraph* had a special relationship with the Conservatives, and a special responsibility. Before the Tories acquired a new leader, the paper acquired a new editor. In early October 2003, Conrad Black took Martin Newland to Downing Street to meet the prime minister (such being the custom of the country), and introduced him to Blair with the words: 'He is taking over from Charles Moore, who is leaving for reasons nothing to do with his performance as editor. Or that is what I have been told to say.' Moore himself said that he was sad to leave, although it meant that he could begin full-time work as Lady Thatcher's official biographer. He added forlornly that the Tories had 'been up the creek, the whole time I've been editor'; it did not occur to him that there was any connection.

That visit was one of Black's last appearances as proprietor of the *Telegraph*. Even then, the ground was crumbling under his feet and he was about to be engulfed by melodramatic financial disaster. In many ways Black had not been a bad proprietor. He had saved the *Telegraph* group at a woeful time, albeit to his own profit, and he had never tried to censor individual writers, preferring to answer back in his own baroque prose. But he had also tried to import a North

American strain of right-wing politics to England, where it did not belong.

If English Conservatism has nothing in common with any of the categories of Continental politics, as Oakeshott said, then it had even less in common with American neo-conservatism; if Toryism is 'not a doctrine but a disposition', neo-conservatism is a doctrine and a half. Toryism is stupid but sensible, stolid, pragmatic, sceptical; the neo-cons are clever but silly. Many of the founders of that movement had begun their political lives on the far left, and as they moved right they retained the very worst old left-wing characteristics, the ideological zealotry, the lack of common sense, the complete detachment from reality.

More neo than con, it might be said, these men exactly illustrate Burke's description.[2] They believe that retrospect is not wise, they do not like to inquire how we got into this difficulty, they consult their invention and reject their experience. And yet even when this met its nemesis in the valleys of Mesopotamia the enthusiasts seemed disinclined 'to take a strict review of those measures, in order to correct our errors if they should be corrigible; or at least to avoid a dull uniformity in mischief, and the unpitied calamity of being repeatedly caught in the same snare'.

As the next two years went by many Tories had an increasing sense of having been taken for a ride over Iraq and having made a mistake; and more and more of them felt that the party had made an even worse mistake when it chose Duncan Smith. No precise moment can be given when his days were numbered, but, so far from being precipitately ejected, he was lucky to last as long as he did. It was not even as though the majority of MPs needed to be disillusioned: two-thirds of them had never been illusioned enough to support him in the first place.

But he cut a poor figure at the despatch box and in meetings of the 1922 Committee, getting worse if anything, before he gave a painful demonstration of his incapacity by picking a quite unnecessary fight with his own party over the question of adoption and homosexuality (both topics which led otherwise sane people to lose balance). The

[2] See p. 27.

Tories might have learned by this time that questions of sexual morality were always best left to individual MPs and a free vote, and that
it was fatal to try to impose a party line. Duncan Smith did just that,
found that numerous MPs, and eminent ones at that, were completely
ignoring him, and then made things worse still by spluttering that 'A
small group of my parliamentary colleagues have decided consciously
to undermine my leadership,' and demanding angrily that the party
should stand by him. As if that were not bad enough, at the party
conference in October he played to his weaknesses, intoning robot-
ically, 'Do not underestimate the determination of a quiet man.'

Appeals for personal loyalty are usually a sign of a weak leader –
see Chamberlain in his sad last moments as prime minister in 1940 –
but in Duncan Smith's case the appeal was ludicrous or even offensive,
as his colleagues had to admit. He had been one of the ringleaders of
the Maastricht rebellion, voting against the Major government more
than forty times in the course of the most prolonged and damaging
defiance of any Tory government by its own MPs since the war. How
could he of all people now in honour demand that the party must
'unite or die'?

Rumblings of discontent were muffled at first, but by November
none other than the author of the 1983 Conservative manifesto
exploded with the rage many MPs were bottling up. 'Iain Duncan
Smith is on the skids or he ought to be by Christmas, if the Conservative party retains a smidgeon of its old instinct for self-preservation,'
Ferdinand Mount wrote. In his fourteen months as leader of the
opposition, he had 'shown as much oratorical oomph as a tran-
quillized vole and as much discretion as the average member of staff
of Diana, Princess of Wales'. He had seemed the wrong choice at the
time, 'but he has failed to live up even to my low expectations'.
Duncan Smith survived this polemic into 2003, but it had made a
mark.

In public at least, MPs bit their tongues until May, when Crispin
Blunt resigned from the opposition team immediately before the local
elections, and said that Duncan Smith should go. Blunt was not by
any means the best known or most popular man on the Tory benches,
and much derision was heaped on him by loyalists in the press, who
mirthfully scanned their rhyming dictionaries to see what they could

make of his surname. But he had at least stabbed Duncan Smith in the front, and this former captain in the 13th/18th Royal Hussars if anything justified what the *Telegraph* said about the simple British soldier: 'when he speaks, you believe him'. Blunt was saying what in their hearts all too many MPs now believed.

Between 1963 and 2003, between the replacement of Macmillan by Home and the replacement of Duncan Smith by Howard, there are indeed many ironical parallels and comical echoes, not least from the sarcastic opening words of Macleod's philippic: there had been within the party 'an unspoken agreement that the less said about the struggle for the Tory leadership the better'. Likewise, the Tories collectively clammed up afterwards about the events of forty years later, but a sequence can be pieced together.

As Duncan Smith's inadequacies became ever clearer, the real question is what held MPs back. There was the difficulty that, as a former minister points out, 'the party members are much more loyal to the existing leader' (adding sardonically that 'if they'd had their way, Ted Heath would still be leader after losing six more elections'). And those party members were likely to feel the more aggrieved if they were deprived of him who was their very own first anointed. Beyond that, MPs felt an acute distaste for the prospect of any further leadership contest, with all its capacity for dissension and recrimination. And there was the sheer difficulty of finding a successor. Of the candidates at the previous two contests in 1997 and 2001, Hague had departed to write what proved a rather good biography of Pitt the Younger, and Portillo to make television programmes. Lilley and Redwood recognized with varying degrees of reluctance that they were out of the game, while the more affable Ancram knew that he could never win except perhaps as a compromise candidate, which left Clarke and Howard.

In the previous two years, Clarke's stock had fallen and Howard's had risen; within the parliamentary party, that is. Clarke was still very much the pet of the liberal chattering classes, Howard still very much not. If the leadership had been decided by *Guardian* columnists Clarke would have won in a canter, but that was of less than no practical use to him. He had provoked some colleagues by his take-it-or-leave-it attitude, and others by his opposition to the Iraq adventure.

There was also Davis, who seemed to colleagues the itchiest: 'David was already quietly mobilizing in the summer' of 2003. It was a delicate game of bluff. No one was in Heseltine's position of acknowledged opposition to the sitting tenant, and anyone who had made a public challenge would have been damned for disloyalty. And yet Duncan Smith's real problem was that he had lost the support (to the extent that he had ever enjoyed it) of his senior colleagues. In particular there was David Maclean, the opposition chief whip. Just as his predecessor Redmayne had decided in 1963 that Macmillan should go, and Renton in 1990 that Thatcher should, now Maclean understood the force of what Macleod had written: a chief whip who is convinced that his leader 'is a major liability to the party would be failing in his duty not to consider alternatives and, if need be, to press for change'. And a major liability was what IDS now seemed to Maclean.

Soon after Blunt's first blast of the trumpet, there was talk of a challenge from Tim Yeo, a genial soul on the left of the party who had resigned in 1994 after amorous complications but who had since worked his way back into favour, while Davis's name was regularly mentioned. And Michael Howard maintained a front of complete loyalty to his leader, while laying into the government in the Commons with a fresh zest which was by way of being a job application. 'We managed to forget how unpopular he'd been as Home Secretary,' one MP recalls, not to say how unpopular he had been with the party in the 1997 leadership election.

Any direct challenge apart, the arcane procedures of the party now allowed for a vote of confidence in the leader to be called if Michael Spicer, the chairman of the 1922 Committee, received confidential letters, requiring one from twenty-five MPs, and the fatal missives began to arrive. If there had been any further question of Duncan Smith's survival by the autumn, it was answered by two speeches. His speech at the conference was a dud, with its bathetically self-conscious words, 'I say this: The quiet man is here to stay and he's turning up the volume.' He was cheered to the echo by the party faithful in a series of Stalinist standing ovations which only made MPs' hearts sink still further. With nothing to lose, Portillo was speaking for most of them when he said briskly that the conference had been 'the worst in living memory'. Duncan Smith raged that his enemies should 'put up or shut up', but his authority was crumbling palpably day by day.

By now Spicer had received his twenty-five letters, and the 1922 was summoned to meet on Tuesday 28 October, forty years and eleven days after that other October day Macleod had described unforgettably. One former minister braced himself to go and see Duncan Smith shortly before the critical meeting to say that he could not support him, and was dismayed to find that the leader was not even writing his speech to address the MPs: 'You can't deliver something as important as that without preparing it.' Predictably, the speech was another embarrassing flop, and the deed was soon done, Duncan Smith losing by 90 votes to 75.

Once he had involuntarily departed, the new magic circle cast its spell. Innumerable private discussions had concluded that most Tory MPs did not want another election, and they did not want Davis, which may have come to the same thing, since it was apprehended that, if a decision went to the perplexed and resentful national party, Davis might win. Clarke now recognized that he could not be the hero of the hour; and that left one man standing. After the customary processes of consultation, as Macmillan might have said, Howard was chosen by the parliamentary party nem. con., and was presented to the national party as the most *accompli* of *faits*. It was the political equivalent of Henry Ford's Model T: the party members could have any candidate they liked so long as it was Howard. As in Biffen's phrase of 1990, a button had been pressed and all the lights lit up, with astonishing effect.

While Howard was not a fantastic choice, he had plainly become leader for negative reasons. When Disraeli reached the top of his greasy pole in 1868, John Bright said that his accession to the Tory leadership was 'a triumph of intellect and courage and patience and unscrupulousness in the service of a party full of prejudices and selfishness and wanting in brains', a remarkably apt description 145 years later. Howard was not an 'old Estonian' in Macmillan's sneer but the son of Jewish immigrants from Romania who had settled in west Wales, and there were many other heavy-handed and scarcely permissible jokes about his Transylvanian heritage and his taste for blood.

He had gone from Llanelli Grammar School to Peterhouse, the epicentre of the Cambridge right, and had prospered at the Bar, but before he won Folkestone in 1983 it had taken him a long time to find a constituency, just possibly because the prejudice Bright spoke of still lingered on. As with Disraeli, the party overcame its prejudice when it found in him a formidable parliamentary hit-man: from the beginning, Howard used his barrister's skills to defend the government, or even sometimes to defend the indefensible.

Ascending through the ministerial ranks, he entered the Cabinet when Major became prime minister, and served as Home Secretary from 1993 to 1997. In that office he had become the darling of the *Daily Mail* (where his 'initiatives' always uncannily appeared the day before parliament heard anything of them) and an ogre to liberals, whom he went out of his way to offend by word as much as deed: 'I know what works. Prison works.' He had been famously evasive when interrogated on television about the departure of his prison chief, declining to answer the same question fourteen times, although on that same matter he had routed Jack Straw, his Labour shadow, in a Commons debate.

And he fell out with the formidable Miss Widdecombe, his junior minister. At the time of the 1997 leadership election, she took her revenge by saying that there was 'something of the night' about Howard. Whether or not because of her phrase, Howard had come fifth of five candidates on that occasion with all three groups, MPs, peers and party chairmen, a fact of which Blair was happy frequently to remind him.

In truth he had not always been a nocturnal reactionary. As a young man, long before he entered parliament, Howard had been chairman of the liberal Bow Group. And after I had published an article once, he sent me a fan letter which is of some little relevance. I had suggested that the best model of how society should operate was the Royal National Lifeboat Institution. It is an autonomous body which performs a literally vital service with no support from the state and no coercion whatever: its brave crews are unpaid volunteers, its income is raised entirely by voluntary donation. This was as much an anarcho-syndicalist as a Tory argument, invoking the principles of mutual aid and co-operation, but Howard said that it was an example he himself liked to use. Alas, he seemed later too often to have forgotten that libertarian impulse.

Another reflection of the way the Tories were now choosing their leaders *faute de mieux* is Howard's age. He belongs to a notable Tory generation who were at Cambridge in the late 1950s and early 1960s, with Parkinson and Clarke, among others. But he was aged sixty-two when he became leader, older than Duncan Smith, who is older than Hague; at this rate the party would soon be choosing an octogenarian. Sometimes his age showed.

At his best Howard is a very good Commons performer, with a nice line in barbs. In an unhappy and quite recent tradition, government 'loyalists' (there are harsher words) are primed by the whips to ask planted questions, to make helpful interventions, or just to remind the prime minister of his immortal greatness. One such trusty is Chris Bryant, the unlikely Labour MP for the famous Welsh mining seat of Rhondda, a former clergyman, and an 'out gay' whose near-naked photograph of himself posted on an exotic dating website caused much merriment among his parliamentary colleagues. After the leader of the opposition had given way for one such grossly sycophantic intervention from Bryant, Howard resumed with the words, 'It's always "Help me, Rhondda, help, help me Rhondda".' This was an excellently amusing put-down, until some of us listening realized with horror that, to get the joke at all, you had to remember the Beach Boys in their heyday – which meant you had, like Howard himself, to be approaching 'bus-pass' age.

One other fascinating development was that the Tories were now a Jewish party. Howard is the son of immigrants from eastern Europe, he chose as his shadow Chancellor Letwin, whose roots are likewise in *der heim*, albeit by way of Chicago and Eton, and if Rifkind, a sometime elder of his Edinburgh synagogue, were in parliament he would be on the front bench also. Howard appointed as a party co-chairman the advertising magus Maurice Saatchi, who was born into the once-famous Jewish community of Baghdad shortly before it vanished for ever. This was all very creditable, to the Tories and to England. Disraeli had suffered from much more bigotry than his earlier biographers acknowledged, but he had percipiently said that the Jews would be a natural conservative element once persecution ceased. This did not stop Howard from launching what seemed a demagogic and nativist campaign against immigration in 2005, and in any case the infusion of talent was still not enough to rescue the party.

After a period of elation following the disposal of Duncan Smith, the Tories had a year of growing despondency as they realized that it had made no difference, at least in terms of polls and the election approaching in 2005. Howard was much better at the despatch box than his predecessor, and the government gave him plenty of opportunities, but that made the failure to dent Blair's lead all the more galling. Although courteous and charming in private, Howard also displayed maybe not unscrupulousness but an incurable appetite for the main chance. If Yasser Arafat, in Abaa Ebau's phrase, never missed an opportunity to miss an opportunity, Michael Howard finds it hard to avoid any occasion for opportunism.

Early in 2004 he opposed the government on its proposed increase of university fees. This looked like a way of embarrassing Blair when large numbers of Labour rebels were also voting against, and it might have appealed to middle-class voters, but anyone with any serious interest in saving British universities from terminal decline knew that the increased fees were essential. Then Howard began to dissociate himself from the Iraq war, saying that he still supported it in some manner but that he had foolishly accepted the prime minister's claims about weaponry, which was almost the worst of both worlds.

Another Tory said that the party's position should be 'Right to fight, wrong to lie', but that was an empty distinction, since the war was not only fought on false pretences but had to be. In Howard's case, the shift looked not only intellectually unconvincing but slippery, with a touch of Macmillan's 'first in, first out' over Suez. Blair did not repeat that phrase, but he silenced Howard in the Commons by saying that the British people would respect those who had honestly supported the war and would respect those who had honestly opposed the war, but would not respect those who had supported and opposed the war in the course of the same newspaper article. The Tory benches winced at this (although another riposte in turn would have been that 'those who had honestly supported the war' did not describe most Labour MPs, or even most members of the Cabinet). Nor did this attempted change of course do the Tories much good: local and European elections suggested ominously that their vote was being squeezed between the Lib Dems on one side and the United Kingdom Independence Party on the other, with whom at least some Tories tried to engage in a fatal competition of Europhobic rhetoric.

As the year wore on, even Howard's strongest supporters lost heart: the number of Tory voters who thought their party might win the next election dwindled and shrank to a small minority as the new year opened. The Italian Marxist Antonio Gramsci advocated 'pessimism of the intellect, optimism of the will'; by 2005 most Tories high and low found within themselves much more of the former than the later.

Behind all these transient Westminster intrigues and caprices lies the far larger question: just why had the Tories declined and fallen? The most absurd explanation of all would be to say that this had been a defeat for 'the right'. To the contrary, the great historical theme of the late twentieth century was quite obviously the universal defeat of the left, throughout the world and as much in England as anywhere. A chronicler of the Conservative party may not be the most detached person to give such a verdict; let him cite two astute witnesses from different sectors of the intelligent left, Martin Jacques and Perry Anderson, the one a former editor of *Marxism Today*, the other of the *New Left Review*.

A year after Howard had become Tory leader, and was making little headway, Jacques wrote that 'the left – in the broadest sense (most certainly including the likes of Roy Hattersley and Denis Healey) – has disintegrated'; the British labour movement 'has effectively disappeared'. Before that, in 2000, while Hague was floundering, the *New Left Review* marked its own fortieth anniversary with a sparkling display of pessimism of the intellect by Anderson. Looking back from the turn of the century, he said

that the only starting-point for a realistic left today is a lucid registration of defeat. Capital has beaten back all threats to its rule, the bases of whose power – above all, the pressures of competition – were persistently underestimated by the socialist movement. The doctrines of the right that have theorized capitalism as a systemic order retain their tough-minded strength; current attempts by a self-styled radical centre to dress up its realities are by comparison little more than weak public relations.

And he added a well-nigh graceful tribute, as well as a swipe at New Labour:

Those who always believed in the overriding value of free markets and private ownership of the means of production include many figures of intellectual substance. The recent crop of bowdlerisers and beauticians, who only yesterday deplored the ugliness of the system they primp, do not.

In British politics the rout of the left is personified by Tony Blair and embodied in New Labour. By any objective historic standards, this party is to the right of centre, having abandoned the minimal definitions of an even mildly progressive left politics for the previous century, the belief in a centrally planned economy and in large redistributive taxation. And it is hard to argue with Jacques that Blair personally stands to the right of every postwar prime minister with the exception of his heroine, Lady Thatcher.

Another observer, closer to Blair than most, is Robert Harris, himself a man of the moderate liberal left who had seen in Blair before almost anyone else a man who could rescue the Labour party and make it electable once more, although like others Harris may not quite have bargained for what he was going to get. On the tenth anniversary of Blair's assumption of the Labour leadership, he paid a memorable tribute of sorts to the man he had once picked out and befriended.

If Blair did have a faction, it would probably not be on the left at all, but located somewhere deep within the Conservative party. Right-wing in his instincts even before he became party leader, Blair has clearly moved further to the right since entering Downing Street. Of all his predecessors, the one with whom he evidently has the closest rapport is Margaret Thatcher. [He had led the Labour party into] an unpopular and possibly illegal war. His prime justification for that war has collapsed in a way that casts doubt on both his judgement and his honesty. He has allied the party of Nye Bevan, Michael Foot and Neil Kinnock with the most reactionary American administration in living memory. He has alienated Labour's natural allies in Europe . . .

On crime, education and health, he has shamelessly filched the rhetoric – and in some cases even the policies – of his Tory opponents.

All of which is true, and truly remarkable. And yet, as David Willetts, one of the cleverer survivors on the Tory benches, has said, there must be a limit to how long any party can go on complaining that its clothes have been stolen by their opponents. That applies in a different form to the historian of the Tories. So what is Blair, apart from merely right-wing?

When James Callaghan met his eventual successor as party leader, he said, 'I don't know what that young man is, but he's not Labour,' which is plainly so. But if Blair is not Labour, he is not Tory either. And that lucid registration of defeat by the left needs to be qualified. Both in academic discourse and in practical politics, class conflict has been superseded by 'culture wars'; and the other great truth of the age is that the right has won politically while the left has won culturally. Blair personifies that also, and thereby comes closer still to explaining the death of Tory England.

Another friend of his has said that 'to understand Tony you must realize that he's really an Aussie'. Indeed, and so is Rupert Murdoch. The intimacy between the two is not merely an alliance of calculation and convenience but a true elective affinity. Murdoch shows that it is possible to combine an intense love of the capitalist system with antipodean contempt for custom, both of which Blair shares: he is a true spiritual Australian. In Ensor's phrase, Blair is ignorant of history and indifferent to English political tradition, and his right-wing political instincts are matched by a fatuous cultural modernity ('I've always been a great Led Zeppelin fan').

One bitter controversy perfectly explains the distinction of political and cultural. Matthew Parris is a sometime Tory MP who worked in the Conservative Research Department before 1979, when Mrs Thatcher became prime minister and he became an MP for eight years, leaving parliament for television and then newspaper journalism. From his different perspective, he saw that great defeat of the left of which Anderson and Jacques wrote, and in November 2004 he asked why the right had 'become associated with gloom and anger about the world'.

The last three decades have seen the collapse of the ideologies of the left across the world. We have won the argument. Britain is an incomparably more right-wing country now than when I was at university in the early 1970s . . . The right should sound like a winner.

This appeared on the very day that parliament passed a law criminalizing fox-hunting; Parris's question could not have been more succinctly or eloquently answered. Hunting had nothing to do with politics, not in the sense of left and right (unless one were to suppose that such a fanatic for the hunting ban as the 'Blairite loyalist' Sir Gerald Kaufman is further to the left of that great fox-hunting man Friedrich Engels, which doesn't seem very likely). It is a cultural question, and one where the Tories are unmistakably and sadly on the losing side.

For all Hailsham's saying about the wiser Tories devoting themselves to religion and the simpler to fox-hunting, not every Tory had always hunted and not every Tory had always been a loyal supporter of the Church of England, any more than every Tory had served in the army, but these were, as Orwell might have said, characteristic aspects of Toryism. And they were all discredited or in decline, along with the values and mores of Macmillan's 'old governing class', the values of fewer and fewer people: only a quarter of a million people hunted; by the new century, the Crown had fewer men under arms than it had had in the 1780s; while services of the national established Church of England are now attended by less than 2 per cent of the population. For a very long time those values of Tory England may have been those of a minority but had a hegemonic force, and were at least formally respected. Now they were openly scorned and despised.

Two great demonstrations were held in London to protest against the hunting Bill, in March 2000 and September 2002, far more people than had ever ridden to hounds marching in the largest such rallies the capital had ever seen, apart from the equally unsuccessful demonstration against the Iraq war. And yet it was audibly a last hurrah. To watch that parade of the rural classes and what was left of the landed gentry was like peering at something from a nature reserve. As Ian Kilbannock might have said, 'Delightful fellows, but the Wrong Period. Hopelessly upper class. "The Fine Flower of the Nation". And it *won't do*.'

Years before, this had been perceived and elegiacally expressed from another angle by a quite different writer from Waugh, the poet

Keith Douglas, who was killed fighting in Normandy. In North Africa a year earlier, he had written a poem called 'Aristocrats', inspired by the death in action of Lieutenant-Colonel J. D. Player, who left £3,000 to the Beaufort Hunt in his will as well as a direction that any incumbent appointed to the living in his gift should be 'a man who approves of hunting, shooting and all the manly sports which are the backbone of the nation'.

> How can I live among this gentle
> obsolescent breed of heroes, and not weep?

But no tears were shed by the new rulers of England. If the forces of capital are everywhere triumphant, old ideals are eclipsed.

No one has made the contrast better than Peter Mandelson, a central figure in the success of Blair's party. It was he who laid down its guiding principle when he said that 'New Labour is intensely relaxed about people getting filthy rich.' But he also quite unconsciously spoke for the new values when he sneeringly referred to the 'chinless wonders' of the Household Brigade. He was trying to ingratiate himself with an Irish audience, at a time when he was Northern Ireland Secretary and permanently protected by the army; he had for the moment forgotten Kipling's line about 'making mock of uniforms that guard you while you sleep'. But he was right, of course. In Blairite England, money is adorable, chivalry is laughable.

When Parris said that the last decades had everywhere seen the collapse of the left he was clearly correct, but when he added that 'we have won the argument' he used exactly the wrong word: battles, yes, arguments, no. Successive Conservative governments had won a devastating series of political – or more precisely economic – victories. In the year Margaret Thatcher became prime minister there were more than 29 million days lost to strikes. In the year that Tony Blair became prime minister, it was 235,000 working days. British economic growth in 1979 was 0.5 per cent against German 4.5 per cent; twenty-five years later the British economy grew at nearly 3 per cent while the German economy was not growing at all but contracting. Before James Callaghan's Labour government fell, both unemployment and interest rates were touching 17 per cent; as Blair approaches his third election, the figures are 2.7 per cent and 4.75 per cent, the latter fractionally above the annual growth rate for average earnings of 4.5 per cent.

Vivid as all those statistics are, they scarcely begin to convey the great social and economic revolution of our time. Life expectancy is far longer, incomes far higher, working hours far shorter than either Marx or any mill-owner could have believed possible 150 years ago. The figures for ownership of houses, motor-cars, mobile telephones, computers (and of course the existence of that last two), would have seemed incredible even when Churchill was prime minister. The British people are property-owning democrats beyond Eden's imagining; they have never had it so good to a degree Macmillan could not have conceived.

Many of the consequences of this revolution have distressed fogeys of the left as well as of the right. In his memoir *Interesting Times*, Eric Hobsbawm writes with comical unconsciousness of how much he loved Spain fifty years ago, when Franco's regime happily kept the country free of 'the mass tourism of the rich'. There is no mass tourism of the rich, as there are no rich masses. There is the tourism of the formerly poor, economically emancipated by the boundless productivity of the competitive market economy. One minor effect of the disaster of December 2004 in the Indian Ocean was to be reminded nightly by those returning that vast numbers of very ordinary British people – 'the lower classes', Essex men, Mrs Thatcher's C2s – now think nothing of taking winter holidays in Thailand. By the end of the twentieth century, the British bought more than 17 million foreign package holidays every year. They were escaping from a damp little island where in 1939 less than half the population spent even one night a year away from home.

Not that Hobsbawm was alone in his puzzled vexation. Although it is statistically demonstrable that most British people were markedly better off when Mrs Thatcher left Downing Street than when she arrived, that had never stopped the chattering classes and the lumpen-intelligentsia from writing as if England in the 1980s were an occupied country. Any historian reading nothing but those writers described in Chapter 8 would have supposed that British people had languished under the iron heel of military dictatorship; they could not possibly have elected such a monster as Mrs Thatcher three times, could they?

And yet those chatterers somehow won the argument. A random glance at the printed word shows how much so. The 'Diaries' of Peter Nichols have already been mentioned, in which that amiable as well as gifted playwright recalled 'how difficult it was at the height of Thatcher's regime to speak out against her'. The 2004 Booker Prize for fiction was won by Alan Hollinghurst with his novel *The Line of Beauty*. It begins in 1983, one of its chief (and most loathsome) characters is a Tory politician, and Mrs Thatcher herself makes an appearance. Apart from elegant prose and lurid descriptions of unsafe sex, the book has a theme which cannot even be called satirical, since that suggests deliberate purpose: the author merely makes the assumption, which he knows his readers will share, that the 1980s had been entirely hateful and contemptible, worse even than the 'low dishonest decade' of the 1930s.

The year 2004 also saw the publication of the magnificent new *Oxford Dictionary of National Biography*. While writing about it with warm appreciation in the *London Review of Books* (always the pure voice of highbrow anti-Thatcherism), the Cambridge don Stefan Collini felt obliged to register his shock or even shame that this great work 'should have been conceived and launched during the sour, bottom-lining years of gutter Toryism'. Even an intelligent young Conservative woman writing a political memoir felt obliged to call it only part-ironically *Too Nice to Be a Tory*. No, this was not a country where the Tories had won the argument. An old line holds that history is written by the victors; that has been confuted in twenty-first century England.

One by one the players in this story have left the stage. Almost all of those concerned in the events of October 1963 are now dead, Macmillan, Home, Macleod, Butler, Powell, leaving varied legacies. Macleod is largely forgotten, though Powell still casts a baleful glance from the grave. Macmillan's stock has fallen further and with reason: the cynicism he showed in larger political matters was reflected in his philistinism which had destroyed the Euston Arch, epitome of the appalling spoliation of town and country under his and later Tory governments. Looking back at this period, it is shameful that Conservatives did so very little to conserve their country.

Most of the cabinet ministers of the 1970s and 1980s are still alive and even kicking, some of them having found the life after politics of Waldegrave's phrase. Three former Tory premiers survive as this book is completed. Sir Edward Heath at eighty-eight is frailer and less curmudgeonly. John Major has sensibly turned away from politics: his only manifesto in 2005 was for membership of the MCC committee and said in his Pooterish way that 'Cricket has given me enormous pleasure throughout my life. I would like to give as much back to the game as the game has given me.'

There has been no happy retirement to the Long Room at Lord's for Margaret Thatcher. Whatever her achievements as prime minister, none of her warmest devotees – not even those who supported her when she won the leadership thirty years ago or those who think she saved the country in the 1980s or the *Telegraph* Maggobites who dreamed of the queen in exile after she was deposed – can believe that her stature has been enhanced since she left office. Even before her eviction she had almost turned herself into a prime minister in opposition, with her inflammatorily anti-European speech at Bruges in September 1988, and after November 1990 she played a relentlessly destructive role. When Baldwin retired from Number 10, he promised not to speak to the man at the wheel or spit on the deck; Lady Thatcher habitually spat on the helmsman's head.

She had accused her colleagues of treachery in November 1990, but over the next decade it was her own disloyalty which came to vex and even appal those who had once served her. Most of us have a kind of mental brake between what we think and what we say, Douglas Hurd observed, but hers wore out, 'So she was saying things that were on her mind, but there was no sort of sieve or filter.' Peter Carrington deplored the way she intervened in every leadership contest after her departure, 'and always with disastrous results'. Chris Patten is even crisper: 'She destroyed the Conservative party.' Instead of acting as a moderating influence, 'she encouraged the suicidal element in the Conservative party and in the media. I think she should have thrown buckets of cold water over people like Charles Moore and discouraged the more rabid commentators of the right. The curiosity about Margaret is she became more radical and fundamentalist out of office than she had been in.'

Before her eightieth birthday in October 2005 approached, she had retired from the public scene, the more so since the death of her husband in 2003, but unhappy memories recurred. General Pinochet, the Chilean dictator she had always called her friend and whom she had entertained at her own home, faces still more charges of torture and murder. And as the new year opened her son Sir Mark Thatcher ('Sir' because an hereditary baronetcy conferred on her Denis was the one favour she sought when she left Downing Street) narrowly escaped prison or worse following a characteristically farcical as well as disgraceful exploit in Africa.

She may not by now be fully able to appreciate the ironies and paradoxes of her career. Her role in helping to defeat Communism should never be forgotten, and will not be in eastern Europe. But that very defeat had grave consequences for conservative parties in the West, hers as much as any, by depriving them of one of their reasons for being, at the same time as allowing the left to slough off a poisonous moral burden. In her own country that was mirrored by her particular problems of success: once she had done the necessary dirty work, others could claim her inheritance, but in ostensibly kinder, gentler guise.

That meant Tony Blair. He enthusiastically claimed all of Lady Thatcher's economic legacy, as he made clear yet again when he began the 2005 election campaign early in the year with the words, 'Everything we do must be for this one central purpose: increased personal prosperity and well-being,' and never mind social justice or equality. And yet he had managed adroitly to shed all the more unattractive aspects of Thatcherism. She could once have been defended on the Viennese saying that if you want the meat you have to pay for the bones; Blair took the meat and left the Tories the bones.

All of which has bequeathed a near impossible position to Lady Thatcher's heirs, and in late 2004 things went from bad to worse for Michael Howard. A trip to Falmouth in front of the television cameras turned into a mild form of humiliation. That was not entirely his fault, but he acted foolishly in sending Boris Johnson on a bizarre mission of penance to Liverpool after the *Spectator* had published a leader of vulgar abuse about that city, and then sacked Johnson from the front bench for an indiscretion in his private life. Admittedly 'private' was not quite the right term, and the leading Tory weekly journal has not lately been an advertisement for the Roman virtues of dignity and authority. In the 1970s, the staff of that magazine may sometimes have behaved very badly (*experto crede*), but the *Spectator* had not yet become part of the Great British Sex Farce. It sometimes seems that Tory journalism, like the party itself, follows another old Viennese joke: not long ago the situation was serious but not hopeless, now the situation is hopeless but not serious.

Chances of a fresh look had anyway been set back at the party conference in October when there was another sighting of the undead. John Redwood appeared on the platform to announce in the most blood-curdling tones, 'I'm back', as indeed he was, on the front bench again to the silent anger of those who thought the party should be moving away from the right. Then at the end of the year, and with the general election looming, Howard made another about turn and said that he now supported the government's proposals to introduce identity cards.

For many Tories this was an awful moment. The arguments for such cards are entirely specious, and there is almost no evidence to suggest that they curb terrorists. An obligation to carry papers used to be thought the one mark of a police state, and it affronts elementary British instincts, harking back to the happy days of a century ago when, in A. J. P. Taylor's words, 'a sensible, law-abiding Englishman could pass through life and hardly notice the existence of the state'. The Tories had returned to power in 1951 not least by campaigning against irksome lingering wartime infringements of freedom, specifically including identity cards.

What is more, this question gives the Tories one of their genuine 'selling propositions' against New Labour. The whole tenor of the Blair government has been relentlessly bossy and authoritarian, fonder than ever of Macleod's nanny state. Blair has been called a man without a libertarian bone in his body, something he almost concedes, since he scorns 'libertarian nonsense' and clung as long as he could to David Blunkett, the most reactionary Home Secretary since William Joynson-Hicks and a man who in turn had sneered at 'the liberati' (those silly stuck-up people who believe in the rule of law and individual freedom). Clever as he is, Howard cannot grasp that there simply is no point in competing with Blair in oppressive rhetoric.

As a final glancing blow, in January 2005 one more Tory deserted the party for the big tent of New Labour. Robert Jackson had been one of the cleverest Tories of his generation, a Fellow of All Souls who had worked as a Eurocrat in Brussels, the author of *The Powers of the European Parliament* and *Reforming the European Budget*, an MP from 1983 and a junior minister in the Thatcher government. As it happened, I bumped into this Oxford contemporary the day after his defection when he was lurking in a little curry snack bar in Covent Garden, where I congratulated him on finding his home in a managerial party of the centre right, or maybe a party for people 'of any particular view'.

He had been quite rightly angered by the Tories' opportunism over university fees, although his other reasons for crossing the floor seem more tenuous, and his personal adoration of Blair is a matter of taste. I reminded Jackson of what his friend Richard Jenkyns, the admirable Oxford classical scholar and literary critic, had said about Blair's 'forces of conservatism' oration: 'in its demonizing of opponents and its aspiration to make the Labour party the political arm of the British people, perhaps the most fascistic speech ever made by a mainstream British politician'. Whatever anyone's opinions or prejudices, there is something truly ominous about the Blairite attempt, genuinely reminiscent of the 1930s, to co-opt all sides and rise above mere party politics.

Despite intermittent flickers in the polls, and for all the disillusionment so many people now felt with the Blair government, there was little serious doubt as to the outcome of the 2005 election. But it was anything but dull, least of all in what it said about the Tories. Howard chose to fight a bare-knuckled or even brutish campaign, importing a mysterious antipodean Svengali called Lynton Crosby who had supposedly won an election for John Howard in Australia by playing populist 'dog-whistle' themes. Not many months before the election Crosby told Howard that – despite the contrary advice of Lord Saatchi – the Tories could not win, but they could still blow those fearful whistles to rally support. And so voters were told to be afraid, very afraid, of dirty hospitals, of undisciplined schoolchildren, of rampant crime, and above all of immigrants and asylum-seekers, coming here 'for nefarious purposes', Howard said. Harking back to the days when he had been Home Secretary and said that 'prison works', one startling poster asked, 'How would you feel if your daughter were attacked by a bloke on early release.'

All this was pleasing enough to part of the Tory press – Charles Moore wrote in the *Daily Telegraph* that, after eight years of Blair, 'the country feels older, crabbier, dirtier, unkinder, ruder, more violent, less British and less free' – but not everyone agreed, or liked the mephitic odour of the campaign. Portillo was now beyond the fray, leaving parliament at last, and free to criticise his old party with asperity. He viewed with displeasure 'a Victor Meldrew manifesto of moans about modern Britain', and recalled the unspoken agreement previously existing that immigration would not treated as an election issue because of the obvious danger that it could become inflammatory. Apart from questions of taste and tone, many voters actually liked immigrants. English agriculture was dependent on them, and large parts of industry too. Kenneth Clarke was not being merely facetious when he said that without the Poles you couldn't find anyone to pour you a drink in a West End bar, and two-income couples who delighted in courteous, willing and honest au pairs from countries like Slovakia contemplated with horror having to employ native products of the British educational system and prevailing culture who were in every respect the opposite.

At the same time Howard exercised a well-nigh Stalinist control over the party when it came to talking candidly about the economy. The fate of two pairs of Tory candidates was instructive. One man faked a photograph to portray himself opposing asylum-seekers, while another campaigned on the slogan 'What part of "send them back" don't you understand, Mr Blair?' The former was rebuked mildly by the party leader, the latter not at all. On the other hand two candidates, Howard Flight, a rich merchant banker and the sitting MP for Arundel, and Danny Kruger, a quick-witted young journalist standing against Blair himself in his Sedgefield constituency, were brutally expelled from the fold, Flight for having thought out loud about the need for deeper cuts in taxing and spending, Kruger for having spoken of the need for 'creative destruction' (a phrase with which Howard was perhaps unfamiliar) in the public services. Flight said that he was astonished at his treatment: 'I urged Michael to rethink, not just for my sake, but for his,' since this summary dismissal was very badly received in his constituency and in the City.

Another new turn was to accuse Blair directly of mendacity: he had 'lied to take us to war'. But the Tory leadership had itself supported the war, and only days before the election Howard weirdly said that he would have supported it even if Saddam had had no weapons of mass destruction. The result of this was to prompt many Labour voters unhappy about the war to vote for the one party which had opposed it: the Lib Dem vote rose – and the Labour vote fell – by more than a million, while the Tory vote only increased fractionally. Some Tories nevertheless claimed to admire Howard for this ruthlessness and brutality. By concentrating on asylum, immigration and crime, he was only doing what Liam Fox among others had already urged him. But hadn't Hague done just that four years earlier? Yes, Fox replied, but he had been merely wrong in his timing: 'William had many of the right issues – it was just the wrong election. We were highlighting trends that voters hadn't yet come to comprehend.'

That was put to the test on 5 May. Alas, the voters still didn't comprehend those trends, and the dogs did not come to heel. It was a curious election result, not so much with something for everyone as nothing for anyone.[3] The Liberal Democrats increased their vote by three percentage points but only picked up ten seats. Labour won a clear majority but a far smaller one. Much more to the point, their share of the poll fell dramatically, to just over 35 per cent. Blair won re-election with the votes of little more than a fifth of the whole electorate, and for the first time in British history those voting for the victorious party were outnumbered by those who did not vote at all.

Not that this was much comfort to the Tories, however much they tried to comfort themselves. On the morrow of the election, Michael Ancram said that 'Overall it has been a very good result for us.' He might have taken a little longer to think about his party's fate. By now, the Tories had lost the popular vote in three successive elections for the first time in fifty years. They had been in opposition for longer than at any time since the Great War. They would shortly have been

---

[3] Labour: 9.6 million votes, 35 per cent, 356 seats; Tories: 8.8 million, 32 per cent, 197 seats; Liberal Democrat: 5.9 million, 22 per cent, 62 seats.

out of office for longer than at any time since the eighteenth century. And this had once been a party of government par excellence. If that was a good result, what would a bad result have been?

Like Ancram, Michael Howard seemed for a moment unable to face reality. When he welcomed the new boys and girls, the first-time Tory MPs, he compared them with the famous vintage of 1950. There were indeed some gifted young men and women among the intake, though time will tell if they measure up to Macleod, Heath, Powell, Deedes, and the other men of '50. But the Tories had won 298 seats in 1950, only 17 behind Labour, and won 43.5 per cent of the vote. In 2005, they had 197 seats, 159 behind Labour, and their share of the popular vote had barely increased, flat-lining after years at a little less than 33 per cent. As Francis Maude, the party chairman (and son of one of that 1950 intake), put it with bleaker self-honesty, at that rate they might well win a majority by 2050.

Even David Davis, as he began his open bid for the leadership (his enemies, not a small group, might have said that he had been quietly bidding for years past), recognized the gravity of the position. For all their successful co-opting of one class after another, down to the lower middle classes and then the C2s, the Conservatives had, at least since they ceased to be 'the gentlemen of England', been first and foremost the party of the commercial and professional upper middle classes. In the latest election, as Davis pointed out, significantly fewer 'ABs', the highest socio-economic sector, voted Tory than had in 1997. We have seen how, after High Tory resistance to the female franchise, women once enfranchised had voted predominantly Tory for most of the twentieth century; by the twenty-first century, only a quarter of women under fifty-five were doing so.

Before he had digested that, Howard resigned. Or rather he said he would resign, but not yet. There was a general sense in the party that Major and Hague had left (not to say that Mrs Thatcher had been evicted) too precipitately, and that a period of reflection was needed before choosing another leader. Howard could have said that he would stay on as long as he was needed, at least to see the party through the referendum on the European constitution then scheduled for May 2006 (although in the event scrapped, conveniently for Blair, in consequence of the rejection of the constitution less than a month after the British election, by the French and Dutch electorates). Instead of that, he announced that he would leave, not in the summer but perhaps before the end of the year. He thereby wilfully made himself a postdated lame duck, he abdicated such authority as he possessed, and he precipitated a crisis for the Tories, who were condemned to months of wrangling and infighting when they should have been pummelling the government. When Howard tried to foist a new scheme for electing the leader, while also announcing insulting and disastrous plans for subjecting MPs to still stricter discipline, even suggesting that their 'work-rate' should be supervised, there was something like a rebellion within the 1922 Committee, and morale was even lower than before the election.

All in all, there was little sign that the party had regained even a little of its old self-confidence. Symptoms of this continuing loss of nerve were more or less serious. As a small but comical sign of social insecurity, party activists were bidden to something which was called 'Evening Glamour' but which was specifically 'not a Black Tie event', so that the unfortunates were told that 'you can wear a Black Tie suit but preferably without the tie.' Less ludicrously, the party had asked the media during the election campaign to avoid calling them the 'Tories', and Andrew Lansley, one of those eyeing the succession, even suggested that the name Conservative should be changed, though to what was not clear; 'Centrica' had already been taken.

When this book was published some weeks before the election, more than one critic said that the theme implied in its title was exaggerated: wasn't it a thriller without a corpse? Portillo took a harsher view, suggesting in a radio discussion with me that Tory England had died forty years earlier, and adding grimly that even if the Tories were to win that coming election 'they won't be out of the woods'. As if to confirm his (and my) grim prognosis, the Tories not only lost the election resoundingly but Howard's conduct before and after polling day suggested that his party was afflicted with a death wish. Ten weeks after the election the hammering of another nail could be heard when the Tories failed at a by-election to recover Cheadle from the Liberal Democrats, to whom they had lost this once-safe Conservative seat in 1997. That meant that the Tories had now failed to gain a set at a by-election since 1982.

By announcing his departure at a later unspecified date, Howard was said to be arranging a beauty contest, but some of the bathing belles were more bashful than others. Despite the Lib Dems' ignoble 'decapitation strategy' for picking off individual Tories, Oliver Letwin guarded his narrow majority, but then said that he was leaving front-bench politics (to spend more time with his merchant bank, as a colleague put it). Of the so-called Notting Hill set of bright youngsters, George Osborne was promoted to shadow chancellor by Howard but said that he would not be standing for the leadership, which left David Cameron as the representative of the thirty-something generation. Of the old guard, Clarke's chances were obviously enhanced by the collapse of the European referendum, in which he would have been on the opposite side to most of his party, but he was a contemporary of Howard's, who said pointedly that he was quitting because he was too old, though 'Ken may prove me wrong'. It was widely believed that Howard's manoeuvres were intended to thwart Davis, who was the clear front-runner almost before Blair was reinstalled in Downing Street, for all that he was unkindly called 'Michael Howard without the charm'. Charming or not, he gave an intelligent analysis of the party's predicament, observing that it was not good enough to ask what the Tories could do to win: they should be asking what they could do for the country. For all his saying that 'we should be a one-nation party' appealing to women and ethnic minorities, Davis was unmistakably the candidate of the Right, whereas Rifkind made his own bid in other terms. In 1964, Macleod had spoken of the need to gain support from outside the party in the centre where elections are won; in 2005, Rifkind said that 'The reality is that winning back the centre ground is not an option, but a necessity for the Conservative Party.' Who became leader was less important than his ability to recognize that truth.

All of which was something Orwell might have understood. He has appeared here before, and although he was a sincere democratic socialist he is also something of a hero to Tory England. Much of the country today would appal him, partly the gross and ostentatious materialism on all sides (but he was a puritan) and partly the brutality and coarseness, all of which is in itself a problem of success that

Conservatives should ponder. At the same time, a kind of Tory manifesto could be compiled from him.

An essential part of our common national culture is 'the privateness of English life', which centres around 'things which even when they are communal are not official'. 'The power-worship which is the new religion of Europe, and which has infected the English intelligentsia, has never touched the common people ... England is perhaps the only great country whose intellectuals are ashamed of their nationality ... The totalitarian idea that there is no such thing as law, there is only power, has never taken root.'

Short of learning from Orwell, the Tories may find themselves at a final dead end. Over the centuries this party has shown a ferocious survival instinct and an endless capacity for re-invention, but it seems to have lost both, with dire prospects. Conservatives have sat around for some years saying to themselves that they will get back one day, but there is no necessary reason why this should be so. No law of history says that any political party has to survive. In 1906, the Liberals won the greatest of landslide elections, and within ten years they had lost office as a party, never to hold power again. Whether the Tories are destined to follow them may depend on humility and a capacity to learn from error.

A few weeks after his diatribe about the magic circle, Iain Macleod observed in his *Spectator* column with a more genial brand of sarcasm that 'The Conservative party always in time forgives those who were wrong. Indeed often, in time, they forgive those who were right.' It might yet find the opportunity to forgive once more.

Some Books

This book is not an academic study and what follows is not a formal bibliography but a list of some of the books I have consulted which readers may want to look at. Here and in the references, the place of publication is London unless otherwise stated.

The unofficial historian in residence to the Conservative party was Robert Blake, a clever and kindly man in whose debt I am and who died just as this book was begun. A useful starting point is his *The Conservative Party from Peel to Major* (1997), the latest of successive editions (... *to Churchill*, ... *to Thatcher*); captious critics have suggested that Lord Blake subtly shifted his interpretation to fit the party line of the moment, but his work is valuable in any case. In his *Last Diaries* (of which more), Alan Clark frequently and sometimes anxiously referred to the 'BB', his big book on the Tory party in the twentieth century he wanted to finish before his death. He was ambitious enough to hope that *The Tories: Conservatives and the Nation State 1922–1997* (1998) would be a great work of history, and honest enough to recognize that it wasn't. It is perhaps most valuable for its personal saltiness and idiosyncrasy. *Conservative Century: The Conservative Party since 1900*, eds. Anthony Seldon and Stuart Ball (Oxford 1994), is a useful collection of essays. Ian Gilmour and M. Garnett, *Whatever Happened to the Tories: The Conservative Party since 1945* (1997) is partisan but informative; John Ramsden, *The Making of Conservative Party Policy: The Conservative Research Department since 1929* (1980), is an excellent study. The many volumes of Ramsden's history of the party are of enormous value to serious students.

More generally, the last two volumes in the old Oxford History of England, R. C. K. Ensor, *England 1870–1914*, and A. J. P. Taylor, *English History 1914–1945*, have by no means been surpassed, especially the underrated Ensor, but there are now also the excellent Peter Clarke, *Hope and Glory: Britain 1900–1990* (1996) and Ross McKibbin, *Classes and Cultures: England 1918–1951* (Oxford 1998).

Fashions in biography change, and the monumental masonry of Victorian artisans like Moneypenny and Buckle has been replaced by less intimidating structures, in the case of their own subject by Robert Blake, *Disraeli* (1966); it's a wonder that Dizzy's reputation survived this ruthless dissection. Blake also edited the enjoyable *Sayings of Disraeli* (1992). The one biography of that age which survives in a class of its own is Lady Gwendolen Cecil's great *Life of Robert Marquess of Salisbury* (4 vols., 1921–1932). It has been substantially supplemented by Andrew Roberts's *Salisbury: Victorian Titan* (1999), enjoyable though also polemical (from its dedication on: 'To Margaret Thatcher: thrice-elected "*illiberal* Tory"').

On Bonar Law there are Robert Blake, *The Unknown Prime Minister* (1955), and R. J. Q. Adams, *Bonar Law* (1999). Baldwin and Chamberlain have had oddly antithetical fates. Baldwin's official biography by his supposed friend G. M. Young was strikingly unsympathetic and even unfair, an imbalance redressed by Roy Jenkins in his (for him rather slight) *Baldwin* (1987). Chamberlain, on the other hand, was treated much better in his official life by Keith Feiling than in Iain Macleod's unsatisfactory 1961 biography.

A whole bibliographical essay could be devoted to Churchill. Apart from his autobiographies disguised as world history (in Balfour's joke) he is the subject of the enormous biography begun by his son Randolph and completed by Sir Martin Gilbert. Its companion volumes are the proverbial goldmine, and were very profitably dug by Roy Jenkins for his excellent *Churchill* (2001). David Reynolds's *In Command of History: Churchill Fighting and Writing the Second World War* (2004), is a brilliant study of how Churchill wrote (or supervised the writing of) his most famous book.

Most prime ministers since him, and many other Tory politicians, have written autobiographies, of very varying quality. In charity I shall not recall which of Mrs Thatcher's ministers it was of whom Hugo Young said that the author deserved to be congratulated on his sheer fortitude in staying awake while he wrote his book, but it might have been said of quite a few. Eden, Macmillan, Heath and Thatcher have all written lengthy autobiographies which lie heavy in the hand, although Eden also wrote a charming memoir about his boyhood, *Another World, 1897–1917* (1976). And Home wrote an admirably brief memoir *The Way the Wind Blows* (1976), engagingly little of it about politics. In all these cases the reader is better served by biographers: D. R. Thorpe's *Eden* (2003) and *Anthony Eden* by D. Carlton (1981). Macmillan has the authorized two volumes by Alistair Horne (1984–8); *The Guardsmen: Harold Macmillan, Three Friends and the World They Made* (2004) by Simon Ball is an illuminating and original multi-biography.

There will be official lives of Heath and Thatcher to come, but Tory history has been luckier still in unofficial biographies, the field led outstandingly by John Campbell with his lives of Heath (1993) and Thatcher (*The Grocer's Daughter* (2000), *Iron Lady* (2001)). Hugo Young's *One of Us* (1989), although unfriendly, is one of the most penetrating studies of the Thatcher premiership and gives much of the flavour of the period. *Maggie and Me: A New Biography of Margaret Thatcher* by John Sergeant (2005) appeared as this book was going to press and is an amusing digestif.

Of the others, Butler wrote *The Art of the Possible* (1971), an autobiography that was much praised at the time and has at least the merit of brevity (although one should not say 'wrote': many of these books, from Churchill's on, have been partly or wholly by other hands; Butler's book – like Macleod's *Chamberlain* – was largely the work of Peter Goldman, while textual critics have pored over Lady Thatcher's memoirs to elucidate which of her team wrote what). The two dissenters of October 1963 are done justice in R. Shepherd, *Iain Macleod* (1994), and Simon Heffer, *Like the Roman: The Life of Enoch Powell* (1998). Anthony Howard, *RAB: The life of R. A. Butler* (1987) is sympathetic and well-informed; while Lewis Baston, *Reggie: The Life of Reginald Maudling* (Stroud, 2004) is hair-raisingly detailed about that gifted but flawed man's decline and fall from grace. Along with memoirs for the early 1970s there is *The Heath Government, 1970–74: A Reappraisal*, eds. Stuart Ball and Anthony Seldon (1997).

In the early years of Mrs Thatcher's leadership, there was a 'battle of the books', with one work after another which might have been called 'My Tory Philosophy (which is also my job application)'. Most of these are now forgotten, but *The Binding of Leviathan* by William Waldegrave (1977) is more than just a period piece. That was the great age of discussion groups and think-tanks, from the Conservative Philosophy Group, by way of the Centre for Policy Studies, which was home to such notable defectors from the left as Hugh Thomas and Alfred Sherman, to the Institute for Economic Affairs, which played a very important part in reviving free-market theory and then practice. Their numerous pamphlets are therefore of far more than ephemeral interest.

Of memoirs from the Thatcher years, several rise above the soporific: James Prior, *A Balance of Power* (1986), Norman Tebbit, *Upwardly Mobile* (1988), Cecil Parkinson, *Right at the Centre* (1992), Nicholas Ridley, *My Style of Government* (1991), and Kenneth Baker, *The Turbulent Years* (1993). Baker also edited the entertaining *Faber Book of English History in Verse* (1988) and the *Faber Book of Conservatism* (1993). *The Chief Whip* by Tim Renton (2004) is a mixed bag, but with new information of historical importance.

The two Chancellors who served, and then fell out with, Mrs Thatcher give their side of events in Geoffrey Howe, *Conflict of Loyalty* (1994) and Nigel Lawson, *The View from No. 11* (1992). Lawson earlier wrote with Jock Bruce-Gardyne *The Power Game* (1976) and with Thérèse Lawson, to show that this rounded personage knows more figures than PSRB and MLR, *The Nigel Lawson Diet Book* (1996).

In a special case is Ian Gilmour. After he helped shape the story in the 1950s and 1960s as owner and editor of the *Spectator*, his political career was by definition none too successful, but he is one of the rare Tories of his age who can be called real writers. That is seen in *Inside Right: A Study of Conservatism* (1977) and the understandably sarcastic *Dancing with Dogma: Britain Under Thatcherism* (1992), but still more in his remarkable books *Riot, Risings and Revolution: Governance and Violence in Eighteenth-century England* (1992) and *The Making of the Poets: Byron and Shelley in Their Time* (1993).

Two very good and very funny pendants to the Thatcher years are by Robert Harris: *Gotcha! The Media, the Government and the Falklands Crisis* (1983) and *Good and Faithful Servant* (1990), a distinctly unauthorized biography of Bernard Ingham. The fall of Mrs Thatcher is the subject of the riveting *A Conservative Coup* (1991), by Alan Watkins, a political journalist who has produced works of real scholarship; his *The Road to Number 10: From Bonar Law to Tony Blair* (1998) describes 'the making of the prime ministers' and demolishes a few myths on the way. Mrs Thatcher's successor had two quick books when he arrived, *The Quiet Rise of John Major* by Edward Pearce and *John Major: The Making of a Prime Minister* by Bruce Anderson (both 1991), and a longer study when he departed: *Major: A Political Life* by Anthony Seldon (1997). All post-war premierships are intelligently assessed in *The Prime Minister: The Office and its Holders since 1945* by Peter Hennessy (2000).

After that come the melancholy tales told in Simon Walters, *Tory Wars: Conservatives in Crisis* (2001) and Hywel Williams, *Guilty Men: Conservative Decline and Fall 1992–1997* (1998). The latter is written intelligently from the inside, although it must be born in mind that the author was a man who actually decided he should abandon all and follow the saviour of his country, in the form of John Redwood.

A considerable and maybe disproportionate role in my story has been played by Alan Clark. His various works of history are of some interest, but are eclipsed by his three volumes of diaries: chronologically rather than in order of publication they are *Diaries: Into Politics* (2000), *Diaries* (1993) and *The Last Diaries: In and Out of the Wilderness* (2002). I have few illusions about Clark's moral character or even the strict veracity of these journals, but the fact is that they give far and away the most readable, and often penetrating, account of politics in those years that we have, and if Clark has thus hogged the limelight then that's why. His great model was *Chips: The Diaries of Sir Henry Channon*, ed. Robert Rhodes James (1967), a wonderful book which needs bringing out in a new, full and unexpurgated edition.

Some other books I enjoyed include Philip Goodhart, *The 1922* (1973), and *Public and Private Doctrine*, ed. Michael Bentley (Cambridge, 1993). This last is a festschrift for Maurice Cowling, a godfather of the intellectual right and author of the imposing if sometimes puzzling testimony to Tory thought, *Religion and Public Doctrine in England* (1980–85). *In Defence of Aristocracy* by Peregrine Worsthorne (2004) is an eloquent last blast of the trumpet (although the title is something of a misnomer: the values of probity and public service Worsthorne rightly esteems are more bourgeois than aristocratic). Jo-Anne Nadler, *Too Nice to be a Tory: It's My Party and I'll Cry if I Want To* (2003) amusingly speaks for itself.

It may be that the Tories will have further time on their hands soon to think things over. They should start by reading two books published in 2004. *The Welfare State We're In* by James Bartholomew and *Mind the Gap* by Ferdinand Mount. Both writers have made the same discovery, of the enormously vital popular – but of course voluntary – system of self-improvement, mutual aid and education which once flourished among the common folk of England, and the way in which this was destroyed by the welfare state, resulting in the demoralization of a large part of the populace and the creation of an underclass. Mount's book in particular is a small classic, which every Tory should read, but probably won't.

Few of the books I have mentioned so far can really be given the hackneyed label 'indispensable'. It properly applies to reference books, from *Who's Who* to *Dodd's Parliamentary Companion* (both of which have regrettably grown in format since I first consulted them: *Dodd's* used to fit into a baggy coat pocket). One book is simply essential: *Twentieth-Century British Political Facts 1900–2000*, by David Butler and Gareth Butler (2000), now after many years in many editions, is a most wonderful work without which my book could not have been written.

At the other end of the scale is that glorious achievement, the *Oxford Dictionary of National Biography*, published in 2004, alas no more than a matter of months before this book was finished; if only it had been earlier. I possess the original *DNB*, and would dearly love to own the fifty volumes of the *ODNB*; until some uncovenanted financial miracle, I shall make do happily enough with the splendid online edition. Anyone with the smallest interest in English political history, or anything else, should subscribe to it.

References

Prologue: Magic Circle

page

2. '... would certainly know': Iain Macleod, 'The Tory Leadership', *Spectator*, 17 Jan. 1964.

3. '... better be generous': Nigel Lawson, 'The Sick PM, his Waiting Successor and the Unexpected Assassin', *Sunday Telegraph*, 3 Oct. 2004.

5. '... adventurer of modern times': J. Colville, *The Fringes of Power: Downing Street Diaries, 1939–1955* (1985), p. 122.

5. 'The chaps won't have you': quoted in Alan Watkins, *The Road to Number 10* (1998), p. 75.

7. '... of matchless skill': Macleod, loc. cit.

8. '... I had ever met': quoted in *Dictionary of National Biography*, s.v. R. S. Churchill.

8. '... fortunes of Butler' ... 'at any rate explicable': Macleod, op. cit.

9. '... had clinched the matter': Lawson, op. cit.

10. '... carried too far': Macleod, op. cit.

10. ' "... to be a king-maker" ': ibid.

12. '... confident a speech as I could' ... 'to the modern Tory party': ibid.

12. '... the 1914 heroes': quoted in Simon Ball, *The Guardsmen* (2004), p. 369.

13. '... shared this view': Macleod, op. cit.

15. '... in the centre of our thinking': Conservative Party Conference Report, 1961, p. 25.

15. '... with the truth' ... 'much more than you think': Lawson, op. cit.

17. '... not heard him use before': ibid.

17. '... of social inferiority': Alan Clark, *The Tories: Conservatives and the Nation State 1922–1997* (1998), p. 331.

18. '... what was happening': Macleod, op. cit.

18. '... went to Eton': ibid.

1 Tory England

23. 'Tory men and Whig measures': B. Disraeli, *Coningsby*, ii, ch. 6.

24. '. . . as though it had never been': Keith Feiling, *A History of the Tory Party 1640–1714* (Oxford 1924), p. 13.

24. '. . . and German princes?': A. J. P. Taylor, 'Tory History', *Rumours of War* (1952), p. 14.

27. '. . . to reject our experience' . . . 'in the same snare': Edmund Burke in House of Commons, 19 April 1774.

30. '. . . as well as himself': Gwendolen Cecil, *Life of Robert Marquess of Salisbury* (1921), i, p. 218.

30. '. . . a British Ministry': Disraeli speech at Mansion House, 10 Nov. 1879.

31. '. . . gin and beer': J. Morley, *Life of Gladstone* (1903), vi, ch. 14.

31. '. . . of the working classes': Robert Blake, *Disraeli* (1966), p. 555.

32. '. . . practically the rule': Fackel, 43 (Vienna 1900), p. 4.

33. '. . . expanding day by day': quoted in R. C. K. Ensor, *England 1870–1914* Oxford 1936), p. 333.

35. '. . . the quarrel sank': Philip Larkin, 'Annus Mirabilis'.

36. '. . . appears to be a practice': Balfour after Carlton Club meeting, 1922, quoted in Watkins, *The Road to Number 10*, p. 10.

38. '. . . sham Augustan prose': Evelyn Waugh, *Men at Arms* (1952), p. 223.

39. '. . . outsiders and amateurs': Ball, op. cit., p. 216.

39. '. . . old bugger's pissed': personal information.

2 Winds of Change

41. '. . . never had it so good': Harold Macmillan at Bedford Conservative party rally, 21 July 1957.

42. '. . . virtuous publisher' . . . 'tender conscience': *Letters of Evelyn Waugh*, ed. Mark Amory (1980), p. 610, letter of 18 July 1963.

46. '. . . no army commander': Alistair Horne, *Macmillan 1957–1986* (1989), p.242.

47. '. . . white heat': Harold Wilson at Labour Party Conference in Scarborough, 1 Oct. 1963.

48. '. . . what you did last night': Roy Jenkins, *Churchill* (2001), pp. 582–3n.

50. '. . . Beatles' first LP': Philip Larkin, 'Annus Mirabilis'.

51. '. . . really serious crime': Jowitt to Goddard, 15 Jan. 1947, PRO, LCO 2/3830.

51. '. . . but of an advocate': Court of Appeal, R. *v.* Derek William Bentley (deceased), 1998.

53. '. . . for the struggle of life': Cyril Connolly, *Enemies of Promise* (1938), ch. 23, 'Glittering Prizes'.

3 Officers and Gentlemen

56. '. . . extreme gentleness' . . . 'crash of boots': George Orwell, *The Lion and the Unicorn*, Part I, 'England Your England', ii.

57. '. . . a naval dictatorship': ibid.

61. '. . . eleven officers killed': Robert Graves, *Goodbye to All That* (1929), ch. 15.

63. '. . . never quite healed': G. M. Young, *Stanley Baldwin* (1951), p. 200.

63. '. . . without admiration': T. B. Macaulay, *The History of England*, ch. 15.

64. '. . . might be exaggerated': George Orwell, 'Looking Back on the Spanish War', (1941), i.

65. '. . . the gang dispersed': Evelyn Waugh, 'Two Unquiet Lives', *Tablet*, 5 May 1951, *The Essays, Articles and Reviews of Evelyn Waugh*, ed. D. Gallagher (1983), p. 395.

66. '. . . in the British Army': E. P. Thompson, *Beyond the Frontier: the Politics of a Failed Mission* (Woodbridge and Stanford, 1997), p. 63.

66. '. . . the Ministry of Supply': Auberon Waugh, 'Douglas Jay, Man of Action', *Sunday Telegraph*, 8 June 1980.

66. '. . . of Economic Warfare': quoted in Ball, *Guardsmen*, p. 389.

69. '. . . from the People': Evelyn Waugh, *Officers and Gentlemen* (1955), Book 1, ch. 10.

4 Unacceptable Faces

69. '. . . how good that can be': quoted in Ball, op. cit., p. 369.

77. '. . . know themselves': Douglas Jay, *The Socialist Case* (1947), p. 258.

79. '". . . with much blood"': Enoch Powell, speech at Conservative Political Centre in Birmingham, 20 April 1968.

79. '. . . hits the buffers' . . . 'own logic': personal information.

81. '. . . return to inequality': Harold Wilson speaking at Greater London Labour party rally, Camden Town Hall, 21 Feb. 1970.

83. '. . . not lame ducks': John Davies in House of Commons, 4 Nov. 1970.

83. '. . . face of capitalism': Edward Heath in House of Commons, 15 May 1973.

84. '. . . to leave the field': Marcia Falkender, *Downing Street in Perspective* (1983), p. 80.

88. '. . . here, are you?' . . . 'political career, then': quoted in Watkins, *Road to Number 10*, p. 189.

89. '. . . an influential ally': B. Disraeli, *The Life of Lord George Bentinck* (4th edn, revised, 1852), p. 499.

92 . '. . . bluff interior': personal information.

5 Rejoice!

95. '. . . No. Fuck off': quoted in Watkins, *Road to Number 10*, p. 139.

95. '. . . continuing economic growth': Roy Jenkins, *Oxford Dictionary of National Biography*, s.v. C. A. R. Crosland.

97n. '. . . without the tomato juice': personal information.

103. '. . . new right-wing policies': James Prior, *A Balance of Power* (1986), p. 118.

106. '. . . with her Keiths': Martin Amis, *Experience* (2000), p. 24n.

108. '. . . no good for anything': Alan Clark, *Diaries: Into Politics* (2000), 2 April 1982.

109. '. . . at the same time': A. J. P. Taylor, *English History 1914–1945* (Oxford 1965), p. 74.

6 Continental Divide

113. '. . . that of baronet': B. Disraeli, *Sybil* (1845), iv, ch. 7.

114. '. . . Frightened? Frit?': Margaret Thatcher in House of Commons, 9 April 1983.

116. '. . . lounges on sofas': quoted in Regenia Gagnier, *Idylls of the Market-place: Oscar Wilde and the Victorian Public* (Stanford 1986), p. 4.

117. '. . . Socialists would propose': George Orwell, review of 'The Soul of Man under Socialism', *Observer*, 9 May 1948.

121. '. . . the labour movement': Scargill at NUM Conference, 4 July 1983, quoted in Hugo Young, *One of Us* (1989), p. 367.

122. '. . . just as dangerous': *Yorkshire Post*, 20 July 1984, quoted in John Campbell, *Margaret Thatcher*, II: *The Iron Lady* (2003), p. 361.

125. '. . . in the butter': Alan Watkins, *A Conservative Coup* (1991), p. 80.

127. '. . . Cabinet minutes . . .' 'fucking well told': Robert Harris, *Good and Faithful Servant* (1990), in *The Media Trilogy* (1994), pp. 759, 763.

128. '. . . in the Cabinet': Clark, *Diaries* (1993), entry for 24 Jan. 1986.

7 Celtic Fringes

134. '. . . dress of a thief': Macaulay, *History of England*, ch. 16.

136. '. . . corner of the empire': *The Crawford Papers: the Journals of David Lindsay, Twenty-seventh Earl of Crawford 1892–1940*, ed. J. Vincent (Manchester, 1984), p. 414.

136. '. . . of the British people': Bonar Law speech at Blenheim, 27 July 1912.

138. '. . . without honour disregard' . . . 'British citizenship': Robert Blake, *The Unknown Prime Minister: The Life and Times of Andrew Bonar Law* (1955), pp. 126–7.

139. '. . . foolish in refusing': ibid., p. 433.

139. '. . . does not include Ulster': John Bowman, *De Valera and the Ulster Question* (Oxford 1982), p. 338.

139. '. . . pulling us to pieces': Kenneth Rose, *King George V* (1983), p. 242.

140. '. . . of Northern Ireland': Taylor, *England 1914–1945*, p. 159.

141. '. . . a Unionist too': Margaret Thatcher, *The Downing Street Years* (1993), p. 385.

141. '. . . bloody awful country!': Lewis Baston, *Reggie: The Life of Reginald Maudling* (Stroud 2004), p. 364.

142. '. . . to the United Kingdom': ibid., p. 367.

145. '. . . the fire extinguishers': Frank Johnson, 'Notebook', *Daily Telegraph*, 18 Sept. 2004.

145. '. . . blearily emerged': Clark, *Diaries*, entry for 12 Nov. 1984.

8 'Not Exactly Vulgar . . .'

150. '. . . for the future': B. Disraeli, *Coningsby*, ii, ch. 5.

150. '. . . only to destroy them': ibid., iii, ch. 5.

151. '. . . who travels alone': Rudyard Kipling, 'The Winners'.

154. '. . . opinion of mankind': Palmerston in House of Commons, 1 June 1829.

155. '. . . ground she treads': quoted in Campbell, *Thatcher*, II: *The Iron Lady*, p. 413.

155. '. . . pushed to one side': Philip Larkin, 'High Windows'.

155. '. . . a quite unlosable game': Larkin, 'Annus Mirabilis'.

156. '. . . this is all right': Larkin, 'Homage to a Government'.

156. '. . . concrete and tyres': Larkin, 'Going, Going'.

158. '. . . the arts budget' . . . 'not philistine': quoted in Geoffrey Wheatcroft '"That Woman" versus the Chattering Classes', *Atlantic Monthly*, December 1991.

158. '. . . present barbarians out' . . . 'and private virtue' . . . 'the swill bucket': quoted in ibid.

159. '. . . but it doesn't matter': quoted in ibid.

161. '. . . bullying, stupid and brutal': quoted in ibid.

162. '. . . hostile to typhoid': quoted in ibid.

163. '. . . out against her': Peter Nichols, *Areté*, xx.

163. '. . . drag us out' . . . 'just low': quoted in Wheatcroft, op. cit.

164. '. . . her version of it' . . . 'noblesse oblige': quoted in ibid.

165 . '. . . grocer's daughter' . . . 'compact bloody discs': quoted in ibid.

167 . '. . . got on so well': Martin Amis, *The Information* (1995), p. 21.

9 November Criminals

169. '. . . fight totalitarianism . . . from Russian Communism': *Erith Observer*, 29 Dec. 1950, quoted in Campbell, *Thatcher*, I, *The Grocer's Daughter* (2000), p. 55.

160. '. . . side of the wall': Thatcher, *Downing Street Years*, p. 263.

174. '. . . of Labour ministers': quoted in M. Sissons and P. French (eds), *Age of Austerity* (1986), p. 11.

176. '. . . erected for him': Harris, *Good and Faithful Servant*, p. 818.

176. '. . . does not think they matter' . . . 'dishonourable conduct' . . . 'end of this year': ibid., p. 819.

178. '. . . to press for change': Macleod, 'The Tory Leadership', *Spectator*, 17 January 1964.

178. '. . . divide between us': Tim Renton, *The Chief Whip: The Role, History and Black Arts of Parliamentary Whipping* (2004), p. 116.

179. '. . . ice at all' . . . 'score by two': Clark, *Diaries*, entry for 19 Nov. 1990.

180. '. . . How could you do it?': Roy Jenkins, *Gladstone* (1995), p. 603.

181. '. . . always been that': personal information.

181. '. . . all the connections lit up': quoted in Alan Watkins, *A Conservative Coup* (1991), p. 213.

182. '. . . to become somebody': personal information.

10 'An Addict of Almost Every Sexual Vice . . .'

185. '. . . classless society': John Major writing in *Today*, 24 Nov. 1990.

187. '. . . practice at the Bar': Raymond Asquith to Robert Ensor, 22 Dec. 1898, Ensor, *England*, p. 239n.

189. '. . . infinitely preferable': Clark, *Diaries*, entry for 17 Nov. 1990.

190. '. . . Marxist sect': Watkins, *A Conservative Coup*, p. 198.

191 . '. . . sleeping together': *Essays, Articles and Reviews of Evelyn Waugh*, ed. D. Gallagher, p. 500.

192. '. . . at ease with itself': John Major at Downing Street, 28 Nov. 1990.

192. '. . . price worth paying': Norman Lamont in House of Commons, 16 May 1991.

192. '. . . appearing once again': Lamont at Conservative Party Conference, 9 Oct. 1991.

197. 'an economic triumph' quoted in 'Grey Wednesday', leading article, *Guardian*, 7 Oct. 2004.

198. '. . . HOUSE OF COMMONS': Clark, *The Last Diaries* (2002), entry for 14 Dec. 1992.

199. '. . . to overturn it': *Daily Telegraph*, 8 Sept. 1999.

201. '. . . over Good Friday': Clark, *Last Diaries*, entry for 28 March 1995.

201. '. . . for a while': Bill Clinton, *My Life* (2004) p. 433.

202. '". . . the morning mist"': speech to Conservative Group for Europe, 22 April 1993.

203. '. . . of the English scene': Orwell, *The Lion and the Unicorn*, Part I, ii.

203. '. . . sight of England': Baldwin speech to Royal Society of St George, Hotel Cecil, 6 May 1924, quoted in Roy Jenkins, *Baldwin* (1987), p. 31.

203. '. . . people and the state': Major speech at Conservative Party Conference, 8 Oct. 1993.

205. '. . . make life intolerable': John Morley, *Life of Gladstone* (1903), III, p. 435.

206. '. . . almost every sexual vice': *Letters of Evelyn Waugh*, ed. Amory, p. 609, letter of 19 June 1963.

210. '. . . coming from?' '. . . out there?': John Major to Michael Brunson, 23 July 1993.

210. '. . . what they've done': personal information.

11 It was the *Telegraph* Wot Lost It

211. '... called Brown and Blair': Clark, *Diaries*, entry for 8 Dec. 1983

213. '... in a word, weird': Robert Harris, 'How do You Beat a Tory PM Running a Labour Government?' *Daily Telegraph*, 21 July 2004.

214. '... too close to the truth for comfort': quoted by Geoffrey Wheatcroft, 'The Paradoxical Case of Tony Blair', *Atlantic Monthly*, June 1996.

217. '... views of its owners' ... 'any such obligation': 'A New Humanism', *Tablet*, 6 April 1946, *Essays, Articles and Reviews of Evelyn Waugh*, p. 306.

218. '... did not direct opinion': A. J. P. Taylor, *England 1914–1945*, p. 283.

219. '... holy is profaned': K. Marx and F. Engels, *The Communist Manifesto*

220. '... a very good one': *The Times*, 22 Sept. 1978.

221. '... is clever, but silly': A. J. P. Taylor, 'Lord Salisbury', *British Prime Ministers and Other Essays* (1999), p. 77.

222. '... younger intellectuals': Dwight Macdonald, *Reporter*, 27 May 1952, *Memoirs of a Revolutionist* (Cleveland and New York 1958), p. 320.

223. '... drift of events': George Orwell, 'Politics vs. Literature', *Polemic*, Sept.–Oct. 1946.

225. '... idle day-dreaming, I know': Charles Moore, 'Kind Hearts and Baronets', *Spectator*, 18 Sept. 1993.

226. '... clean an ending?' ... 'to the grave': A. E. Housman, *A Shropshire Lad*, XLIV.

227. '... dubious credentials': Watkins, *Road to Number 10*, p. 235.

228. '... a garden suburb': Evelyn Waugh, *Brideshead Revisited*, ch. 1.

230. '... fucking *Mail* readers!': personal information.

12 Things Fall Apart

237. '... for the leadership': Clark, *The Last Diaries*, entry for 21 Dec. 1996.

238. '... candidates the best': *The Times*, 8 May 1997.

240. '... in the Commons': *The Times*, 19 June 1997.

240. '... alliance of opposites' ... 'Hague': ibid.

242. '... posted nonetheless': quoted in Geoffrey Wheatcroft, 'Annus memorabilis', *Prospect*, January 1998.

243. '... farce and satire': W. H. Auden, *For the Time Being* (1945), pp. 115–16.

245. '. . . poor brave Serbs' . . . 'where it is going' Clark, *Last Diaries*, entries for 4 April and 16 Feb. 1999.

Epilogue: Full Circle

247. '. . . hash of things': Clark, *Last Diaries*, 25 April 1999.

248. '. . . a better way': *Sunday Times*, 13 May 2001.

250. '. . . cricket on Friday': *Guardian*, 9 June 2001.

251. '. . . that they need': ibid.

252. '. . . man with children': *Guardian*, 12 June 2001.

253. '. . . poisoned our party': *Guardian*, 18 July 2001.

253. '. . . sold in Vietnam': Boris Johnson, 'The Optimist's Case for Ken Clarke', *Daily Telegraph*, 28 June 2001.

254. '. . . outside the Tory party': Macleod, 'The Tory Leadership', *Spectator*, 17 Jan. 1964.

254. '. . . drove off the road': *Daily Telegraph*, 23 June 2001.

254. '. . . to that soldier': *Daily Telegraph*, 16 July 2001.

255. '. . . with the 1950s?': personal information.

256. '. . . folly and crookedness': *Observer*, 4 Nov. 1956.

257. '. . . political leader . . . any Clintonian': 'Diary', *Spectator*, 2 March 2002.

258. '. . . moral basis for war': Douglas Hogg in House of Commons, 24 September 2002.

260. '. . . not to like?': Michael Gove, *The Times*, 25 Feb. 2003.

260. '. . . Michael Gove, *The Times*, 2 Nov. 2004.

262. '. . . my low expectations': Ferdinand Mount, 'Out with IDS and in with the Tory Unifier', *Sunday Times*, 10 Nov. 2002.

263. '. . . leadership the better': Macleod, op. cit.

263. '. . . six more elections': personal information.

264. '. . . as Home Secretary': personal information.

265. '. . . without preparing it': personal information.

266. '. . . something of the night': *Sunday Times*, 11 May 1997.

269. '. . . has effectively disappeared': Martin Jacques, 'The Only Show in Town', *Guardian*, 20 Nov. 2004.

270. '. . . weak public relations' . . . 'primp, do not': Perry Anderson, 'Renewals', *New Left Review*, Jan.–Feb. 2000.

270. '. . . of his Tory opponents': Robert Harris, 'How do you Beat a Tory PM Running a Labour Government?' *Daily Telegraph*, 21 July 2004.

271. '. . . sound like a winner': Matthew Parris, 'The Right has Won the Argument, so Why is it so Angry and Sour?': *Spectator*, 20 Nov. 2004.

273. '. . . getting filthy rich': quoted in Nick Cohen, *Pretty Straight Guys* (2003), p. 135.

274. '. . . tourism of the rich': Eric Hobsbawm, *Interesting Times* (2003), p. 345.

274. '. . . out against her': Peter Nichols, 'Diaries 1989', *Areté*, Autumn 2004.

275. '. . . of gutter Toryism': Stefan Collini, 'Our Island Story', *London Review of Books*, 20 Jan. 2005.

276. '. . . sieve or filter': John Sargeant, *Maggie: Her Fatal Legacy* (2005), p. 273.

276. '. . . disastrous results': ibid., p. 10.

276. '. . . the Conservative party': ibid., p. 11.

276. '. . . She had been in': ibid., p. 365.

277. '. . . and well-being': *International Herald Tribune*, 14 Jan. 2005.

278. '. . . existence of the state': A. J. P. Taylor, *English History 1914–1945*, p. 1.

279. '. . . mainstream British politician': Richard Jenkyns, 'Mother Tongue', *Prospect*, Jan. 2005.

280. '. . . who were right': 'Quoodle', *Spectator*, 21 Feb. 1964.

Index